JOURNAL FOR THE STUDY OF THE OLD TESTAMENT SUPPLEMENT SERIES
186

Sheffield Academic Press

Three Faces of a Queen

Characterization in the Books of Esther

Linda Day

Journal for the Study of the Old Testament
Supplement Series 186

Copyright © 1995 Sheffield Academic Press

Published by Sheffield Academic Press Ltd
Mansion House
19 Kingfield Road
Sheffield, S11 9AS
England

Typeset by Sheffield Academic Press
and
Printed on acid-free paper in Great Britain
by Bookcraft
Midsomer Norton, Somerset

British Library Cataloguing in Publication Data

A catalogue record for this book is available
from the British Library

ISBN 1-85075-517-5

CONTENTS

ACKNOWLEDGMENTS

The present work, minus minor revisions, was originally submitted as a PhD dissertation to Princeton Theological Seminary in March 1993. As one who has just recently completed her formal education, I am acutely aware of my great debt to innumerable persons, especially those individuals who shared my journey while there. I am particularly grateful to those on the faculty who served at one time or another on the dissertation committee, not least for their willingness to work with a topic and methodology which was somewhat unconventional. Dennis T. Olson, my advisor, assisted me through all stages of the project. I appreciate his extremely close and thoughtful readings of the various drafts and the benefits which his expertise in literary studies brought to the work. J.J.M. Roberts offered helpful advice and criticism, particularly on the Greek portions of the work. And especially to Katharine Doob Sakenfeld and Patrick D. Miller, Jr, I will always be greatly indebted. They have modelled how one can integrate rigorous scholarship and excellent teaching, and both have taught me much throughout my years in their company.

The staff at Speer Library at Princeton Seminary were also helpful in finding the material needed for research and in their willingness to fulfill requests to purchase for their holdings yet another book on Esther. And a special recognition is due to my fellow students in Hebrew Bible while there, Carolyn J. Pressler and Nancy R. Bowen, for our surviving together through the ups and down of the doctoral program. It is an unexpected and fine thing when one's colleagues become one's friends.

Finally, above all, I wish to thank my parents, Janet and Mike Day, for their unfaltering faith in me and their many types of support for my academic pursuits.

ABBREVIATIONS

AJSL	*American Journal of Semitic Languages and Literatures*
ASTI	*Annual of the Swedish Theological Institute*
BA	*Biblical Archaeologist*
BR	*Biblical Research*
BTB	*Biblical Theology Bulletin*
BZ	*Biblische Zeitschrift*
CBQ	*Catholic Biblical Quarterly*
HAR	*Hebrew Annual Review*
HTR	*Harvard Theological Review*
HUCA	*Hebrew Union College Annual*
JBL	*Journal of Biblical Literature*
JETS	*Journal of the Evangelical Theological Society*
JES	*Journal of Ecumenical Studies*
JQR	*Jewish Quarterly Review*
JRAS	*Journal of the Royal Asiatic Society*
JSOT	*Journal for the Study of the Old Testament*
JTS	*Journal of Theological Studies*
PAAJR	*Proceedings of the American Academy of Jewish Research*
RB	*Revue biblique*
RSR	*Recherches de science religieuse*
SEÅ	*Svensk exegetisk årsbok*
TZ	*Theologische Zeitschrift*
USQR	*Union Seminary Quarterly Review*
VT	*Vetus Testamentun*
WZKM	*Wiener Zeitschrift für die Kunde des Morgenlandes*
ZAW	*Zeitschrift für die alttestamentliche Wissenschaft*

Chapter 1

Introduction

The biblical book of Esther is a compelling story. It has long fascinated Jewish and Christian readers, as a book within the Writings of the Hebrew Bible and as the Scroll which is read during the yearly celebration of Purim. The book's basic story line is simple but captivating. The plot first heightens suspense and then releases it with a dramatic reversal of a seemingly unavoidable disastrous fate. The elements of the story have been joined together well, and the book evidences the literary artistry of its composers. The book of Esther utilizes irony, pathos, suspense, humor, intrigue, and serendipity. It contains all of the elements of which good literature is made. Simply put, the Esther story makes a 'good read'.

A great deal of the enjoyment we get from the story depends upon its characters. The primary protagonists of the work are few—Esther, Mordecai, Ahasuerus, and Haman—and on the surface they appear simple and transparent. Yet they hold our interest. We are intrigued by the beautiful orphan who makes good in the king's court, the proud and stubborn Jew who refuses to lower himself, the good-hearted king who never seems quite in control, and the egotistical and evil manipulator. The characters of the book are artfully, yet subtly, crafted. They evidence a power and influence beyond their straightforward portrayal.

However, the story of Esther with which we are most familiar, the book in the Hebrew Bible, is not the only version of the story. This work presents a textual situation unique in the Bible. The book of Esther exists in three ancient witnesses to the story, the Hebrew Masoretic text and two Greek texts, the B text (which is part of the Septuagint) and the A text. Significant differences exist among these three versions of the story. Most notable are the extended portions and the endings. Six extended passages in both of the Greek versions report elements of the plot which are not present in the Hebrew. These passages include a dream experienced by Mordecai and its interpretation, long prayers from Esther and Mordecai, more detailed accounts of Esther's approach to the king, and verbatim copies of the royal edicts of Haman and Mordecai. The ending of the A text is shorter than the other two versions, with different actions assigned to Esther and Mordecai. In addition, there are numerous differences in details of plot, ordering and wording of the material, and overall length.

The effect of these variations in the two Greek versions is to create stories which differ from the Hebrew version. Although many similarities remain with regard to plot, characterization, and literary devices, the variations must also be acknowledged and taken into account. One of the consequences arising from the variant versions of the story is a difference in the manner in which the story's main characters appear.

The objective of this study is to consider the differences in characterization presented in the three texts. I will concentrate upon those differences that lie beneath the overarching, and sometimes more obvious, similarities in character among the versions. In so doing, I have chosen to concentrate upon the characterization of Esther in particular for two reasons. First, Esther is the character in the story who is changed most by the variant versions. Her differing approaches to the king and variant roles at the conclusion of the stories, as well as differing speeches, responses, actions, and appearances throughout the story, make her appear as quite a different type of person and queen. Second, Esther is a focal point for the action. Esther is the most engaging character, the one in whom readers most readily become interested, and she is portrayed in the greatest depth by all three of the versions. And she is the only character who really changes throughout the course of the story. Esther alone is not static, but grows and develops in response to the challenges posed to her. She is the book's main character, and the one who is to serve as an example for its readers.

Past Scholarship

The book of Esther has fostered curiosity, discussion, and even opposition within both Jewish and Christian religious communities throughout the centuries. From the time of disagreements about its canonical status, the book has proven controversial, engendering widely divergent interpretations of its meaning, purpose, and worth for religious edification. And especially during the last two or three decades it has been the recipient of a wealth of scholarly attention. Discussion has focused around questions of the historical accuracy of the events and characters, genre, original purpose, layers of composition, theological meaning (or lack thereof), thematic elements, literary style, and connection to other biblical materials.

Two areas within the breadth of recent scholarship on the book of Esther impact this present study: interpretation of the figure of Esther as she appears in the story, and assessment of the Greek materials and their connection to the Masoretic text. Yet there remain certain limitations of the work which has been done, areas left unexplored. In the following two sections, I will briefly discuss the contributions of recent scholarship to the interpretation of the book of Esther.

The Figure of Esther

When addressing the question of the portrayal of Esther in the book, some have seen her presented as only a 'flat' character, according to E.M. Forster's categories.[1] Esther has been perceived as lacking in depth and difficult for the reader to identify with by even as knowledgeable an interpreter of the book as Carey A. Moore.[2] Others have highlighted how she, along with the other characters in the story, act as only a type and not as a unique individual.[3] The argument that the author of the book is primarily interested in plot and action, not characterization, is frequently provided as a reason for Esther's flatness and typological aspect.[4]

Certain interpreters of the book have noted a generally negative portrayal of Esther. Lewis Bayles Paton,[5] and also Bernhard W. Anderson

---

1. E.M. Forster, *Aspects of the Novel and Related Writings* (London: Edward Arnold, 1974), pp. 46-54.

2. C.A. Moore, *Esther* (Garden City, NY: Doubleday, 1971), pp. liii-liv. Also note A. LaCoque, *The Feminine Unconventional: Four Subversive Figures in Israel's Tradition* (Minneapolis: Fortress Press, 1990), p. 49, who agrees with Moore about Esther's characterization as superficial.

3. B.W. Anderson, 'Introduction and Exegesis to Esther', in G.A. Buttrick *et al.* (eds.), *The Interpreter's Bible* (Nashville: Abingdon Press, 1954), III, p. 831; M. Gendler, 'The Restoration of Vashti', in E. Koltun (ed.), *The Jewish Woman* (New York: Schocken Press, 1976), p. 242.

4. Moore, *Esther*, p. liii; Anderson, 'Esther', p. 831; R. Gordis, 'Studies in the Esther Narrative', *JBL* 95 (1976), p. 45.

5. L.B. Paton, *A Critical and Exegetical Commentary on the Book of Esther* (New York: Charles Scribners & Son, 1908), p. 96.

to a lesser extent,[1] find Esther to be lacking in virtues. In fact, these two determine that not only Esther but none of the characters of the story are admirable examples of moral or godly persons. The major proponents of an understanding of Esther as not a particularly positive figure include the aforementioned Moore, Solomon Zeitlin, Alice L. Laffey, Mary Gendler, and Esther Fuchs, in addition to Paton and Anderson. These scholars tend to interpret Esther as one who is weak,[2] immoral or unreligious,[3] selfish,[4] passively obedient,[5] manipulative,[6] and who only gets ahead by using her beauty and 'feminine charms'.[7] She also has been compared with other characters in the story who act in a more exemplary manner: Mordecai[8] and Vashti.[9] And some of those scholars working from a feminist perspective find in Esther a woman who acts in compliance with a patriarchal system, as a stereotypical woman and hence one who should not be emulated.[10]

Other scholars have viewed the figure of Esther more sympathetically. They have refuted both of these two schools of opinion,

---

1. B.W. Anderson, 'The Place of Esther in the Christian Bible', *JRelS* 30 (1950), pp. 38-39.

2. S. Zeitlin, 'The Books of Esther and Judith: A Parallel', introduction to M.S. Enslin, *The Book of Judith* (Leiden: Brill, 1972), p. 15; E. Fuchs, 'Status and Role of Female Heroines in the Biblical Narrative', *Mankind Quarterly* 23 (1982), p. 153; M.A. Portney, 'Ahasuerus is the Villain', *JBQ* 18 (1990), pp. 188-89.

3. Zeitlin, 'Esther and Judith', p. 13; Anderson, 'Place', p. 39; Fuchs, 'Female Heroines', p. 150.

4. Anderson, 'Place', p. 39; Fuchs, 'Female Heroines', pp. 153-54.

5. C.A. Moore, *Daniel, Esther and Jeremiah: The Additions* (Garden City, NY: Doubleday, 1977), p. 220; Gendler, 'Restoration', p. 245; Fuchs, 'Female Heroines', pp. 153-55, 157; Portney, 'Ahasuerus', p. 188.

6. Fuchs, 'Female Heroines', p. 155.

7. Paton, *Esther*, p. 96; Anderson, 'Esther', p. 831; *idem*, 'Place', pp. 38-39; A.L. Laffey, *An Introduction to the Old Testament: A Feminist Perspective* (Philadelphia: Fortress Press, 1988), p. 216; Gendler, 'Restoration', p. 243; Fuchs, 'Female Heroines', pp. 155-56, 157. Also, in a more complimentary sense, LaCoque, *Feminine Unconventional*, p. 72.

8. Moore, *Additions*, p. 220; Gendler, 'Restoration', p. 246; Fuchs, 'Female Heroines', p. 154. In addition, note the views of M.V. Fox, *Character and Ideology in the Book of Esther* (Columbia: University of South Carolina Press, 1991), pp. 185-91, 196.

9. Laffey, *Introduction*, pp. 213-15; Gendler, 'Restoration', p. 246; Fuchs, 'Female Heroines', p. 156.

10. Laffey, *Introduction*, p. 216; Gendler, 'Restoration', p. 242.

demonstrating that the book presents Esther as a full-fledged character who retains the reader's attention and whose positive qualities outweigh her limitations. Almost a century ago, Elizabeth Cady Stanton and Lucinda B. Chandler, in *The Woman's Bible*, saw in Esther a woman who possesses wisdom and courage and who acts in only a self-sacrificing and queenly manner.[1] Arthur C. Lichtenberger notes these qualities as well, but emphasizes that, despite initial hesitance, she gives her own life for the sake of her people.[2] Others have further highlighted particular admirable aspects of Esther's character: S. Talmon views Esther as embodying wisdom qualities as a courtier, surpassing even Mordecai;[3] John F. Craghan sees Esther as one who expresses liberation and liberates others;[4] and Bruce William Jones argues that the book proposes a positive evaluation of the status of women through humor and its portrayal of Esther's initiative, wisdom, and authority.[5]

Sidnie Ann White's recent essay has proven influential in the latest scholarship in Esther studies. Finding Esther to be the main character and true heroine of the story, she argues that Esther's character and actions must be assessed according to women's standards, not men's. In so doing, the traits which Esther displays are those necessary to live successfully in the diaspora setting, traits which Mordecai lacks. Thus, on the whole she acts as a positive model for the Jewish community.[6] Both Katheryn Pfisterer Darr and Michael V. Fox depend upon White's assessment. Darr argues further that Esther, as well as Vashti, deserves

1.   E.C. Stanton and L.B. Chandler, 'Comments on the Book of Esther', in *The Women's Bible* (New York: European Publishing Company, 1898; repr. Seattle: Coalition Task Force on Women and Religion, 1974), pp. 84-92 (page references are to reprint edition).

2.   A.C. Lichtenberger, 'Exposition to Esther', in G.A. Buttrick *et al.* (eds.), *The Interpreter's Bible* (Nashville: Abingdon Press, 1954), III, pp. 841-47.

3.   S. Talmon, '"Wisdom" in the Book of Esther', *VT* 13 (1963), pp. 437-53.

4.   J.F. Craghan, 'Esther: A Fully Liberated Woman', *Bible Today* 24 (1986), pp. 7-10.

5.   B.W. Jones, 'Two Misconceptions about the Book of Esther', *CBQ* 39 (1977), pp. 172-77.

6.   S.A. White, 'Esther: A Feminine Model for Jewish Diaspora', in P.L. Day (ed.), *Gender and Difference in Ancient Israel* (Minneapolis: Fortress Press, 1989), pp. 161-77. She reiterates many of these same ideas in her entry on Esther in the recent *Women's Bible Commentary* ('Esther: A Feminine Model for Jewish Diaspora', in C.A. Newsom and S.H. Ringe [eds.], *The Women's Bible Commentary* [London: SPCK and Louisville: Westminster Press /John Knox, 1992]), pp. 124-29.

the respect of feminist thinkers and serves as a model of appropriate behavior for women.[1] Fox takes much the same approach to Esther as does White, also disagreeing with those who see Esther as a negative character in the story.[2] He more fully develops an argument earlier mentioned by several other scholars, that Esther's character and the types of actions she performs change during the course of the story.[3] Fox views Esther as at first displaying only passivity, a characteristic which turns into activity, and at last changes to authority.[4]

These most recent interpreters have made accurate assessments of the figure of Esther in general.[5] Esther's strength of character, her wisdom and resourcefulness, and her development to a position of importance within the Persian court system and for the Jewish people have been well observed and articulated. Still, there has been a lack of attention to the characterization of Esther as she is portrayed in the two other versions of the story. Those observations which have been made about her character and actions, though correct and beneficial, have been based solely upon the Masoretic version of her story. And White limits her textual base even further, to only the first eight chapters of the book.[6] Analysis of the figure of Esther in these other narratives has yet to be undertaken in any comprehensive or systematic fashion.

We can note two primary limitations to this sole concern with the Masoretic Esther in past Esther studies. The first is the inadequacy of conclusions based upon the Masoretic text for the other two versions of the story. Much of what has been suggested about the figure of Esther does indeed apply to her portrayals in the two Greek versions. But many of those qualities noted do not apply equally well to the A and B texts. The assessments of Esther's character provided thus far, excellent though many have been, are inadequate to describe all three Esthers accurately and satisfactorily. And second, those aspects of character

1.   K.P. Darr, *Far More Precious than Jewels: Perspectives on Biblical Women* (Louisville: Westminster Press/John Knox, 1991), pp. 188-93.

2.   Fox, *Character*, pp. 205-11. But in contrast with White's argument, Fox thinks that Mordecai, and not Esther, is the dominant figure of the book and the one meant to be emulated (pp. 185, 196).

3.   Jones, 'Misconceptions', p. 176; LaCoque, *Feminine Unconventional*, p. 67; Craghan, 'Esther', p. 8; Lichtenberger, 'Exposition', pp. 843-45.

4.   Fox, *Character*, pp. 196-205.

5.   Particular places during the story at which I disagree with specific arguments will be noted throughout the analysis of the following two chapters.

6.   White, 'Feminine Model', p. 164.

unique to the A and B texts which are not found in the M text have not
been represented at all. These alternate presentations of Esther, which
differ in significant ways, have not been part of the recent discussions on
the figure of Esther. All in all, the distinctions between Esther as she can
be understood in the story in general and Esther as she appears particularly in the Masoretic text have been obliterated, and the Greek
presentations of her have been neglected. The goal of this present study
on the characterization of Esther among all three of the primary
versions of the story is to address this deficiency in Esther scholarship. It
is my contention that the results from a closer look at the two Greek
Esthers as well as the Masoretic Esther will prove fruitful to Esther
studies in general.

The Greek Versions and Their Relationships to the Masoretic Text

The past decade has seen considerable activity within the field of Esther
studies involving the Greek versions of the book, most notably in the
three extensive treatments by David J.A. Clines (*The Esther Scroll: The
Story of the Story,* 1984), Charles V. Dorothy (*The Books of Esther:
Structure, Genre, and Textual Integrity,* 1989) and Michael V. Fox (*The
Redaction of the Books of Esther,* 1991). It was Charles C. Torrey's
work in 1944 which initiated this modern interest in the two Greek
versions of the story. He deduced a longer Semitic (Aramaic) original,
which differed from the present Masoretic text, underlying the two
Greek versions. Torrey argued that the bulk of the original beneath the
A text was earlier, but dependent upon the Septuagint, the B text, for its
first chapter and ending (8.17 on).[1] Though Elias J. Bickerman later
argued for only one translation of the book into Greek, and the other
witnesses (the A text, Josephus, Old Latin) being only later revisions of
it,[2] subsequent scholarship has demonstrated his view to be in error.
Moore postulated, in contrast to Lagarde's opinion, that the A text is
not Lucianic in character and reflects a Hebrew original very different at
points from the Masoretic text.[3] He further argued that some of the

---

1. C.C. Torrey, 'The Older Book of Esther', *Harvard Theological Review* 37
(1944), pp. 9, 15-16.
2. E.J. Bickerman, 'Notes on the Greek Book of Esther', *PAAJR* 20 (1950),
pp. 108-13.
3. C.A. Moore, 'A Greek Witness to a Different Hebrew Text of Esther', *ZAW*
79 (1967), pp. 352-58.

more extensive material in the Greek versions but not in the Masoretic text are translations from Semitic originals (Additions A, C, D, F) and others are of original Greek composition (Additions B and E).[1] The work of both Herbert J. Cook and R.A. Martin have reinforced Moore's conclusions by differing means, the former adding further evidence of the A text's textual distance from the Masoretic text[2] and the latter providing a statistical study of the syntax of the Additions in the Greek versions.[3]

Clines and Fox have advanced the discussion on the relationships of the versions of the book in significant ways. Clines concentrates upon the redactional history and literary shape of the story. Analyzing the Masoretic text, he argues that its ending includes two later secondary additions to an earlier story (9.1-19; 9.20–10.3). He provides further argumentation, usually based upon literary criteria, for the A text as a translation of a story differing from the Masoretic text. Clines considers the differences among the versions of the story beneath these texts and hypothesizes five stages of the Esther story which modified the story as a whole.[4] Fox likewise performs a redactional study and concentrates upon the A text and the Masoretic text. He writes in essential agreement with Clines's outline of the formulation of the Esther story, though he differs on minor particulars. Fox's focus is to determine the purpose and goals of those who worked earlier versions of the story into what we now have in the A and Masoretic texts, and his method is to analyze specific passages, often by means of statistics and charts.[5] The contributions of

1.   Moore, 'Greek Witness', pp. 382-93; *Additions*, p. 155.

2.   H.J. Cook, 'The A Text of the Greek Versions of the Book of Esther', *ZAW* 81 (1969), pp. 371-76.

3.   R.A. Martin, 'Syntax Criticism of the LXX Additions to the Book of Esther', *JBL* 94 (1975), pp. 65-72.

4.   D.J.A. Clines, *The Esther Scroll: The Story of the Story* (Sheffield: JSOT Press, 1984). Note the helpful chart on p. 140. Clines also provides a translation of the A text.

5.   M.V. Fox, *The Redaction of the Books of Esther* (Atlanta: Scholars Press, 1990). Chapters I–III are the most pertinent to the questions of the formation of the Esther story. In the latter part of the monograph (chs. IV–V) he takes up issues that have more far-ranging implications, using his method for the books of Esther as a model for redaction criticism as a whole. See also his more recent article ('The Redaction of the Greek Alpha-Text of Esther', in M. Fishbane and E. Tov [eds.], *Sha'arei Talmon: Studies in the Bible, Qumran, and the Ancient Near East Presented to Shemaryahu Talmon* [Winona Lake, IN: Eisenbrauns, 1992], pp. 207-

Lawrence M. Wills and Charles V. Dorothy, while their goals are likewise to determine the origins and redaction of the versions of the Esther story, vary in method. Wills's focus is source critical, using the A text to try to isolate the bottommost layer of the story, which he sees as an example of a wisdom court legend.[1] Dorothy applies form critical methods to the versions, using conclusions from structural, redactional, and canonical analysis. He concludes that under all three present texts lie versions of a rescue novella which have been formed into feast etiologies, and that the structure of the A text and the Septuagint differ significantly and are the work of two different religious communities.

What becomes apparent from this brief outline of the most significant recent scholarship is that study of the Greek versions and their relationships with the Masoretic text has been primarily redactional, source critical, or text critical in focus. The overriding concern has been with the origins and textual history of the story, the only (partial) exception being Dorothy's structure analysis of the final forms of the A text and the Septuagint. While the new insights gained from these recent excellent studies, particularly those of Clines and Fox, are indeed important for our understanding of the three versions, the almost sole focus upon redactional history has left many other areas yet unexplored. The unique portrayals of the characters by the three versions is one of these areas. When characterization has been considered, it has been done so only sporadically, only at earlier levels of the story, and only within the context of redactional questions as the primary objective.[2] Even though it has been well noted how different the three primary versions are, and it has been well argued that they evolved from different origins

20), in which Fox presents many of the same ideas of his longer redactional study.

1.   L.M. Wills, *The Jew in the Court of the Foreign King: Ancient Jewish Court Legends* (Minneapolis: Fortress Press, 1990), pp. 153-91.

2.   Fox, in his monograph on the character and ideology represented by the Masoretic text (*Character*), very briefly addresses differences in Esther in the Proto-A level (pp. 261-62, 264-65) and the LXX (pp. 271-72), and, also briefly, the changes made by the redactor of the MT within his redaction study (*Redaction*, pp. 122-23). His assessment is far from comprehensive in scope. And Esther appears quite different in what can be determined as the Proto-A level from the final A text, with its additional material and changed ending. White also, in her otherwise excellent analysis, does not deal with the final form of the Masoretic text, but only the first eight chapters. Her study is similarly limited to an earlier level of the text ('Feminine Model', p. 164). As will become apparent, Esther's action of writing a letter at the conclusions of the story significantly affects her overall appearance.

and through different formative processes incorporating different ideologies and objectives, any resulting differences in how they present their characters has not been adequately addressed. This present study will look closely at the textual variations among the versions of the Esther story, but with literary objectives rather than redactional.

Recent scholarship of the Greek versions affects the present analysis in two ways. First, I accept the basic consensus on the formation of the three texts.[1] It has been thoroughly and persuasively demonstrated that the bulk of the A text arose from an alternate stratum of the early Esther story which differed from the Masoretic text, that the Septuagint (B text) reflects the translation of a Hebrew version much like the Masoretic text except for six extended additions, and that the A text is dependent upon the same source as the B text for these six passages. Though smaller differences exist among the various appraisals, it will not be necessary to resolve these individual points decisively for the assessment of character portrayal, the objective of the present study. Secondly, I agree with Dorothy that there is a need to study variant forms of a text holistically as well as text critically.[2] With regard to the versions of the Esther story, scholarship needs to consider the integrity of each textual tradition. We must look at what the ancient redaction processes produced, their final documents, as well as the bits and pieces of the story which were integrated at various points during these processes. Respect must be given to the reasons each of the three versions was formed into what we now have. Hence, the final form of the versions of the Esther story will be the primary focus of conclusions about the portrayal of Esther.

---

1.   Tov is the only recent scholar who dissents from this hypothesis. He suggests instead that the A text is a translation based on the LXX but corrected towards a Semitic text different from the Masoretic text (E. Tov, 'The "Lucianic" Text of the Canonical and Apocryphal Sections of Esther: A Rewritten Biblical Book', *Textus* 10 (1982), pp. 1-25). Clines, though, notes that Tov's argument of the A text's dependence upon the LXX relies on verses secondary to the A text (*Story*, pp. 75, 85-92). Fox also convincingly refutes Tov's claim (*Redaction*, pp. 14-17), particularly in questioning the motive for changing the LXX.

2.   C.V. Dorothy, 'The Books of Esther: Structure, Genre, and Textual Integrity' (PhD dissertation, Claremont Graduate School, 1989), pp. 7-10, 450-55.

Characterization as a Literary Quality[1]

Characters in literature are an element of the text of the story. They do not exist autonomously as independent constructs, but are linked with the other elements in any given work of literature. As part of the surface structure, characters are intimately interlocked with a story's other elements, especially its plot and its other characters. They function through action and are revealed through the progression of the events of the plot. As Henry James recognized in his now-famous essay, characters and actions are interdependent for each other's existence.[2] That is, we know the characters of a story primarily as we see them act. And secondly, we know them through their connections with the other characters. All the characters in a literary work, and all the actions they undergo with each other, serve to illuminate one another. Hence, any individual character is a part of the impression and meaning of the work as a whole.

There are, admittedly, certain limitations to these human figures in literature. Characters exist in a limited context, that of the story, and function only within that context. And as an element of the structure of a text, they do not even exist of themselves but only as a reader understands and retrieves them. We are given only a selected amount of information about characters, and this information is highly organized.

1. Included in this section is only the bare minimum of what can be said about character in literature. For more detailed considerations of the theory and techniques of characterization, consult the thorough discussions in S. Chatman, *Story and Discourse: Narrative Structure in Fiction and Film* (Ithaca, NY: Cornell University Press, 1978), pp. 96-145; B. Hochman, *Character in Literature* (Ithaca: Cornell University Press, 1985); W.J. Harvey, *Character and the Novel* (London: Chatto & Windus, 1965), pp. 11-99 and *passim*; Forster, *Aspects*, pp. 30-57; R. Scholes and R. Kellogg, *The Nature of Narrative* (London: Oxford University Press, 1966), pp. 160-206; and J. Phelan, *Reading People, Reading Plots: Character, Progression, and the Interpretation of Narrative* (Chicago: University of Chicago Press, 1989), pp. 1-26 and *passim*. Their insights have been instrumental in helping to formulate the following suggestions about character.

2. 'What is character but the determination of incident? What is incident but the illustration of character?...It is an incident for a woman to stand up with her hand resting on a table and look out at you in a certain way; or if it be not an incident I think it will be hard to say what it is. At the same time it is an expression of character'. H. James, 'The Art of Fiction', in M. Roberts (ed.), *The Art of Fiction and Other Essays* (New York: Oxford University Press, 1948), p.13.

And unlike real people, we cannot think to influence or change them in any way.

Yet characters in some sense refuse to be limited to the written text. Even if we do not see in them the same freedom as does Baruch Hochman, in their being able to be actually removed from their texts,[1] characters do indeed take on lives of their own. We can recognize individual characters because they look and act like real people. Characters somehow do function as more than words on a page or the actants of plot events. They experience conflict within the plot line and with other characters and undergo development through their conflict. Characters are not static. And they often invite our response to their stories, especially in biblical literature.

As readers, we analyze characters in literature as if they were alive. Such is the mimetic aspect of literature in general, to reflect life back to us. We understand characters according to human experience, using the same process and criteria for apprehending a person in literature as we do for persons in real life. And, in a sense, we can know the characters in literature better than we can ever hope to know our fellow human beings. Though we know a character only in a certain context, we know that one completely in that context. We, as readers, are given all the information we need to understand that individual in that situation. Even though we can gather more data about real people, it is more difficult to synthesize this information and provide a coherent portrait.[2]

The means by which characters in literature are known is one in which the reader must participate. To do so, the reader does not merely read the text, but must interact with it—a 'reading out' of the story. In narrative, we are given certain data about a character.[3] However, this information is not complete (that is, telling everything about a character) but selective. Realizing character is a process of piecing the data together, filling in the gaps between the details with which we are provided. In essence, the reader needs to make sense of the actions of a story. And to do so, the reader looks for motivational, emotional, or

---

1. Hochman, *Character*, pp. 49, 168-76, and *passim*.

2. Forster goes as far as to suggest that, for this reason, the ability to know characters perfectly, they are more satisfying to know than are real people (*Aspects*, p. 44).

3. Unlike modern fiction, when interpreting the story of Esther in particular, we can assume a reliable narrator, and therefore trust the veracity of the information the narrator provides.

psychological reasons for the characters to act as they do. We register the data given and then begin to organize its fragments into recognizable and coherent patterns and traits, checking our preliminary conclusions against further information as the plot progresses. The reader must determine such patterns for the characters themselves, relationships between the characters, and any other object with which they are associated in the story. It is in this fashion that the understanding of character in literature is not static but progressive, a 'process of discovery'.[1] Narrative, and especially biblical narrative, does not comprehensively and exhaustively describe its characters from the beginning, but their personalities and motives emerge gradually throughout their appearances in the story and within the interaction between the text and its readers.

Reading character is never done in a vacuum. How we view character in literature is dependent upon our own individual experience and our own situation in real life. Our understanding of any particular character is unavoidably influenced by our personal understanding of what people are like and how they act, and also by how we understand ourselves. We validate the patterns of details in literature that are proposed by the text, but we do so only by recognizing similar patterns in our own experience and in the world around us. And as in life, where two persons never see a third in precisely the same way, opinions about particular characters also vary. Like the interpretation of the actions and motives of the persons we see in our own world, interpreting character in literature is ultimately a process containing a subjective element.

Particularly useful for this present study is Chatman's conceptualization of character as a 'paradigm of traits'. In his view, characters are understood in their literary contexts by means of a set of traits which belong to the character. The paradigm is a constant construct formulating a character, extending throughout the narrative and not dependent upon the fluctuating moods and situations of the character. The trait in characterization is a 'relatively stable or abiding personal quality', and as readers we extrapolate a paradigm of such qualities from the cumulative data of the text. An actual descriptive adjective need not, and usually will not, occur in the text. But we must infer the trait to be able to understand the narrative, to account for a character acting as she does. Within such a paradigm, traits can overlap or may even conflict with another.

---

1. In the terminology of M. Sternberg, *The Poetics of Biblical Narrative: Ideological Literature and the Drama of Reading* (Bloomington: Indiana University Press, 1985), p. 323.

Any given trait may unfold early or late in a story, or it may disappear
and be replaced by another.[1]

Whereas the determination of character by means of a set of traits
may prove limiting for the consideration of other types of literature,[2]
Chatman's theory is well suited for the consideration of different formu-
lations of the same character. The character Esther, in general, can be
seen to possess certain qualities, certain traits, in all three versions of her
story, as well as traits unique to each version. It is within such categories,
such traits, that a greater or lesser degree of the trait can be read in the
different narratives. Thus a stable ground for comparison is provided
within the general paradigm.

Assessment of Character

A variety of techniques is used to reveal character in literature. Simply
expressed, reading character is a recognition of these techniques
employed by a narrative and assessment of the overall portrait of an
individual character that they provide. In biblical literature in general we
tend to be told less about the characters directly by the narrative, their
inward feelings and thoughts or their outward appearances, than in more
modern types of narrative literature. Yet biblical characterization must
not be deemed inferior for this reason, for it often displays recognizable

---

1.   Chatman, *Story and Discourse*, pp. 116-34. Those characters which exhibit a
paradigm of a variety of traits correspond to the 'round' classification. Chatman
describes them as 'open constructs'. That is, their behavior is not predictable and they
are capable of changing throughout the narrative and/or surprising the reader. They
live beyond the text and influence how we live in the world, an attribute which is
important for the portrayal of Esther and her continuing significance for faith
communities, as will be discussed in the final chapter. 'We come to anticipate, indeed
to demand, the possibilities of discovering new and unsuspected traits ... The
character may haunt us for days or years as we try to account for discrepencies or
lacunae in terms of our changing and growing insight into ourselves and our fellow
beings. The great round characters seem virtually inexhaustible objects for contem-
plation. We may even remember them as presences with (or in) whom we have lived,
rather than as separate objects' (pp. 132-33).

2.   For instance, in contemporary narrative literature or even nineteenth-century
novels. Hochman, though finding Chatman's formulation illuminating in some
aspects, goes beyond its dependence upon the verbal surface of the text (*Character*,
pp. 34-38). Phelan, though not addressing Chatman's ideas directly, prefers to speak
in terms of 'dimensions' and 'attributes' of characters (*Reading People*, p. 9).

artistry in the combination of techniques it uses and the significance it imparts to the information about its characters which it does provide.

The following is a listing of the techniques which can be deemed useful for the assessment of character in the Esther story.[1] Some techniques, in general, provide information that is more significant or reliable for the overall characterization of Esther than others. I have therefore categorized them according to primary and secondary classifications.[2] Generally speaking, primary criteria involve details about the individual character herself, and secondary criteria provide information about the character's interaction with other characters or the contrast between her and other characters. In addition, for the assessment of Esther among the versions, I have listed the criteria according to gradation of significance in each of these two categories, from greatest to least importance.[3] That is, the information ascertained from the techniques noted toward the top of this listing is, generally speaking, more determinative for Esther's character than is information from the techniques described further down.

---

1.   I here present these techniques in only the most abbreviated manner. For fuller discussions, see especially A. Berlin, *Poetics and Interpretation of Biblical Narrative* (Sheffield: Almond Press, 1983), pp. 33-42; S. Bar-Efrat, *Narrative Art in the Bible* (Sheffield: Almond Press, 1989), pp. 48-92; and R. Alter, *The Art of Biblical Narrative* (New York: Basic Books, 1981), pp. 114-30.

2.   In the primary category I include techniques which Bar-Efrat places in both his classifications of direct shaping (outward appearance and inner personality) and indirect shaping (speech and actions).

3.   At least for Esther's characterization, I consider the criteria of inward speech and the narrator's direct statements in reverse order of significance than does Alter, according to his scale of certainty of information (*Art*, pp. 116-17). I do this for two reasons which reflect the particularities of the Esther narratives and their portrayal of her. First, Esther's inward speech is relatively rare throughout the stories. When it does occur, it tends to illuminate her thoughts and feelings more than do the narrators' statements and descriptions. Second, Esther's mental activity is generally accurate in the information it conveys about her. Such is not the case for the inner speech of all the other characters; for instance, Haman's inner thoughts arguably do indeed exhibit self-delusion. Esther's inward thoughts occur primarily during her praying. Because of the nature of this situation—a person pouring out her heart before a God who she confesses to know everything—Esther's inner expressions are honest reflections of her feelings and are reliable for ascertaining information about her character.

Primary Means

Inward Speech. Character and personality are determined by what a character thinks and says about herself. Interior expressions include the character's own thoughts and any interior monologue, but also what she expresses in prayers, dreams, and visions. Of course, care must be taken when using inward speech to elucidate character, for the possibility that a character is deluding himself always exists.

Description. A character can be described either by other characters or by direct statements of the narrator. Information given by description is wide-ranging, including mental states, character traits, and outward appearances. When not the statement of the narrator, point of view must also be considered when using such data to determine its reliability for an accurate reflection of the character in question. Within this category is the naming of character, the way by which a character is named by the narrator or by other characters. Naming both describes a character directly and hints at the role of that character in the present scene and in actions to come.[1]

Direct Speech. All speech reflects the speaker to a certain degree. Often, in narrative, an individual's own words characterize him and show his personality. But the manner in which it is said is as determinative as what a character says. It is important to note the style of direct speech and to compare the information spoken with that provided by the narrator. How a character addresses other characters hints at the relationship between them. And even noting at what times a character decides to speak and when to keep silent reveals her personality.

Actions. The actions an individual performs serve to shape their character. A character's inner nature and motives can be determined by observing outer behavior. Often a character's actions work in conjunction with direct speech. The gestures a character uses, reactions to information learned, and the repetition of certain behaviors can be illuminating. And as with speaking, the contrast between when a character chooses to act and the times of inaction determines character.

---

1.   Sternberg has more intricately developed ideas regarding naming, in what he terms 'proleptic epithet' (*Poetics*, pp. 328-41).

Secondary Means
Relationships with Other Characters. The ways in which a character
relates to another or to a group of people aids in that one's portrayal.
Though interaction between two or more characters lies in the realm
between their characterizations, it also works to provide an impression
of an individual character.

Comparison with Other Characters. A narrative's comparison of one
character with another, whether they actually interact with each other or
not, makes the particular traits of each character stand out more clearly.
Sometimes such comparisons are stated explicitly by the narrator, and
sometimes they are suggested more implicitly. A character can show
significant similarities and differences with another character in the story.
In the case of biblical literature, a character may even be compared with
another character in an entirely different biblical narrative.

Contrast with Expectations. Often a character, by nature of being in a
particular situation, is expected to be a certain type of person or to
behave in accordance with an expected norm. Such expectations may be
expressed by other characters or the narrator, or a character may simply
act in a way different from how any average person would be expected
to behave in such a situation. Points at which a character distinguishes
himself from such expectations highlights those differences.

As will become apparent through the following chapters, I do not find
character analysis to be always straightforward nor based upon hard and
fast rules and precise procedure. Reading character includes the mixing
and weighing of the data provided by this spectrum of techniques. It
often requires the use of the reader's best judgment and, at times,
intuition.

Selection of Episodes

Certain events within the Esther story are more illuminating for an
assessment of her character than others. The scenes in which she herself
appears and the places at which she is mentioned are obviously most
important. Therefore, those portions of the story will serve as the focus
for the present study. When details not in these sections affect the figure
of Esther, they will be included in the analysis at the appropriate points.

The episodes of the story which will be examined are as follows:

Episode 1	2.7-20	Selection of new queen
2	4.4-17	Conversation with Mordecai
3	14.1-19	Prayer
4	15.1-16	First approach to the king
5	5.3-8	Invitation and first banquet
6	7.1-8	Second banquet and revelation of Haman
7	8.1-8	Second approach and petition
8	9.11-15	Decision for retribution and results
9	9.21-32	Letter
Minor references	2.22; 16.3; 9.24-25; 11.10; 10.6	

Analysis of the varying character of Esther will be of two types, which might be thought of as horizontal and vertical. First, in discussions of each individual episode, comparison will be made among the versions from that material (Chapter 2). This comparison will be an across the board look at how Esther is portrayed in that particular scene. However, any conclusions will remain only provisional. Second, the characterization of Esther will be considered in each of the three versions throughout the whole of the story (Chapter 3). These overall conclusions will be dependent upon the results of the first level of analysis.

Attention to Textual Details

Assessment of differences in Esther's characterization among the versions requires a detailed examination of the texts of the story. That two of the versions are in Greek and the other one in Hebrew complicates the process. Additionally, at certain places throughout the story two or all three are quite different, and at other places they are remarkably similar in details. For these reasons, it is only at the textual level that the differences among the versions can be properly noted and the data important for the characterization of Esther be deduced. Thus the method for this study will involve a consideration of the similarities and differences among the Greek and Hebrew texts. Larger conclusions will be drawn upon what can be seen on the textual level.

Nomenclature

No consistent system of nomenclature has been used in Esther studies to refer to the three primary versions. The Hebrew version alone has remained consistent, as the Masoretic text (MT). The more well-known of the Greek versions, the textual tradition represented by Codex Vaticanus, has most often been referred to as the Septuagint (LXX or LXXᴮ),[1] but also as the B text (Εσθηρ β)[2] or as ό.[3] However, the facts that there is another significant textual tradition of the book which is also Greek and that both the Larger Cambridge[4] and the Göttingen editions of the Septuagint include both of these traditions renders it confusing and inaccurate to use the expression 'Septuagint' to refer to only one of the textual traditions. The other Greek tradition, represented by five minuscules,[5] has been variously called the Lucianic text, in erroneous connection with the Lucian text type (L),[6] or the Alpha text (Εσθηρ α) or A-Text (AT).[7] For the sake of simplification of terminology and to aid in a comparison of these three texts on an equal footing, this study will employ the following nomenclature for these texts: 'M text' will refer to the Hebrew Masoretic text, 'B text' will refer to the dominant Greek text (according to the textual tradition of Vaticanus), and 'A text' will refer to the shorter Greek textual tradition.

The terminology used to refer to the portions of the Greek texts not reflected in our current Masoretic text has been somewhat more consistent. These six extended passages have typically been spoken of as 'Additions' and provided with the letters A through F. The NRSV translation broke with this modern tradition in its presentation of Greek Esther, using instead the numbers for the chapters which reflect Jerome's placement of this material at the conclusion of his Latin translation of the book. (The Cambridge edition also notes the chapter numbers, in parentheses, in addition to the letters.) The correspondences are as

1.   In most of the recent redactional and textual studies.

2.   By Lagarde's edition of the LXX (P. de Lagarde, *Liborum Veteris Testamenti Canonicorum Prior Graece* [Göttingen: Arnold Hoyer, 1883]); hereafter referred to as 'Lagarde's edition'.

3.   By the Göttingen edition of the LXX (R. Hanhart [ed.], *Septuaginta*, VIII.3 [Göttingen: Vandenhoeck & Ruprecht, 1983]; hereafter referred to as 'Göttingen edition') and Dorothy, 'Books'.

4.   A.E. Brooke, N. McLean, and H. Thackeray (eds.), *The Old Testament in Greek*, III (London: Cambridge University Press, 1940); hereafter referred to as 'Cambridge edition'.

5.   As categorized by Robert Hanhart, in his introduction to the Göttingen edition of the LXX (pp. 15-16, 91; also cf. pp. 87-95).

6.   By the Göttingen edition of the LXX and Dorothy, 'Books'.

7.   By the Cambridge edition of the LXX, Lagarde's edition of the LXX, and in most of the recent textual and redactional studies.

follows: Addition A = 11.2–12.6; Addition B = 13.1-7; Addition C = 13.8–14.19; Addition D = 15.1-16; Addition E = 16.1-24; Addition F = 10.4-13 and 11.1. These passages are integrated into each of the Greek texts, and they are not indicated as separable portions of the story nor as having any different textual origins than the portions reflected by the Masoretic tradition. Because a numbering system reflects their integral connection at the textual level better than a system based upon letters, this present study will designate this material by chapter numbers 11 through 16.

Chapter 2

COMPARATIVE ANALYSIS

Explanation of Procedure

Format

In this chapter, each of the nine episodes will be analyzed according to its bearing upon the character of Esther. The sections dealing with each episode will first place that scene within its context in the story of Esther and summarize the general movement of the plot during that episode. Any major variations among the three versions in the events of the episode and any adjustments made in versification will be indicated as well. Then, each section will be composed of three parts: text, notes, and analysis.

The 'Text' section will consist of the three texts presented in a side-by-side format, in the order of A text, B text, and M text from left to right. The texts used for the Greek versions will be those produced by Hanhart's Göttingen edition of the Septuagint. For this purpose, a critical edition is to be preferred to the Cambridge edition (which does also provide a version of the A text). The Hebrew text used will be the Leningradensis of BHS.[1] For each verse, the Greek and Hebrew texts will be provided first, then an English translation. These translations will be kept quite literal in order to discern more precisely the vocabularic differences among the texts. The details which are unique to each version will be underlined in the Greek and Hebrew texts. In so doing, difference will be determined not on exact grammatical agreement but on whether the sense of the information is essentially synonomous with regard to its effect upon the portrayal of Esther. The choice of what warrants underlining is not an exact procedure and often will reflect my best judgment in the matter.

---

1. K. Elliger and M. Rudolph (eds.), *Biblia Hebraica Stuttgartensia* (Stuttgart: Deutsche Bibelgesellschaft, 1977).

In the 'Notes' section, comments will be made on the variations in order to highlight the differences which can be seen among the three texts. The notes will proceed verse by verse. The discussion will focus only upon those differences in details which are relevant for the characterization of Esther. Any differences which do not affect her will not be addressed. Variant readings from other manuscript evidence will be brought into the discussion only when pertinent to Esther's characterization.

The 'Analysis' section will include considerations of the overall effects which the differences throughout the whole episode have on the portrayal of Esther in each of the three texts. Not every difference in detail will necessarily prove significant at this point. These conclusions will remain preliminary to the composite portrait of Esther in each version.

Versification

The system for numbering verses in the book of Esther varies among the versions. For the sections of the book with which this study will deal, the chapter and verse numbers of the B and M texts correspond quite closely throughout the portions in which they have parallel material (that is, everything except Esther's prayer and her extended approach to the king). If one follows the chapter and verse numbers in parentheses in Göttingen's A text, it agrees with that of the B and M texts relatively closely throughout the greater part of the story, although it does not contain parallel material for every verse of the other two texts. Because the A text's conclusion to the narrative is significantly different, its versification there diverges from that of the B and M texts. At those places (Episodes 7 and 8), the system of the B and M texts will be taken as the standard. The versification of the A text will be adapted to the B and M texts as closely as possible for comparative purposes. Details on any changes in versification will be noted in the analyses of the episodes. As a general rule, where there is divergence in numbering, the text of the A text will be adjusted to the numbering system of the other two texts for the objectives of this study. All of these details will become clear as they are worked out in the following analyses.

Episode 1 (2.7-20)

It is in this section that the reader is first introduced to Esther. The sequence of the Esther story prior to this narrative includes Mordecai's dream (in the A and B texts), Mordecai's report of the eunuchs' plot against the king (in the A text), the banquets given for the Persian people by the king and queen, Vashti's refusal to follow the king's desire and her consequent banishment, and the king's decree regarding the place of men within their households. The scene has been set for the rise of a new queen. Esther and her relationship to her relative Mordecai are named, and we are told of the procedure of gathering women to the capital city of Susa so that one might be selected. Esther is also gathered in, and she quickly wins the approval of the king's servant and receives special treatment at his hand. The process for preparation and selection is described, and Mordecai's concern for Esther throughout this time and her silence about her ethnic heritage are reported. Esther then goes in to the king for assessment. He selects her to be the new queen, she is crowned, and he holds a celebratory banquet. The scene concludes with the narrator's report that Mordecai is in a place of proximity to the king and that Esther's way of life in the Persian court has not changed from that of her upbringing.

The A text is considerably shorter at this point and does not contain all the details of plot which are presented by the B and M texts. In particular, it does not exhibit narrative which corresponds to vv. 10-13, 15-17, and 19-20 in the other two versions, and it is abbreviated in some of the remaining verses as well. The primary material not found in A includes the process of the preparation of the women, notation about Esther's concealing her ancestry, and Mordecai's actions throughout these events.

Text

καὶ ἦν ἐκτρέφων *πιστῶς* τὴν Εσθηρ θυγατέρα ἀδελφοῦ τοῦ πατρὸς αὐτοῦ· καὶ ἦν ἡ παῖς καλὴ τῷ εἴδει *σφόδρα* καὶ ὡραία τῇ ὄψει.

καὶ ἦν τούτῳ παῖς *θρεπτὴ* θυγάτηρ Αμιναδαβ ἀδελφοῦ πατρὸς αὐτοῦ, καὶ ὄνομα αὐτῇ Εσθηρ· ἐν δὲ τῷ μεταλλάξαι αὐτῆς τοὺς γονεῖς *ἐπαίδευσεν* αὐτὴν ἑαυτῷ εἰς *γυναῖκα·* καὶ ἦν τὸ κοράσιον καλὸν τῷ εἴδει.

7 ויהי אמן את‏‏‎‎‏‎‏‏‏ַ‎‎‏‎‏‎‎‏‎‏‎‏ַה‎‎ַד‏‎ַס‎‎ַה היא אסתֹר בת־
דדו ‏‎‎כי אין לה אב ואם‎‎ והנערה יפֹת־
ת‏‎אֹר‎‎ ומובת מראה ובמות אביה ואמה
לקחה מרדכי לו ‏‎‎לבת‎‎

And he was faithfully bringing up Esther, the daughter of the brother of his father. And the child was exceedingly beautiful to see and lovely to behold.

And he had a foster child, the daughter of Aminadab his father's brother, and her name was Esther. When her parents passed away, he raised her up into a wife for himself. And the girl was beautiful to see.

He supported Hadassah, or Esther, the daughter of his uncle, for she did not have father or mother. And the girl was beautiful in form and lovely in appearance. And when her father and her mother died, Mordecai took her as a daughter.

καὶ ἐλήφθη τὸ κοράσιον εἰς τὸν οἶκον τοῦ βασιλέως· καὶ εἶδε Βουγαῖος *ὁ εὐνοῦχος* ὁ φυλάσσων τὸ κοράσιον, καὶ ἤρεσεν αὐτῷ *ὑπὲρ πασας τὰς γυναῖκας*.

καὶ ὅτε ἠκούσθη τὸ τοῦ Βασιλέως πρόσταγμα, οννήχθησαν κοράσια πολλὰ εἰς Σουσαν *τὴν πόλιν* ὑπὸ χεῖρα Γαι, καὶ ἤχθη Εσθηρ πρὸς Γαι τὸν φύλακα τῶν γυναικῶν.

8 ויהי בהשמע דבר־המלך *ודתו* ובהקבץ
נערות רבות אל־*שושן הבירה* אל־יד
הגי ותלקח אסתר אל־בית המלך אל־
יד הגי שמר הנשים

And the girl was taken into the house of the king, and Bougaios, the eunuch who guarded, saw the girl. And she pleased him above all the women.

And when the decree of the king was heard, many girls were gathered in Susa the city under the hand of Gai. Also Esther was led out to Gai, the guardian of the women.

And when the word of the king and his command were heard, and when many girls were gathered to Susa the fortress, to the hand of Hegei, also Esther was taken to the house of the king, to the hand of Hegei, the guardian of the women.

καὶ εὗρεν Εσθηρ χάριν *καὶ ἔλεον* κατὰ πρόσωπον αὐτοῦ, καὶ ἔσπευσε *προστατῆσαι αὐτῆς* καὶ ἐπέδωκεν *ὑπὲρ τὰ ἑπτὰ κοράσια*, τὰς ἄβρας αὐτῆς. ὡς δὲ εἰσήχθη Εσθηρ πρὸς τὸν βασιλέα, *ἤρεσεν αὐτῷ σφόδρα*.

καὶ ἤρεσεν αὐτῷ τὸ κοράσιον καὶ εὗρεν χάριν ἐνώπιον αὐτοῦ, καὶ ἔσπευσεν *αὐτῇ δοῦναι* τὸ ομῆγμα καὶ τὴν μερίδα καὶ τὰ ἑπτὰ κοράσια τὰ ἀποδεδειγμένα αὐτῇ ἐκ βασιλικοῦ *καὶ ἐχρήσατο αὐτῇ καλῶς* καὶ ταῖς ἄβραις αὐτῆς ἐν τῷ γυναικῶνι.

9 *תיטב* הנערה *בעיניו* ותשא חסד לפניו
ויבהל את־תמרוקיה ואת־מנותה לתת
לה ואת שבע הנערות הראיות לתת־לה
מבית המלך *ישנה* ואת־נערותיה *לטוב*
בית הנשים

And Esther found favor and mercy before him, and he hastened to take charge of her and gave, beyond the seven girls, her own servants. When Esther was taken in to the king, she pleased him very much.

And the girl pleased him and found favor before him, and he hastened to give her ointments and her portion and seven girls chosen from the palace. And he treated her well, and her servants, in the harem.

And the girl was good in his eyes, and she bore favor before him. And he hastened to give to her ointments and her portions, and seven girls chosen out to give to her from the house of the king. And he changed her (place) and her girls to a good one in the house of women.

καὶ οὐχ ὑπέδειξεν Εσθηρ τὸ γένος αὐτῆς οὐδὲ *τὴν πατρίδα·* ὁ γὰρ Μαρδοχαῖος ἐνετείλατο αὐτῇ μὴ ἀπαγγεῖλαι

10 לא־הגידה אסתר את־עמה *ואת־מולדתה*
כי מרדכי צוה עליה אשר לא־תגיד

And Esther had not indicated her people nor her country, for Mordecai had charged her not to report (them).

Esther had not reported her people or her ancestry, for Mordecai had put charge upon her not to report (them).

καθ᾽ ἑκάστην δὲ ἡμέραν ὁ Μαρδοχαῖος περιεπάτει κατὰ τὴν αὐλὴν τὴν γυναικείαν *ἐπισκοπῶν* τί Εσθηρ *συμβήσεται.*

וּבְכָל־יוֹם וָיוֹם מָרְדֳּכַי מִתְהַלֵּךְ לִפְנֵי 11 חֲצַר בֵּית־הַנָּשִׁים *לָדַעַת אֶת־שְׁלוֹם* אֶסְתֵּר וּמַה־*יֵּעָשֶׂה בָּהּ*

Each day Mordecai walked around the courtyard of the women's area to oversee what would happen to Esther.

And day by day Mordecai walked about in front of the court of the house of women, to know the welfare of Esther and what was being done to her.

οὗτος δὲ ἦν καιρὸς κορασίου εἰσελθεῖν πρὸς τὸν βασιλέα, ὅταν ἀναπληρώσῃ μῆνας δεκαδύο· οὕτως γὰρ ἀναπληροῦνται αἱ ἡμέραι *τῆς θεραπείας*, μῆνας ἕξ *ἀλειφόμεναι* ἐν σμυρνίνῳ ἐλαίῳ καὶ μῆνας ἕξ ἐν τοῖς ἀρώμασιν καὶ ἐν τοῖς ὀμήγμασιν τῶν γυναικῶν,

וּבְהַגִּיעַ תֹּר נַעֲרָה וְנַעֲרָה לָבוֹא אֶל־ 12 הַמֶּלֶךְ *אֲחַשְׁוֵרוֹשׁ* מִקֵּץ הֱיוֹת לָהּ *כְּדָת* *הַנָּשִׁים* שְׁנֵים עָשָׂר חֹדֶשׁ כִּי כֵּן יִמְלְאוּ יְמֵי *מְרוּקֵיהֶן* שִׁשָּׁה חֳדָשִׁים בְּשֶׁמֶן הַמֹּר וְשִׁשָּׁה חֳדָשִׁים בַּבְּשָׂמִים וּבְתַמְרוּקֵי הַנָּשִׁים

And the time for a girl to go in to the king was when twelve months was fulfilled. Thus the days of service are fulfilled; six months of anointing with oil of myrrh and six months with spices and ointments of women.

And the turn came, girl by girl, to enter in to the king Ahasuerus, as the end of (her time) came under the regulation of the women; twelve months that thus fulfill the days of their cleansing, six months with oil of myrrh and six months with perfumes and ointments of women.

καὶ τότε εἰσπορεύεται πρὸς τὸν βασιλέα· καὶ ᾧ ἐὰν εἴπῃ, *παραδώσει* αὐτὴν συνεισέρχεσθαι αὐτῷ ἀπὸ τοῦ γυναικῶνος ἕως τῶν βασιλείων.

וּבָזֶה *הַנַּעֲרָה* בָּאָה אֶל־הַמֶּלֶךְ אֵת כָּל־ 13 אֲשֶׁר תֹּאמַר *יִנָּתֵן* לָהּ לָבוֹא עִמָּהּ מִבֵּית הַנָּשִׁים עַד־בֵּית הַמֶּלֶךְ

And then she goes in to the king. And whatever she might signify, he will give to her to enter with it from the women's area to the palace.

And at that (time) when the girl went in to the king, everything which she requested is given to her, to enter in with her from the house of the women to the house of the king.

καὶ ὅταν *ἐγένετο* ἑσπέρα, *εἰσήετο*, καὶ τὸ πρωὶ *ἀπελύετο.*

δείλης εἰσπορεύεται, καὶ πρὸς *ἡμέραν ἀποτρέχει* εἰς τὸν γυναικῶνα τὸν δεύτερον, οὗ Γαι ὁ εὐνοῦχος τοῦ βασιλέως ὁ φύλαξ *τῶν γυναικῶν,* καὶ οὐκέτι εἰσπορεύσεται πρὸς τὸν βασιλέα, ἐὰν μὴ κληθῇ ὀνόματι.

בערב היא באה ובבקר היא <u>שבה</u> 14
אל־בית הנשים שני <u>אל־יד</u> שעשגז
סריס המלך שמר <u>הפילגשים</u> לא־תבוא
<u>עוד</u> אל־המלך כי אם<u>־חפץ בה</u>
<u>המלך</u> ונקראה בשם

And when evening came, she was led in, and in the morning she was dismissed.

In the afternoon she goes in, and in the day she departs to the second women's area, where Gai the eunuch of the king, the guardian of the women, is. And she does not go in to the king unless she is called by name.

In the evening she went in, and in the morning she returned to the second house of women, to the hand of Shaashgaz, the eunuch of the king, the guardian of the concubines. She would not go in again to the king unless the king was pleased with her and she is called by name.

ἐν δὲ τῷ ἀναπληροῦσθαι τὸν χρόνον Εσθηρ τῆς θυγατρὸς Αμιναδαβ ἀδελφοῦ πατρὸς Μαρδοχαίου εἰσελθηεῖν πρὸς τὸν βασιλέα, οὐδὲν *ἠθέτησεν* ὧν *ἐνετείλατο* ὁ εὐνοῦχος ὁ φύλαξ τῶν γυναικῶν· ἦν γὰρ Εσθηρ εὑρίσκουσα χάριν παρὰ πάντων τῶν βλεπόντων αὐτήν.

ובהגיע תר־אסתר בת־אביחיל דד 15
מרדכי <u>אשר לקח־לו לבת</u> לבוא אל־
המלך לא <u>בקשה</u> דבר כי אם את־אשר
<u>יאמר</u> הגי סריס־המלך שמר הנשים
ותהי אסתר נשאת חן בעיני כל־
ראיה

When the time was fulfilled for Esther, the daughter of Aminadab the brother of the father of Mordecai, to go in to the king, she did not reject those things the eunuch, the guardian of the women, had commanded. For Esther was finding favor with all who saw her.

When the turn drew near for Esther, the daughter of Abihail the uncle of Mordecai, who took (her) for himself as a daughter, to go in to the king, she did not seek any article except that which Hegei the eunuch of the king, the guardian of the women, said. And Esther was bearing favor in the eyes of all who saw her.

16

καὶ *εἰσῆλθεν* Εσθηρ πρὸς Ἀρταξέρξην τὸν βασιλέα τῷ δωδεκάτῳ μηνί, ὅς ἐστιν Αδαρ, τῷ ἑβδόμῳ ἔτει τῆς βασιλείας αὐτοῦ.

ותלקח אסתר אל־המלך אחשורוש
אל־בית מלכותו בחדש העשירי הוא־
חדש טבת בשנת־שבע למלכותו

And Esther went in to Artaxerxes the king in the twelfth month, which is Adar, in the seventh year of his reign.

And Esther was taken to the king Ahasuerus, to the royal palace, in the tenth month, which is the month of Tebeth, in the seventh year of his reign.

17

ὡς δὲ *κατεμάνθανεν* ὁ βασιλεὺς πάσας τὰς παρθένους, *ἐφάνη ἐπιφανεστάτη* Εσθηρ, καὶ εὖρε χάριν καὶ ἔλεον κατὰ πρόσωπον αὐτοῦ, καὶ ἐπέθηκε τὸ διάδημα τῆς βασιλείας ἐπὶ τὴν κεφαλὴν αὐτῆς.

καὶ *ἠράσθη* ὁ βασιλεὺς Εσθηρ, καὶ εὖρεν χάριν παρὰ πάσας τὰς παρθένους, καὶ ἐπέθηκεν αὐτῇ τὸ διάδημα *τὸ γυναικεῖον.*

ויאהב המלך את־אסתר מכל־הנשים
ותשא־חן וחסד לפניו מכל־הבתולת
וישם כתר־מלכות בראשה וימליכה
תחת ושתי

When the king had carefully considered all the virgins, Esther appeared magnificent, and she found favor and mercy before him. And he placed the diadem of royal power upon her head.

And the king chose Esther, and she found favor above all the virgins. And he placed the woman's diadem upon her.

And the king loved Esther more than all the women, and she bore favor and kindness before him, more than all the virgins. And he placed the diadem of royal power upon her head and he made her reign instead of Vashti.

18

καὶ *ἤγαγεν* ὁ βασιλεὺς τὸν γάμον τῆς Εσθηρ *ἐπιφανῶς* καὶ ἐποίησεν ἀφέσεις *πάσαις* ταῖς χώραις.

καὶ ἐποίησεν ὁ βασιλεὺς πότον πᾶσιν *τοῖς φίλοις αὐτοῦ καὶ ταῖς δυνάμεσιν ἐπὶ ἡμέρας ἑπτὰ* καὶ *ὕψωσεν* τοὺς γάμους Εσθηρ καὶ ἄφεσιν ἐποίησεν τοῖς ὑπὸ τὴν βασιλείαν αὐτοῦ.

ויעש המלך משתה גדול לכל־שריו
ועבדיו את משתה אסתר והנחה
למדינות עשה ויתן משאת כיד המלך

And the king celebrated the marriage of Esther in splendor, and he gave remission to all regions.

And the king gave a banquet for all his friends, and it lasted for seven days. And he raised up the marriage festivities of Esther, and he gave remission to those under his kingdom.

And the king gave a large banquet for all his princes and officials; the banquet of Esther. And he granted (a time of) rest to the provinces, and he gave gifts with royal hand.

19

ὁ δὲ Μαρδοχαῖος *ἐθεράπευεν* ἐν τῇ αὐλῇ.

ובהקבץ בתולות שנית ומרדכי ישב
בשער המלך

Then Mordecai was serving in the courtyard.

Now when the virgins were gathered together a second time, Mordecai was sitting by the gate of the king.

ἡ δὲ Εσθηρ οὐχ ὑπέδειξεν τὴν πατρίδα αὐτῆς· οὕτως γὰρ ἐνετείλατο αὐτῇ Μαρδοχαῖος, *φοβεῖσθαι τὸν θεὸν καὶ ποιεῖν τὰ προστάγματα αὐτοῦ*, καθὼς ἦν *μετ' αὐτοῦ· καὶ Εσθηρ οὐ μετήλλαξεν τὴν ἀγωγὴν αὐτῆς.*

20 אין אסתר מגדת מולדתה וְאֶת־עַמָּהּ
כאשר צוה עליה מרדכי ואת־מאמר
מרדכי אסתר עשׂה כאשר היתה
בְאָמְנָה אִתּוֹ

But Esther did not indicate her country, for thus had Mordecai charged her, fearing God and doing his commands, just as when she was with him. And Esther did not change her discipline.

Esther had not reported her ancestry or her people, just as Mordecai had put charge upon her. And the word of Mordecai Esther did, just as when she was in her upbringing by him.

Notes

Verse 7. With regard to the descriptive nomenclature used to introduce Esther, B uses two terms: παῖς and κοράσιον. The former is used in what could be a more technical sense, within the expression παῖς θρεπτή ('foster child'). M employs נערה, 'girl', which can be considered a parallel to B's κοράσιον. In A is found only the gender-neutral παῖς, 'child'.

Only in B is the name of Esther's father given (Αμίναδαβ). A notes nothing about the deaths of her parents, but M mentions this fact twice.

Esther is introduced by her Hebrew name, Hadassah (הדסה), only in M.

B includes the odd detail that Esther was to become Mordecai's wife ('he raised her into a wife for himself', ἐπαίδευσεν αὐτὴν ἑαυτῷ εἰς γυναῖκα). Many commentators have noted the incongruity of a betrothed relationship between Esther and Mordecai within the events of the story (Paton, *Esther*, p. 171; Moore, *Additions*, pp. 184, 186; Fox, *Character*, pp. 275-76). As has been variously suggested, it is likely that an error of some sort was made in the translation of the Greek at this point.

A uses the adverb πιστῶς to refer to Esther's upbringing by Mordecai. However, the text remains ambiguous concerning the object of his faithfulness or loyalty (Persian legal regulation? Jewish religious tradition? civic responsibility for orphaned children?). M alone suggests that Esther becomes like a daughter (לבת) to Mordecai.

Esther's beauty is accentuated in A through the term σφόδρα, and in M it is noted that she posesses a beautiful figure ('beautiful in form', יפת־תאר). B has only one, rather than two, descriptive phrases regarding her visual attractiveness.

Verse 8. A includes no mention of either a king's command nor a kingdom-wide gathering of women to the capital city.

B mentions that the women were taken to the city of Susa (εἰς Σουσαν τὴν πόλιν); M more specifically suggests the fortress or castle (בירה). In 8b, Esther herself is described in M as being taken to the palace ('the house of the king', בית המלך); this detail is found in 8a of A (τὸν οἶκον τοῦ βασιλέως), but not at all in B.

It is mentioned in A that the servant is pleased with Esther. He first 'sees' her (εἶδε), a possible allusion to her physical appearance. It is only in A that Esther is found better than all other women ('above all the women', ὑπὲρ πάσας τὰς γυναῖκας), though it is unclear against which other women Esther is being judged or by what criteria her superiority is being assessed. A's notation of Esther's pleasing the servant (ἤρεσεν) has parallels in v. 9 of B (ἤρεσεν) and M ('she was good ... in his eyes', ותיטב ... בעיניו).

Verse 9. A notes that Esther finds mercy (ἔλεον) as well as the favor (χάριν) expressed by both it and B. M's statement, 'and the girl was good in his eyes' (ותיטב הנערה בעיניו), is not quite the same; even though the verb יטב is in the qal, this first phrase suggests that Esther has been judged good by the servant rather than attaining approval by her own more direct action, as suggested by ἤρεσεν αὐτῷ (v. 8 in A, v. 9 in B) as well as the following phrases in B and M ('and she found favor before him', καὶ εὗρεν χάριν ἐνώπιον αὐτοῦ, ותשא חסד לפניו).

In A, Esther already has seven woman servants, and the eunuch of the king gives her more ('beyond the seven girls', ὑπὲρ τὰ ἑπτὰ κοράσια). It makes no mention of her being given ointments and portions as well.

M suggests that the place, status, or opinion of Esther and the servants within the palace is changed ('and he changed her (place?) and her girls to a good (one)', וישנה ואת־נערותיה לטוב). B less specifically reads that Esther was well-treated ('he treated her well', ἐχρήσατο αὐτῇ καλῶς).

The latter part of v. 9 in A, relating Esther's being taken to the king, best corresponds to vv. 16-17 in B and M. It will be compared with them in the notes to those verses.

Verse 10. Both B and M note Esther's concern with her people (τὸ γένος αὐτῆς, את־עמה). B's use of τὴν πατρίδα suggests concern with a political country as well as the ethnic group; M's use of מולדתה suggests instead her ancestral family or her progeny.

Verse 11. In M, Mordecai is concerned to know whether Esther is doing well ('to know the welfare of Esther', לדעת את־שלום אסתר), a detail not present in B.

B's use of ουμβήσεται is a middle, and not active, form of ουμβαίνω ('to happen, to befall, to come to pass'); however, it does not intimate to the extent that M's use of the niphal imperfect (יעשה, 'it will be done') does of Esther's experience in the women's quarters consisting of actions done upon her by others.

Verse 12. M suggests that this year-long process is some sort of official decree or regulation which applies to these women ('the regulation of the women', דת הנשים). The phrase 'girl by girl' (נערה ונערה) also lends to the idea of a more formal or ordered procedure.

In B, the purpose of this process is stated to be one of service or attendance (τῆς θεραπείας); in M, it is one of cleansing or purification (מרוקיהן—from מרק, 'to scour, polish, rub').

Verse 14. In A and M, the woman goes in to the king late in the day, in the evening (ἑσπέρα, ערב), and returns early the next day, in the morning (πρωΐ, בקר). In B, the woman goes in during the afternoon (δείλης), and returns at an unspecified time during the following day (ἡμέραν). She spends a longer time with the king.

A suggests that the woman is more passively involved in her traveling, employing middle indicative forms of the verbs εἰσάγω ('to lead in') and ἀπολύω ('to dismiss').

M describes the second group of women over which the eunuch has control as concubines (הפילגשים), thus providing a more sexually based reference.

Only M includes a double criteria for the woman returning to the king; she returns not only if he calls her by name, but also if he is pleased with her or has taken delight in her ('unless the king [was] pleased with her', כי אם־חפץ בה המלך).

Verse 15. M repeats (cf. v. 7) that Mordecai had raised Esther as a daughter ('he took [her] for himself as a daughter', לקח־לו לבת), in addition to stating her parentage, as also does B.

B uses the more specific and forceful ἐνετείλατο ('he commanded') for the eunuch's action towards his recommendation to Esther. M uses the more general יאמר ('he said'), which does not necessarily convey the same sense of power, though its semantic range does include the possibility of being interpreted in a similar way.

Verse 16. B expresses the movement of Esther to the king as being of her own accord and through her own power (εἰσῆλθεν, 'she went in'). The active voice is used. Both M and A use a passive voice instead: תלקח (niphal of לקח, 'to be taken') and εἰσήχθη (aorist passive of εἰσέχω, 'to be taken in') (v. 9 in A).

M notes that Esther is taken to the palace of the king (בית מלכותו) as well as to the king himself.

Verse 17. A notes that first Esther pleases the king immensely ('she pleased him very much', ἤρεσεν αὐτῷ σθόδρα) before he makes his choice (v. 9).

The king is shown to have differing actions and attitudes in the consideration of the women and in the choice of Esther. In A, his action is a logical, calculated choice based on studious and thorough examination (κατεμάνθανεν, 'he carefully considered'). B notes simply that the king prefers Esther (ἠράσθη, 'he chose'), without stating the reason for his choice. In M, the king instead chooses Esther for emotional reasons (ויאהב, 'and he loved').

M alone states that the king prefers Esther to all other women (מכל־הנשים), as well as to all the virgins. (This designation is not necessarily limited to only those girls [נערות] who had just been gathered, as Paton has suggested [*Esther*, p. 184].)

In A, Esther's splendid aspect and superiority is stressed (ἐφάνη ἐπιφανεστάτη, 'she appeared magnificent').

Both A and M name Esther's new crown with specific reference to its royal quality ('the diadem of royal power', τὸ διάδημα τῆς βασιλείας, כתר־מלכות). B does not describe her crown with similar regal terminology ('the women's diadem', τὸ διάδημα τὸ γυναικεῖον).

Only in M is there reference to Esther's replacement of Vashti ('and he made her reign instead of Vashti', וימליכה תחת ושתי).

Verse 19. M includes a plot detail of women being gathered for a second time ('and the virgins were gathered together a second [time]', ובהקבץ בתולות שנית), though nothing further is explained about this gathering nor its purpose in the text. Various possible explanations and textual emendations have been suggested by commentators to understand this somewhat puzzling verse (cf. Paton, *Esther*, pp. 186-88; Moore, *Esther,* pp. 29-30; Fox, *Character,* pp. 38, 276-77).

Verse 20. According to M, Esther does not report the identity of her people (עמה) in addition to the familial or native ties she does not identify in both it and B (מולדתה, πατρίδα).

M specifically recalls Esther's being raised by M ('her upbringing by him', אמנה אתו). B more vaguely suggests Esther's being with Mordecai ('she was with him', ἦν μετ' αὐτοῦ).

B includes significant and unique details at the end of this verse. It states that Esther is 'fearing God' (φοβεῖσθαι τὸν θεὸν) and 'doing his commands' (ποιεῖν τὰ προστάγματα αὐτοῦ). And it also notes that Esther does not change her lifestyle ('and Esther did not change her discipline', καὶ Εσθηρ οὐ μετήλλαξεν τὴν ἀγωγὴν αὐτῆς). However, the ambiguity in these phrases must be highlighted. It is not clear in the text whether Esther continues to do God's commands or Mordecai's commands. The third person masculine singular pronoun (αὐτοῦ) could legitimately refer to either. Similarly, it could also be understood that Esther retained her disciplined lifestyle from a time of being with God instead of with Mordecai (μετ' αὐτοῦ). And Esther's disciplined or instructed lifestyle (τὴν ἀγωγὴν αὐτῆς) could refer to her continuing to follow either Jewish legal traditions or the responsibilities and instruction of Mordecai's household.

Analysis
A Text. Esther is initially introduced to the reader by her exceptional beauty as well as her relationship to Mordecai. These two attributes are the only details about her first provided by the narrative. However, the process by which Esther is selected queen is not a beauty contest nor an elaborate procedure. The process gives the impression of being conducted rather quickly, including no kingdom-wide gathering of prospective

female candidates nor prolonged preparation with cosmetic substances. Women, including Esther, are acceptable for the king as they are, and do not need any augmentation or improvements to their natural selves. Moreover, there is no mention that those women who have had their experience with the king are returned to a separate dwelling. An air of equality is suggested.

Esther appears consistently to please people in this narrative. She meets with the pleasure of Bougaios immediately. His initial positive response is quite probably because of her beauty, which had just been mentioned. He sees her and is then reportedly pleased with her. The narrative states again that Esther wins his favor, and then twice that she also pleases Ahasuerus, to which he responds by choosing her. An identical phrase is used to express Esther's involvement first with Bougaios and then with the king. For each, she 'finds favor and mercy before him'. Such a repetition of her favored status is significant, in that this narrative is missing in vv. 7-9 many of the other details found in the other two versions.

Esther is portrayed with dependent status. In the beginning of this episode, her youth is stressed. She is introduced to the reader as a child, and she, as a girl, is contrasted with the women to whom Bougaois prefers her. In general, in the first two verses of this episode, the narrative tends to refer to her primarily in terms of her childhood or girlhood rather than by proper name. The male protagonists also assert their authority over her. After she wins Bougaios's favor, his first response is to quickly take charge over her. She is also a recipient of mercy from both him and Ahasuerus. Such terminology suggests a situation of inferiority, that of a person from a higher class bestowing compassion or pity upon a person of a lower rank. And Esther is portrayed as passive in their hands, in being led by others in to and out from the king.

Yet Esther exhibits a certain relative autonomy and freedom, even within her dependency. Throughout the selection process, she is not as much under the servants' daily watchful eyes and their recommendations as in the other two versions. Nor is she observed by Mordecai while she is in the court, though this detail also contributes to the picture of her isolation from family during this time.

In contrast to the other two texts, Esther's Jewishness is not important to this narrative, as there is no outright reference to it.[1] First

---

1. Dorothy finds Esther's not concealing her nationality when in the Persian court to accentuate her Jewishness in the A text ('Books', p. 92). But, in contrast, the

of all, Esther's relationship to her family is left ambiguous. This narrative does not state that her parents had died. And because there is no mention throughout that she concealed her Jewish ancestry, we are left to surmise that Esther was recognized as a Jew by the Persians of the court. Thus her ethnicity must not have been viewed as a hindrance to her excelling in the court and attaining the throne.

The reader is led to understand that Esther must be an outstanding person, superior to all others. She is first preferred by Bougaios not only over all the virgins but over all women in general. In making his choice, it is not explicitly stated that Ahasuerus bases his selection upon emotional affection, physical beauty, or whim, but upon what he discerns by careful consideration. And he also clearly finds her to be magnificent. As the only experience which he has had up to this point has been a night in bed, it is likely that it is Esther's sexual performance which causes him to view her as splendid above all others. It is also significant to note that the episode concludes with her being crowned and given royal power in this narrative. Unlike the other two narratives, this text does not conclude with a report of her obedience to Mordecai and/or God. The final view is of Esther in a position of royal splendor and authority, if not yet acting out that authority.

B Text. This narrative finds it important to include Esther's relationship within her family and her people. She is first introduced in connection with her father's familial line. Her father's name, Aminadab, is provided at this point only in this version. But from the start, Esther's position in Mordecai's household is likewise important. The narrative first names her as a foster child of Mordecai, though also being raised to become his wife. Thus, Esther's place within her patrilineal heritage is established from the start. Later in this episode she is portrayed as part of the Jewish nation as well as of her own people, and these two relationships comprise the pertinent information about her identity which she conceals from the Persian court.

The description of the selection process in this narrative implies a choice based upon more than mere sexual ability. The time of day when each woman is to go in to meet the king is during the afternoon, and she leaves his presence during the daytime of the following day. The woman

opposite conclusion is more likely. The fact that this text does not choose to mention Esther's Jewish identity at all, not reporting that she either conceals it or reveals it, suggests that this aspect of Esther's character is not important to the A text.

spends a longer time with the king than just the night suggested by the other two narratives. Staying only overnight suggests that the primary manner by which the king becomes acquainted with each woman is through sleeping with her. In contrast, in this narrative the reader may expect that the activities of the king and each woman would not be limited to sexual activity. Their longer time together might be expected to include meals, conversation, perhaps an evening's entertainment or a tour of the palace, as well as a sexual encounter during the night. In this more leisurely procedure, Artaxerxes is given a chance to get to know the women among whom he adjudicates. However, in this narrative, it is also unclear for what reasons Artaxerxes actually chooses Esther. It states only that he chooses her, but not why.

Esther is here obedient. This trait is first suggested when she takes the articles from Gai. The narrative states that he had commanded these things, and we are left to assume that he had actual command over other areas of Esther's life and actions as well. However, the most interesting aspect of her obedience is found in the narrative's statement at the conclusion of this episode. Esther's obedience to Mordecai's command is recounted, but also, in the same breath and with ambiguous terminology, her obedience to God's commands. Mordecai's authority over her is connected with God's authority. In one sense, it seems that the roles of God and Mordecai are combined for Esther; obedience to Mordecai is obedience to God. The Esther–Mordecai and Esther–God relationships are confused and thus fused.

We also see more minor details regarding the characterization of Esther exhibited by this narrative. In her choice not to reject what Gai has charged her to take in with her to the king, she shows diplomacy as well as obedience. It is good court strategy not to refuse a courtier's suggestion. And when she enters in to Artaxerxes, she goes of her own accord and is not led by others. Esther is shown to be somewhat less passive at this point and more in charge of her own actions.

M Text. Esther's familial ties and her status within her family and people are also significant aspects of her character in this narrative, as we see from the very first verse of the episode. Esther's Jewishness is integral to her identity, for the reader is introduced to her by her Hebrew name even before her Persian one. Immediately following this introduction, her status as an orphan is mentioned twice. We are then told of Esther's role within Mordecai's household, that of daughter. She has been transferred from being the daughter of Mordecai's uncle to being Mordecai's own daughter. Familial relationship and position are further emphasized throughout the entire episode. When the narrative reports her turn to go in to Ahasuerus, it reiterates that she was taken by Mordecai as his own daughter, and for the first time the name of Esther's birth father is provided. We also find that Esther acts as a part of the Jewish people as a whole. When the narrative mentions Esther's concealing of her identity, at both times it indicates that she did not reveal both her people and her lineage.[1] Esther's family connections remain strong throughout the events of this episode.

The first verse of the episode establishes her place as a member of Mordecai's household. However, this version highlights the transfer of households which Esther undergoes throughout the episode. In the very next verse we are specifically told that Esther is taken from Mordecai's household to the house of the king, the palace, as well as more generally to the capital city. And when Esther is taken in to Ahasuerus, it again indicates that she enters the royal house. Esther's rise to queenship thus also signifies a change in family household from that of Mordecai to that of Ahasuerus. However, at the end of this episode she is still strongly connected to Mordecai even within her new habitation. She follows Mordecai's commands in the same manner as she had when she was being raised by him as his daughter. But the reference to Mordecai's raising her and continuing in this relationship of parenting suggests that Esther still remains in a childlike position at this point in the story.

In this version, the selection of a new queen includes the most explicit aspect of sexuality, though all the narratives include the sexual element. Each woman spends little time with Ahasuerus, only overnight. Thus sexual activity is probably the most important aspect of his impression of her. The woman then goes to the servant who is entrusted with the care of the concubines. After their night with the king, it appears that the women then hold the status of concubine, or sexual paramour, in the palace. Two requirements are also given for Ahasuerus to summon back a woman: if he calls her name, or if she has given the king pleasure. Pleasure of a sexual nature would be anticipated from such a situation.

---

1.   The accumulation of all of these details about Esther's family and people draws into question Moore's opinion that Esther's family ties are not important in this scene. He states that 'apart from establishing Esther as Mordecai's cousin, the author is not concerned with her genealogical lines; rather it is the lines of her face and figure (v. 7) that are most important' (*Esther*, p. 26).

We can assume that Esther's own experience with Ahasuerus was with the same sexual intent. However, this narrative also more directly states why he chooses her. Here his selection is based on emotion. Ahasuerus loves Esther, and then we find that he has been caused to feel a sort of devotion or kindness for her as well. But his choice of Esther for reason of affection suggests a lesser emphasis upon her own role in ascending to the throne. Esther appears somewhat more passive in attaining her favored status.[1] She first is described not as pleasing Hegei (which would hint at a certain degree of activity on her part) but as being deemed good by him. Only secondarily are we told that she actively attains his favor. Then Esther is assessed as superior by Ahasuerus primarily because of his emotional response to her, a response over which she would not have had much control.

Finally, Esther's status and relationship with other women is more often expressed. First, Hegei shows concern for her position among the women in the palace. He changes things around in some manner, most likely her social status or position, so that all would go well for her. Then when the narrative reports Ahasuerus's selection of her, it states that he found her superior to two categories of women in the kingdom, all the virgins and all the women. And there is also a reference to Esther's relationship to Vashti. She is contrasted with the former queen when taking her place, a comparison which expresses a hope that Esther would turn out to be a different type of queen than was Vashti. Thus, this narrative determines that Esther's place in Persia is not only as its queen, but also as superior to all its women.

Episode 2 (4.4-17)

The portion of the story between Esther's coronation and this episode relates the actions of Mordecai, Haman, and the king. These events include Mordecai's hearing of the eunuchs' plot against the king (in the B and M texts), Haman's promotion, Mordecai's refusal to bow down before Haman, Haman's proposal to destroy the Jews and his casting of lots, the king's approval of the plan, Haman's writing and sending out an announcement of the edict as well as a verbatim copy of the decree (in the A and B texts), and the Jews' response of confusion and

---

1. Though Esther does exhibit a certain amount of passivity in this first episode, it is not quite to the degree of the pliancy and docility proposed by Fox (*Character*, pp. 37, 197-98).

mourning. Out of the people's grief, Mordecai then consults with the queen Esther. This episode relates their conversation. Esther hears of what Haman has done and is distressed. She sends clothes to Mordecai, but he will not remove his garments of lamentation. Speaking through servants who are sent back and forth with messages, Mordecai provides Esther with more complete information of what had happened and how the Jews outside the court are responding. He requests that she go to the king in an attempt to change the situation. She reminds him of the king's rule against coming to him without first being called, but Mordecai continues to urge her. Esther decides to attempt an approach, requesting all the Jews to pray or fast for her success. The episode concludes with Mordecai carrying out Esther's commands.

The M text is the longest for this section. The B text is slightly shorter than the M text, not exhibiting the material represented by the M text's v. 6, but including details of v. 8 not appearing in the M text. In general, the B and M texts are fairly similar with regard to the primary events of the plot. The A text is shorter than both for this episode, not providing the details given by vv. 5-8a and 12 of the other two. The primary way in which it differs significantly is in not indicating that Mordecai tells Esther specifically of Haman's promise nor that he sends her a copy of the official edict.

Text

καὶ *ἐκάλεσεν* εὐνοῦχον *ἕνα* καὶ *ἀπέστειλε πρὸς Εσθηρ*, καὶ εἶπεν ἡ βασιλίσσα Περλέλεσθε τὸν σάκκον καὶ *εἰσαγάγετε αὐτόν·* ὃς δὲ οὐκ *ἤθελεν*

καὶ εἰσῆλθον αἱ ἄβραι καὶ οἱ εὐνοῦχοι τῆς βασιλίσσης καὶ ἀνήγγειλαν αὐτῇ, καὶ ἐταράχθη *ἀκούσασα τὸ γεγονὸς* καὶ ἀπέστειλεν στολίσαι τὸν Μαρδοχαῖον καὶ ἀφελέσθαι αὐτοῦ τὸν σάκκον, ὁ δὲ οὐκ *ἐπείσθη*.

ותבואינה נערות אסתר וסריסיה ויגידו   4
לה ותתחלחל המלכה <u>מאד</u> ותשלח בגדים
להלביש את־מרדכי ולהסיר שׂקו מעליו
ולא <u>קבל</u>

And he called a certain eunuch and sent to Esther. And the queen said, 'Remove the sackcloth and bring him in.' But he was not willing.

And the servants and the eunuchs of the queen came in and brought report to her, and she was troubled by what she heard had happened. And she sent clothes to Mordecai, so to take off the sackcloth from him, but he was not persuaded.

And when the girls of Esther and her eunuchs came in and reported to her, the queen was greatly anguished. And she sent garments to clothe Mordecai, to take his sackcloth off from upon him. But he would not accept (them).

ἡ δὲ Εσθηρ
προσεκαλέσατο
Αχραθαῖον <u>τὸν εὐνοῦχον</u>
<u>αὐτῆς</u>, ὃς παρειστήκει
αὐτῃ, καὶ <u>ἀπέστειλεν</u>
μαθεῖν αὐτῇ παρὰ τοῦ
Μαρδοχαίου <u>τὸ ἀκριβές</u>.

ותקרא אסתר להתך <u>מסריסי המלך</u> 5
אשר העמיד לפניה <u>תצוהו</u> על־מרדכי
לדעת <u>מה־זה ועל־מה־זה</u>

Then Esther summoned Hachratheus, her eunuch who stood before her. And sent (him) to learn for her accurate information from Mordecai.	And Esther called to Hathach, from the eunuchs of the king, who stood before her. And she commanded him to Mordecai, to learn what this was and on account of what this was.

ויצא התך אל־מרדכי אל־רחוב 6
העיר אשר לפני שער־המלך

And Hathach went out to Mordecai, to the open plaza of the city, which was in front of the gate of the king.

ὁ δὲ Μαρδοχαῖος
ὑπέδειξεν αὐτῷ τὸ
γεγονὸς <u>καὶ τὴν</u>
<u>ἐπαγγελίαν</u>, ἣν
ἐπηγγειλατο Αμαν τῷ
Βασιλεῖ εἰς τὴν γάζαν
<u>ταλάντων μυρίων</u>, ἵνα
<u>ἀπολέσῃ</u> τοὺς Ιουδαίους.

ויגד־לו מרדכי את <u>כל־</u>אשר קרהו ואת 7
<u>פרשת הכסף</u> אשר אמר המן לשקול על־
גנזי המלך ביהודיים <u>לאבדם</u>

Then Mordecai indicated to him what happened and the promise, that Haman had promised ten thousand talents to the king, into the treasury, that he might destroy the Jews.	And Mordecai indicated to him all that had happened to him and the exact amount of silver which Haman had promised to pay into the treasury to the king for the Jews, to destroy them.

ἀλλ' εἶπεν <u>Οὕτως ἐρεῖτε</u>
<u>αὐτῇ</u> Μὴ <u>ἀποστρέψῃς τοῦ</u>
<u>εἰσελθεῖν πρὸς τὸν</u>
<u>βασιλέα</u> καὶ
<u>κολακεῦσαι</u> τὸ
πρόσωπον αὐτοῦ ὑπὲρ
<u>ἐμοῦ</u> καὶ τοῦ λαοῦ
μνησθεῖσα ἡμερῶν
ταπεινώσεώς σου ὧν
ἐτράφης ἐν τῇ χειρί μου.
ὅτι Αμαν ὁ δευτερεύων
λελάληκε τῷ βασιλεῖ
καθ' ἡμων εἰς θάνατον.

καὶ τὸ ἀντίγραφον τὸ ἐν
Σούσοις ἐκτεθὲν ὑπὲρ
τοῦ ἀπολέσθαι αὐτοὺς
ἔδωκεν αὐτῷ δεῖξαι τῇ
Εσθηρ καὶ <u>εἶπεν αὐτῷ</u>
ἐντείλασθαι αὐτῇ
εἰσελθούσῃ
παραιτήσασθαι τὸν
βασιλέα καὶ <u>ἀξιῶσαι</u>
<u>αὐτὸν</u> περὶ τοῦ λαοῦ
μνησθεῖσα ἡμερῶν
ταπεινώσεώς σου ὡς
ἐτράφης ἐν χειρί μου,

ואת־פתשגן כתב־הדת אשר־נתן בשושן
להשמידם נתן לו להראות את־אסתר
<u>ולהגיד לה</u> ולצוות עליה לבוא אל־
המלך <u>להתחנן</u>־לו ולבקש מלפניו על־
עמה

ἐπικαλεσαμένη <u>οὖν</u> τὸν
<u>θεὸν</u> λάλησον περὶ ἡμῶν
τῷ βασιλεῖ καὶ ῥῦσαι
ἡμᾶς ἐκ θανάτου.

διότι Αμαν ὁ δευτερεύων
<u>τῷ βασιλεῖ</u> ἐλάλησεν
καθ' ἡμῶν εἰς θάνατον·
ἐπικάλεσαι τὸν <u>κύριον</u>,
<u>καὶ</u> λάλησον· τῷ
βασιλεῖ περὶ ἡμῶν καὶ
ῥῦσαι ἡμᾶς ἐκ θανάτου.

8

But he said, 'Thus you
will say to her, "Do not
turn away from going in to
the king to flatter before
him, concerning me and the
people. Remember the days
of your low estate, being
supported by my hand. For
Haman, who is second, has
spoken to the king against
us for death. Therefore,
calling upon God,
speaking concerning us to
the king, then save us from
death."'

And an official copy of
what was declared forth in
Susa about destroying
them, he gave to him, to
show to Esther. And he
told him to command her
that she might go in to
entreat the king and to
honor him, with regard to
the people. 'Remember the
days of your low estate,
being supported by my
hand. For Haman, the
second to the king, spoke
against us for death.
Calling upon the Lord, and
speaking to the king
concerning us, then save us
from death.'

And a copy of the written decree,
which was given in Susa to
annihilate them, he gave to him, to
show to Esther and to inform her,
and to command her to go in the
the king to implore him and to
make request in his presence on
account of her people.

καὶ ἀπήγγειλεν αὐτῇ
<u>τὴν ὀδύνην τοῦ Ισραηλ</u>

εἰσελθὼν δὲ ὁ
Αχραθαῖος ἐλάλησεν
αὐτῇ <u>πάντας</u> τοὺς
λόγους τούτους.

ויבוא התך ויגד לאסתר את דברי 9
<u>מרדכי</u>

And he proclaimed to her
the sorrow of Israel.

So Hachratheus went in;
he told her all of these
words.

And Hathach went and told to
Esther the words of Mordecai.

καὶ <u>ἀπέστειλεν</u> <u>αὐτῷ</u>
κατὰ τάδε λέγουσα

εἶπεν δὲ Εσθηρ πρὸς
Αχραθαῖον Πορεύθητι
πρὸς Μαρδοχαῖον <u>καὶ</u>
<u>εἶπον</u>

ותאמר אסתר להתך <u>ותצוהו</u> אל־ 10
מרדכי

And she sent to him; thus
she said:

And Esther said to
Hachratheus, 'Go to
Mordecai and say,

And Esther spoke to Hathach and
she commanded him to Mordecai:

Σὺ γινώσκεις <u>παρὰ</u>
<u>πάντας</u> ὅτι ὃς <u>ἂν</u>
εἰσέλθῃ πρὸς τὸν
βασιλέα ἄκλητος, ᾧ οὐκ
ἐκτενεῖ τὴν ῥάβδον
<u>αὐτοῦ</u> τὴν χρυσῆν,
θανάτου ἔνοχος ἔσται.

ὅτι <u>Τὰ ἔθνη πάντα τῆς</u>
<u>βασιλείας</u> γινώσκει ὅτι
πᾶς ἄνθρωπος ἢ γυνή, ὃς
εἰσελεύσεται πρὸς τὸν
βασιλέα εἰς τὴν αὐλὴν
τὴν ἐσωτέραν ἄκλητος,
<u>οὐκ ἔστιν αὐτῷ</u>

<u>כל־עבדי המלך ועם־מדינות המלך</u>
יודעים אשר כל־איש ואשה אשר יבוא־
אל־המלך אל־החצר הפנימית אשר
לא־יקרא <u>אחת דתו</u> להמית לבד
מאשר יושיט־לו המלך את־שרביט הזהב
<u>וחיה</u> ואני לא נקראתי לבוא אל־המלך
זה שלושים יום

καὶ ἐγὼ οὐ κέκλημαι πρὸς αὐτόν, ἡμέραι εἰσὶ τριάκοντα· *καὶ πῶς εἰσελεύσομαι νῦν ἄκλητος οὖσα.*

σωτηρία· πλὴν ᾧ ἐκτείνει ὁ βασιλεὺς τὴν χρυσῆν ῥάβδον, *οὗτος σωθήσεται.* κἀγὼ οὐ κέκλημαι εἰσελθεῖν πρὸς τὸν βασιλέα, εἰσὶν αὗται ἡμέραι τριάκοντα.

11

'You know, like everyone, that one who would go in to the king uncalled, if he does not extend his golden rod, will be subjected to death. And I myself have not been called to him; it is thirty days. And how will I go in now, being uncalled?'

that, "Every nation of the kingdom knows that any man or woman who will go in to the king, to the inner court, uncalled, there is no salvation to that one—except the one to whom the king extends the golden rod, that one will be saved. And I myself have not been called to go in to the king; it is these thirty days."'

'All the servants of the king and the people of the provinces of the king know that any man or woman who will go in to the king, to the inner court, who is not called—his decree is unilateral, to be killed. Only the one to whom the king extends the golden sceptre will live. And I myself have not been called to go in to the king these thirty days.'

καὶ ἀπήγγειλεν *Αχραθαῖος* Μαρδοχαίῳ *πάντας* τοὺς λόγους Εσθηρ.

ויגידו למרדכי את דברי אסתר

12

And Hachratheus reported to Mordecai all the words of Esther.

And they reported to Mordecai the words of Esther.

καὶ *ἀπέστειλε* πρὸς αὐτὴν Μαρδοχαῖος καὶ εἶπεν αὐτῇ

καὶ εἶπεν Μαρδοχαῖος *πρὸς Αχραθαῖον Πορεύθητι καὶ εἶπον αὐτῇ* Εσθηρ, μὴ εἴπῃς σεαυτῇ ὅτι σωθήσῃ *μόνη ἐν τῇ βασιλείᾳ* παρὰ πάντας τοὺς Ιουδαίους·

ויאמר מרדכי להשיב אל־אסתר אל־
תדמי בנפשך להמלט בית־המלך מכל־
היהודים

13

And Mordecai sent to her and said to her,

And Mordecai said to Hachratheus, 'Go and say to her, "Esther, do not say to yourself that you will be saved, remaining in the kingdom, out of all the Jews.

And Mordecai said, to return to Esther, 'Do not think to yourself to be delivered (in) the house of the king more than any of the Jews.

Ἐὰν *ὑπερδῇς τὸ ἔθνος*
σου τοῦ μὴ βοηθῆσαι
αὐτοῖς, ἀλλ' ὁ θεὸς ἔσται
αὐτοῖς βοηθὸς καὶ
σωτηρία, σύ δὲ καὶ ὁ
οἶκος τοῦ πατρός σου
ἀπολεῖσθε· καὶ τίς οἶδεν
εἰ εἰς τὸν καιρὸν τοῦτον
ἐβασίλευσας;

ὡς ὅτι ἐὰν *παρακούσῃς*
ἐν τούτῳ τῷ καιρῷ,
ἄλλοθεν βοήθεια καὶ
σκέπη ἔσται τοῖς
Ἰουδαίοις, σὺ δὲ καὶ ὁ
οἶκος τοῦ πατρός σου
ἀπολεῖσθε· καὶ τίς οἶδεν
εἰ εἰς τὸν καιρὸν τοῦτον
ἐβασίλευσας;

כי אם ‏_החרש תחרישי_‏ בעת הזאת רוח 14
והצלה ‏_יעמוד_‏ ליהודים ממקום אחר ואת
ובית־אביך תאבדו ומי יודע אם־לעת
כזאת הגעת למלכות

'If you disregard your country, not to help them, then God will be to them help and salvation. But you and the house of your father will be destroyed. And who knows if for this time you have ruled.'

Thus if you fail to listen at this time, from another place help and protection will be for the Jews, but you and the house of your father will be destroyed. And who knows if for this time you have ruled."'

For if you indeed hold to silence at this time, relief and salvation will arise for the Jews from another place, but you and the house of your father will die. And who knows if for a time such as this you have attained royal authority'.

καὶ ἀπέστειλεν ἡ
βασίλισσα λέγουσα

καὶ ἐξαπέστειλεν Εσθηρ
τὸν ἥκοντα πρὸς αὐτὴν
πρὸς Μαρδοχαῖον
λέγουσα

ותאמר אסתר ‏_להשיב_‏ אל־מרדכי 15

And the queen sent, saying,

And Esther sent forth the one who had come to her, to Mordecai, saying,

And Esther said, to return to Mordecai,

Παραγγείλατε
θεραπείαν καὶ δεήθητε
τοῦ θεοῦ ἐκτενῶς κἀγὼ
δὲ καὶ τὰ κοράσιά μου
ποιήσομεν οὕτως, καὶ
εἰσελεύσομαι πρὸς τὸν
βασιλέα *ἄκλητος*, εἰ
δέοι καὶ ἀποθανεῖν με.

βαδίσας ἐκκλησίασον
τοὺς Ἰουδαίους τοὺς ἐν
Σούσοις καὶ νηστεύσατε
ἐπ' ἐμοὶ καὶ μὴ φάγητε
μηδὲ πίητε ἐπὶ ἡμέρας
τρεῖς νύκτα καὶ ἡμέραν·
κἀγὼ δὲ καὶ *αἱ ἄβραι*
μου ἀσιτήσομεν, καὶ τότε
εἰσελεύσομαι πρὸς τὸν
Βασιλέά παρὰ τὸν
νόμον, ἐὰν καὶ
ἀπολέσθαι με ᾖ.

לך כנוס את־כל־היהודים ‏_הנמצאים_‏ 16
בשושן וצומו עלי ואל־תאכלו ואל־תשתו
שלשת ימים לילה ויום גם־אני ונערתי
אצום כן ובכן אבוא אל־המלך אשר לא־
כדת וכאשר אבדתי אבדתי

'Command a service and earnestly beseech God. And I also and my girls will do so. And I will go in to the king uncalled, if it is necessary for me to die'.

'To proceed, summon forth the Jews in Susa, and fast on behalf of me, and do not eat nor drink during the day for three nights and days. And I also and my servants will abstain from food. And after that I will go in to the king, contrary to the law, even if I am destroyed.'

'Go, assemble all the Jews who are found in Susa, and fast for me, and do not eat and drink (for) three days, night and day. And I also will fast thus, and my girls. And after this I will go in to the king, which is not according to decree. And when I die, I die.'

καὶ ἐποίησεν οὕτως Μαρδοχαῖος.	Καὶ βαδίσας Μαρδοχαῖος ἐποίησεν ὅσα ἐνετείλατο αὐτῷ Εσθηρ.	‏17 ויעבר מרדכי ויעש כֹּל אשר־צוּתה‎ ‏עליו אסתּר‎
And Mordecai did thus.	And going, Mordecai did that which Esther had commanded to him.	And Mordecai went and did according to all which Esther had commanded to him.

Notes

Verse 4. A represents Mordecai as the initiator of the communication between Esther and Mordecai; it is he who first sends a eunuch to tell Esther of the events which have transpired. In M and B, Esther is the one who acts first, by sending clothes to Mordecai. Her eunuchs and female servants are not necessarily sent to her by him, but just come by to tell her the news.

M uses a more general term נערות ('girls, damsels, maids') to speak of Esther's attendants, in contrast to the more specific and rare term αἱ ἄβραι ('favored slaves, female servants') of B, which makes more clear their status as servants. A does not include mention of Esther as having such an entourage of attendants.

In B and M, Esther's emotions are presented. B notes her general anxiety ('and she was troubled', καὶ ἐταράχθη), but M's adverb מאד intensifies its description. A does not attribute any emotional reaction to her.

Only B states the reason for Esther's response; she is disturbed 'by what she heard had happened' (ἀκούσασα τὸ γεγονὸς). However, even this additional phrase leaves it ambiguous as to exactly what of that which had occurred upsets her. (There is no indication whatever in the text that Esther is upset at Mordecai's sackcloth, as Moore suggests [*Esther*, p. 48]. Rather, B presents her as disturbed by the events in general. It is most likely that she asks Mordecai to put on acceptable clothes in order to enter the palace and speak with her face to face, as is stated more clearly by A.) This notation also has the effect of rendering Esther as seeming more removed from the action, highlighting that she herself is not experiencing the events first hand but only hearing about them from afar.

A portrays Esther as more authoritative and vocal. She does not merely send articles in silence but speaks directly. She is also more directive, commanding Mordecai (presumably through the eunuch) to take off (περιέλεσθε) his sackcloth and come in (εἰσαγάγετε) with imperative verbs (though, oddly, in the plural). Only in A does Esther explicitly desire direct communication with Mordecai, in requesting that he come in to her in the palace, presumably to discuss the situation at hand.

In A, Esther offers no gift of clothing to Mordecai. She does not try to take care of him, but expects him to find his own clothing that will make him presentable for entrance into the palace.

All three narratives provide a different response of Mordecai to Esther's actions. A notes that he is not willing or inclined (οὐκ ἤθελεν), but leaves it ambiguous whether this attitude is a response to Esther's command that he remove the sackcloth, be brought into the palace, or both. B states that Mordecai is not convinced (οὐκ ἐπείσθη), and thus suggests that Esther had tried to get him to act with logical argumentation. M states that Mordecai would not take or accept (לֹא קִבֵּל), presumably Esther's offer of clothing.

Verse 5. In B, it is specifically Esther's own servant (τὸν εὐνοῦχον αὐτῆς, 'her eunuch') whom she calls, but in M it is one of the king's servants (מִסָּרִיסֵי הַמֶּלֶךְ, 'from the eunuchs of the king').

M presents Esther as somewhat more authoritative than does B. She orders or commands Mordecai (תְּצַוֵּהוּ) through the servant, rather than merely sending him out (ἀπέστειλεν).

In M, Esther dictates more explicitly what type of information she needs from Mordecai (מַה־זֶּה וְעַל־מַה־זֶּה, 'what this [is] and on account of what this [is]'). In B, she instead stresses that it must be accurate (τὸ ἀκριβές).

Verse 6. This verse is represented only by M. The additional details it provides have the effect of showing Esther's authority, through demonstrating the eunuch's implementation of her command and emphasizing Mordecai's official position in the court as one who sits at the king's gate. It also highlights the physical distance between Esther and Mordecai (as noted also by Fox, *Character*, p. 59).

Verse 8. B's version of this verse is the most complete, for it combines elements unique to M (Mordecai's request of the eunuch) and to A (a direct quotation of what Mordecai wants to be said to Esther). The correspondence between the last part of the quotation in A and B is almost exact.

In A, the eunuch does not show Esther a copy of Haman's decree, nor is it explicitly stated that Mordecai commands (ἐντείλασθαι and לצוות, in B and M) her.

M shows Esther's actions to be more independent and autonomous. It does not include Mordecai's reminder to Esther about being raised by him and her former low social status as an orphan, the death decreed for the Jews, or reliance upon God. Here Esther does not so much choose to act because of any past obligation she feels towards Mordecai, nor is she dependent upon God in her actions. There is less emphasis on Mordecai's persuading Esther and Esther's expected obedience to him.

B assumes Esther's intelligence. Whereas in M the eunuch is to do two actions, to show a copy of the decree to her (להראות את־אסתר) and then to explain it to her (ולהגיד), in B the eunuch is to do only one corresponding action, to show Esther the decree (δεῖξαι τῇ Εσθηρ). It is assumed that, with reading the decree, Esther will understand it by herself and not need the eunuch's announcement of its contents or its effects upon the Jews.

Differing actions on the part of Esther towards the king are given. In M, the emphasis is upon her asking something from the king; two verbs of request are used (hithpael of חנן, 'to seek or implore favor', and the piel of בקשׁ, 'to seek, request'). In B, Esther is also to ask (παραιτέομαι, 'to entreat, beg off'), but also to honor (ἀξιῶσαι) the king. (The verb ἀξιόω has a primary meaning of 'to deem worthy, esteem, honor', though it can also refer simply to asking.) And in A, Esther is to make her request in a manner which flatters him (κολακεύω, 'to flatter, be a flatterer').

A and B, by their grammatical structure, stress Esther's action of delivering the people over her actions of calling upon God and speaking to the king. In A, the final phrase has a sequence of three verbs, two participles (ἐπικαλεσαμένη, 'invoking, calling upon', and λάλησον, 'speaking') followed by an active imperative (ῥῦσαι, 'rescue, save, deliver'). These participles act here in a circumstantial manner. As Esther calls upon God and speaks to the king, these two actions will be necessary to meet the objective of what is specified by the finite verb, that is, to save the people. B uses a similar sequence of the same verbs, the only difference being the infinitive ἐπικάλεσαι rather than the first participle. (That A's use of ἐπικαλέω is in the middle voice and B's use of it is in the active voice does not indicate a significant difference in the meaning of this verse, as the active and middle voices of λἐπικαλέω render similar meanings.)

In M, Esther is presented more as a part of the Jewish population. She is to act for 'her people' (עמה), not just 'the people' in general (τοῦ λαοῦ in A and B).

Verse 9. Only in A does this verse give new information. B and M merely report that Mordecai's request is carried out.

In A, it is the grief and pain of the Jews ('the sorrow of Israel', τὴν ὀδύνην τοῦ Ἰσραηλ) that the eunuch tells Esther after he has related Mordecai's request (v. 8). Mordecai expects Esther's decision of whether to risk going in to the king to be based upon the fact that the Jews are grieving in addition to the reasons he gave in the previous verse.

M states that it is explicitly what Mordecai said ('the words of Mordecai', דברי מרדכי) which the eunuch tells Esther. The reference to Mordecai here emphasizes his command to her and suggests that obedience to Mordecai's speech is what will influence her to decide to act. In B, Esther is told a more general announcement of everything that has happened ('all of these words', πάντας τοὺς λόγους τούτους), without reference to Mordecai himself.

Verse 10. In B, Esther appears somewhat more directive and commanding to the servant. Only B quotes Esther's direct speech to him, and she uses the imperative forms of the two verbs (πορεύθητι, 'go' and εἶπον, 'say').

In M, it is ambiguous whether Esther commands Hathach or 'it' (referring to what she says in the following verse) to Mordecai. The third person masculine singular suffix of תצוהו ('she commanded it/him') could refer to either. It is not clear whether this statement expresses Esther's authority over her servant or over Mordecai.

Verse 11. M stresses significantly more than A and somewhat more than B that absolutely everyone knows of this rule. By the phrase כל־עבדי המלך ועם־מדינות המלך ('all the servants of the king and the people of the provinces of the king'), Esther includes categories of people both inside and outside the court system. B speaks only of the outside realm, the nations within the kingdom (τὰ ἔθνη πάντα τῆς βασιλείας), and A refers only generally to all people (πάντας).

In A alone, Mordecai himself is explicitly addressed. By beginning her statement with a direct reference to what Mordecai knows of the procedure in the court (Σὺ γινώσκεις, 'you know...'), Esther places responsibility upon Mordecai for the result of her actions.

In B and M, the hypothetical individual who dares to disregard the king's rule goes in to two places: to the king (πρὸς τὸν βασιλέα, אֶל־הַמֶּלֶךְ) and to the inner court (εἰς τὴν αὐλὴν, אֶל־הֶחָצֵר הַפְּנִימִית). In A, this person goes to only one place, just in to the king (πρὸς τὸν βασιλέα), without any certain place specified.

In B, Esther speaks in terms of salvation rather than of death. She first describes no deliverance for the one who would disobey ('there is no salvation to that one', οὐκ ἔστιν αὐτῷ σωτηρία) and then salvation if the king decides to extend the sceptre ('that one will be saved', οὗτος σωθήσεται).

M puts this procedure in the realm of government policy, as an actual law ('his decree', דָּתוֹ).

A alone has the final rhetorical question to conclude Esther's message to Mordecai. It stresses the improbable nature of Esther's faring well when going to the king. And the repetition in her question of her uncalled (ἄκλητος) status emphasizes that she is no longer the favored one of the king.

Verse 12. The occurrence in M of the verb form יַגִּידוּ, a plural, is peculiar here, as there has been mention of only the one eunuch, Hathach, who has been travelling between Esther and Mordecai. It cannot logically refer back to the girls and the eunuchs of v. 4. BHS notes that it has been proposed that the verb should be read as a singular form (יַגֵּד).

This is the final time that M explicitly refers to an emissary or intermediary in Esther and Mordecai's conversation or to the action of sending. From now on the two appear to speak more directly to each other. Moore is correct in noting that their direct address after this point heightens the drama of the scene (*Esther*, p. 49).

Verse 13. There is a differing sense of distance between Esther and Mordecai in this verse. In B, Esther seems quite distanced from Mordecai. She is only the recipient of his commands to Hachratheus to go and to speak to her (although addressing her by her proper name, through the servant, tends to temper this feeling of distance a bit). In M, there is the sense that Mordecai is speaking more directly to Esther, without the inclusion of the servant in the action. But A makes them appear very close, as if they were conversing normally, especially by means of the second phrase εἶπεν αὐτῇ, 'he said to her'.

In M and B, Esther is expected to be passive. It is suggested not that she will act to save herself but that she will be delivered by an outside agency. The terminology used is the niphal of מלט, which can have a passive sense in later Hebrew (for instance, cf. a similar usage in Dan. 12.1), and the passive voice of σώζω.

M emphasizes Esther's high position in the house of the king, which would cause her to be singled out from the overall destruction of Jews. B really gives no reason why Esther might think to be treated differently. And A's lack of this prohibition of Mordecai does not make Esther appear to be one who expects that she can avoid the coming destruction.

Verse 14. In A, Mordecai's speech suggests that Esther's decision is national in scope. If she chooses not to act, in addition to herself being killed, she will actually be a traitor to her people ('to disregard your country', ὑπερίδῃς τὸ ἔθνος σου). Also here she is warned to avoid two things—not considering her country and not helping it (τοῦ μὴ βοηθῆσαι). M and B each only mention one thing which she is not to do (not listening in B and not speaking in M). Neither of them directly consider Esther to be a possible helper of the people.

In B, Esther's decision lies within the realm of obedience to Mordecai. He warns her not to fail to pay attention to the commands and arguments he has presented ('if you hear amiss' or 'if you neglect to obey', ἐὰν παρακούσῃς). M instead presents Esther's actual act of speaking as the key to the Jews' salvation; what is crucial now is that she not keep silent ('if you hold to silence', אם־החרש תחרישי).

In A, Esther's connection to the people is emphasized in that they are not just referred to as Jews but specifically as her people.

God is mentioned only in A, and in a manner which makes God's action appear to be an alternative to salvation through Esther's hand. In B and M, Esther's action at this time is not seen in terms of God at all. The ambiguity of the phrase 'another place' (ἄλλοθεν, מקום אחר) makes the stress of Mordecai's message fall upon the indestructability of the Jewish people rather than upon Esther's response to what is suggested to be God's own desire for Esther's action of salvation.

Verse 15. M suggests the reciprocal actions of Esther and Mordecai. The wording of this verse is exactly parallel to that of v. 13a, where

Mordecai sends to Esther. The parallel makes these two characters appear on equal terms by this point in their conversation.

This verse represents a turning point in the A narrative. Esther is not referred to by personal name, but by her rank as queen. She is now acting with regal authority. There is also no mention of who, what, or to whom the queen sends (ἀπέστειλεν), just that she sends out her word. Her speaking is no longer part of a private conversation between just her and Mordecai, in the manner introduced by vv. 10 and 13, but a message that Esther, from her position as queen, sends out generally to all the Jews.

Verse 16. In A, Esther is no longer working primarily through Mordecai to carry out her desires. She begins by speaking directly to the people herself, as indicated by the plural imperatives παραγγείλατε ('[you all] command') and δεήθητε ('[you all] beseech'). In B and M, the first two verbs are singular (βαδίσας and εκκλησίασον, לך and כנוס). In them Esther addresses all the people only when she later speaks of fasting, switching over to plural imperatives at that time in her announcement (νηστεύσατε, צומו).

A shows Esther to be more concerned with worship and prayer than doing pious works. Her command to the people is for them to hold a worship service (θεραπείαν) and to pray (δεήθητε). Also, God is again referred to only by A. This command is in contrast to B and M, in which Esther instead requests everyone to fast and there is no explicit mention of God.

A again uses the term ἄκλητος, 'uncalled', to describe Esther (cf. v. 11, where this adjective was earlier used twice).

B again uses αἱ ἄβραι to refer to Esther's attendants (cf. v. 4).

A portrays Esther as not so much concerned with herself or her own survival. It does this in two ways. First, in contrast to M and B, Esther here does not ask the Jewish people to fast, worship, or pray especially for her own sake. And second, Esther's final phrase, 'if it is necessary for me to die' (εἰ δέοι καὶ ἀποθανεῖν) suggests her willingness to sacrifice herself even more than do B and M. With the use of δέοι, 'it is necessary', A gives the impression that it is a higher good for which Esther finds it proper and needful to give up her own life.

In M, the final phrase, 'and when I die, I die' (וכאשר אבדתי אבדתי) gives more the sense of passive resignation. (The conjunction כאשר can have a temporal sense, which which we might see as fitting best in this instance, as well as the conditional sense with which the term has been more commonly translated.) It appears here that Esther already accepts her death as a foregone conclusion to her decision to go in to the king. She appears even less hopeful of escaping death than Paton suggests (*Esther*, p. 226).

B's final phrase depicts the violence Esther anticipates by means of the verb ἀπολέσθαι, 'to be destroyed, brought to naught'. Earlier in this episode, the verb ἀπόλλυμι is also used to describe how the Jews would be destroyed under Haman's plan (vv. 7, 8) and that Esther and her family would be destroyed if she chose not to go in to entreat the king (v. 14). B's repetition of this verb suggests that violent death and destruction will come to all the Jews, Esther included, regardless of what she or they do.

Verse 17. A is quite brief. It does not tell what it is that Mordecai does, nor does it express Esther's authority over him.

In A, as Esther did not specifically tell Mordecai to lead the Jews in any way (v. 16), he here acts as only a representative of the people and not as their leader (as is the case in B and M). He, as we expect all other individual Jews to do, is following Esther's orders for the Jewish community as a whole.

Analysis

A Text. Esther exhibits a good deal of authority in this narrative, evidenced particularly by her commanding presence. She holds authority over the Jews and, to a certain extent, over Mordecai as well. At the beginning of this episode, Mordecai does initiate their conversation by sending a eunuch to her, but the very next thing that Esther does is to issue a direct command back to him. And later in this narrative, it is not told explicitly that Mordecai commands her to go in to speak with Ahasuerus. His authority over her does not appear strong, nor is her obedience to him important. By the conclusion of this episode, Esther is shown in full queenly authority. She has moved past her involvement with Mordecai alone and is now commanding the Jewish people as a whole.

This narrative shows Esther to be a person with knowledge and common sense. She is practical and unemotional. Living in the palace, she is well-informed on the happenings of the kingdom. Esther must already have known of the situation of Haman's actions against the Jews and have seen and understood his decree, for Mordecai does not report to her these details as he does in the other two narratives. Later in the conversation, Esther even challenges his own logic, in questioning how Mordecai can suggest such a plan when he himself certainly knows the dire consequences which would result from it. Part of the characteristic of Esther's good sense is her quality of not making decisions based solely upon emotion. She is not presented as feeling certain emotions in this episode, which is especially significant in that the A text in general tends to portray the inner thoughts of its characters more than the other two versions. And even being told outright of the Jews' sorrow does not move her to decide to act, for her very next statement questions the sense of such a decision.

Esther and Mordecai are not separated by as much distance. From the very first, we see Esther wanting Mordecai to come in to the palace, supposedly so that she might speak with him face to face. This narrative, overall, includes fewer references to servants carrying messages back and forth, which makes the two appear to be communicating with each other more directly. Moreover, no large group of attendants, girls and eunuchs, surrounds Esther.

This narrative highlights Esther's status as one who is not favored by the king. She often describes herself as 'uncalled', emphasizing that, in her mind at least, Ahasuerus has not paid much attention to her recently. And Mordecai asks her to go in specifically to flatter the king. Perhaps he knows that she is not, for some reason, in the king's good graces and he suggests that she pour on the charm to win the king's favor again.

This episode marks the point in the story at which Esther is portrayed as most involved with the Jewish people in the A text. Even in the court, she knows what is going on outside of the palace walls, and she continues to act on the part of the people. This characteristic becomes most clear towards the end of Esther and Mordecai's conversation. His argument to her, the one which finally convinces her to confront Ahasuerus, accuses her of being a traitor, of disregarding what is termed as explicitly her country, if she decides not to act. But if she does act, her effort will be that of a helper to her country, just as God's character is to help and to save the Jews. By the end of this episode, Esther is speaking directly to the Jews. She obviously feels political responsibility, if not a great deal of affection, towards the people. And in her working for them she is not concerned for her own welfare. She does not ask them to pray for her but for the situation in general.

Esther's influence and leadership, however, is not only political but also religious. This narrative frequently refers to God. Mordecai first tells Esther to call upon God as well as to speak to Ahasuerus. He later tells her that God will save the Jews if Esther does not, and then Esther herself commands the people to pray to God. Esther shows herself to be a pious person, concerned not with the religious activity of fasting but with the more spiritual and liturgical activities of worship and communication with God through prayer. All in all, this narrative gives the impression that these events are occurring within a larger plan which is based upon God, though such is never stated explicitly. Esther's action is linked with God's action; if she fails, God will intervene to save. She and Mordecai also expect God to be moved by her and the people's prayers. The request of their prayers is God's cause, not just Esther and Mordecai's or the Jews' cause. And her concession to die 'if it is necessary' hints that there is something greater for which Esther's sacrifice would be deemed essential.

B Text. From the beginning of this episode, this narrative is concerned with the sending of information. It highlights a particular interest in correct and complete messages. Esther asks Hachratheus to obtain accurate information from Mordecai, and Mordecai responds by telling even the details of how much money Haman had paid to the king. Later, the narrative describes Hachratheus as specifically reporting the whole of Mordecai's message to Esther and of her message to him. And Esther becomes more and more active in her sending as the episode progresses. This narrative first tells of her summoning Hachratheus, getting information from Mordecai only indirectly. But later it uses direct discourse to report Esther's actual words to each of them, which makes her appear more active in the process.

Such an emphasis upon the sending of information creates an impression of verbal distance between Esther and Mordecai, making it always clear that they are communicating only through intermediaries. Yet, throughout this episode they move from being more to less estranged from each other. At first Esther seems far away from Mordecai and the Jews, as she only hears what is happening and thus does not actually experience it herself. But later in their conversation, Mordecai addresses Esther by her proper name, suggesting more close communication. And by the final time Esther sends information to Mordecai, the messenger is no longer mentioned by name, which renders him less visible and hence less intrusive.

In this narrative Esther is especially obedient. This obedience is seen most clearly when Mordecai urges her to approach Artaxerxes. The key to her decision is to listen to, or obey, the words of Mordecai. However, earlier in the scene there are also references to Esther's expected obedience. In the first message from Mordecai, he commands her and reminds her that he raised her, both in the same breath—an obvious expectation on his part that Esther will obey him now as she did when under his parentage. We also see here how Esther's obedience is linked with her subservience and her low social status as a (former) orphan. Only in this narrative is Esther instructed to honor the king, as one would do to a person of higher social class.

Esther begins this episode with a positive, optimistic outlook. When explaining to Mordecai the king's rule, she speaks in terms of salvation rather than of death. Instead of seeing the king as a possible extermi-nator, she sees him as a possible savior. And when Mordecai suggests that she herself expects to be delivered in the coming destruction, he provides no reason for this expectation. Thus it must be based only upon Esther's own high hope. However, Esther's initial outlook on the situation contrasts with Mordecai's more pessimistic outlook. Instead of Esther's peaceful hopes for life and salvation, Modecai speaks of violence. His remarks about Haman's working for the Jews' death and how Haman himself will kill them, and his descriptions of how Esther and her family will be destroyed, heighten his negative, fear-inspiring message. Mordecai's language affects Esther, for in her next, and last, message she uses the same term of violent destruction and applies it particularly to herself. From the optimism of hoping for salvation for the hypothetical individual who might go in to the king without being called, Esther's outlook has shifted to the pessimism of expecting her own annihilation when she herself will go before the king.

M Text. Esther begins this episode by not being sure how to act effectively, especially with regard to Mordecai. At first she shows extreme emotion; she is greatly anguished and disturbed. Out of her pain, she tries to take care of Mordecai by sending him clothes. This way of dealing with the situation and her pain does not work, as Mordecai refuses her gift. After this exchange, Esther changes her tactics, and she decides to ask Mordecai for information. Her second response to the situation proves more successful. This narrative even reports how

Hathach goes out to do Esther's commands and how receptive Mordecai is to her desire, in that he gives her all the types of information she requests, what happened and why. However, the information which Esther receives is not objective observation but specifically from Mordecai's perspective. Mordecai's first response is to tell her what had happened to him, not just what had occurred in general. And Hathach is then careful to tell her particularly the actual words and concerns of Mordecai himself. Esther continues to repeat her action of commanding to get the information and the results she desires. During the first part of this episode she commands Hathach, but then she shifts to commanding Mordecai himself, seen most explicitly in the final verse.

An interesting progression occurs between this episode and the previous episode. In the first episode, Mordecai twice told Esther not to speak of her ancestry or her people while in the palace (2.10, 20). Here, however, Mordecai insists that she *must* speak. In this narrative it is precisely her failure to speak, her keeping silent about her people, that will be her downfall. The two episodes also make the same distinction between the people whom Esther's actions affect. Earlier she was told not to tell about her ancestry and her people. Here the narrative uses the same two categories in their relationship to her, her ancestry (the house of her father) and her people (the Jews in general). It is only Mordecai's advice which changes. Esther is getting mixed commands from Mordecai, first to be silent, and now a warning not to be silent.

This narrative emphasizes Esther's position in the court. Only here does Mordecai refer to her place in the house of the king, that her new position should not lead her to the expectation that her life will be spared. And we see later that it does not include reference to her former position of low social status or of being an orphan in Mordecai's household. This narrative makes it clear that Esther is no longer so much connected to her past but fully moved from his household and parentage to the king's household. Mordecai's position outside the palace at the gate of the king furthers the idea of physical separation between their two lives now.

This narrative does not portray Esther in a saving role. Her actions on behalf of the people are seen in a more limited scope. In Mordecai's first statement encouraging her to approach Ahasuerus, he does not speak of the result of her action as being the salvation of the people from death. He mentions no anticipated result here at all. However, Mordecai commands her in two ways: to implore the king and to make request from the king. The key to Esther's actions is not saving the people but making a request to the king. Mordecai also later speaks of Esther in a passive sense with regard to salvation, suggesting that she is expecting to *be* saved, not to save the people herself.

Finally, God is not of explicit concern. Esther is not presented as dependent upon God for success. Mordecai does not suggest that she call upon God when going in to Ahasuerus. Nor does this narrative propose that if Esther does not act, God will still help the Jews; it is only stated that deliverance will come from another place. Mordecai, at least, is assured that the Jews will be saved, but not necessarily that their salvation will be through divine causality. And even though Esther tells the Jews to fast, this narrative does not mention devotion to God as the basis for their fasting.

Episode 3 (14.1-19)

Immediately following the past episode, in which Esther and Mordecai converse with each other, Mordecai goes away and begins to pray to God. He prays about God's power and sovereignty over the universe, the reasons for his decision not to bow down to Haman, and the actions of the Jews' enemies towards them. He then asks God to change the situation. After the conclusion of Mordecai's prayer, this episode begins and focuses upon Esther's prayer to God. Esther first prepares to pray by changing her clothing. She then begins to pray, mentioning her feelings about the Jews' predicament, her family heritage, the actions of those who oppose the Jews, and what she has done in the Persian court. She asks God to come to help the Jewish people and to give her success before the king.

This episode of the story is present in only the Greek narratives, the A and B texts. It is represented by the versification C.12-30 in the Göttingen edition. These narratives align more closely in their textual character here than in other parts of the story, as is the case in general throughout the material that exists only in the Greek versions of the book. Nonetheless, there are differences between the two narratives which significantly affect the characterization of Esther portrayed by them in this episode.

The format for the analysis of this episode will vary from that of the previous two episodes. The A and B texts will be analyzed as before: consideration of the effects of textual differences upon the characterization of Esther in these two narratives. Because the M text does not have material corresponding to this episode of the story, it will not be included. Instead, the primary ways in which this Greek material affects what we know of Esther's actions and her overall character will be noted.

The two prayers, Mordecai's and Esther's, function as parallel entities in the Greek narratives. Yet their content differs in significant ways which affect the overall characterization of Esther. Therefore, Esther's prayer will be examined in light of Mordecai's prayer. For these final two comparisons, those of the Greek Esther and of her prayer, only those details which both the A and B texts include will be considered.

Text

Καὶ Εσθηρ ἡ βασίλισσα κατέφυγεν ἐπὶ τὸν κύριον ἐν ἀγῶνι θανάτου κατειλημμένη

And Esther the queen fled for refuge to the Lord, seized with agony of death.

Καὶ Εσθηρ ἡ βασίλισσα κατέφυγεν ἐπὶ τὸν κύριον ἐν ἀγῶνι θανάτου κατειλημμένη,　　1

And Esther the queen fled for refuge to the Lord, seized with agony of death.

καὶ ἀφείλατο τὰ ἱμάτια τῆς δόξης *ἀφ᾽ ἑαυτῆς καὶ πᾶν σημεῖον ἐπιφανείας αὐτῆς* καὶ ἐνεδύσατο στενοχωρίαν καὶ πένθος καὶ ἀντὶ ὑπερηφανων ἡδυσμάτων σποδοῦ καὶ κόπρου ἔπλησε τὴν κεφαλὴν αὐτῆς καὶ τὸ σῶμα αὐτῆς ἐταπείνωσε σφόδρα καὶ πᾶν *σημεῖον* κόσμου *αὐτῆς καὶ* ἀγαλλιάματος *τερπνῶν* τριχῶν ἔπλησε *ταπεινώσεως*

And she removed the garments of glory from herself and every mark of her manifested rank, and she put on anguish and sorrow. And instead of extravagant perfumes she covered her head (with) ashes and dung, and she utterly debased her body. And every mark of her ornamentation and exultation of (her) pleasing hair she covered (with) humiliation.

καὶ ἀφελομένη τὰ ἱμάτια τῆς δόξης *αὐτῆς* ἐνεδύσατο *ἱμάτια* στενοχωρίας καὶ πένθους καὶ ἀντὶ τῶν ὑπερηφάνων ἡδυσμάτων σποδοῦ καὶ κοπριῶν ἔπλησεν τὴν κεφαλὴν αὐτῆς καὶ τὸ σῶμα αὐτῆς ἐταπείνωσεν σφόδρα καὶ πάντα *τόπον* κόσμου ἀγαλλιάματος *αὐτῆς* ἔπλησεν *στρεπτῶν* τριχῶν *αὐτῆς*　　2

And removing the garments of her glory, she put on garments of anguish and sorrow. And instead of extravagant perfumes she covered her head (with) ashes and dung, and she utterly debased her body. And every area of her exultant ornamentation she covered (with) her tangled hair.

καὶ ἐδεήθη τοῦ κυρίου καὶ εἶπεν Κύριε βασιλεῦ, σὺ εἶ μόνος *βοηθός·* βοήθησόν μοι *τῇ ταπεινῇ* καὶ οὐκ ἐχούσῃ βοηθὸν *πλὴν σοῦ,*

And she prayed to the Lord and said, 'Lord, king, you alone are a helper. Come help me who am debased and not having a helper besides you.

καὶ ἐδεῖτο κυρίου *θεοῦ Ισραηλ* καὶ εἶπεν Κύριέ *μου* ὁ βασιλεὺς *ἡμῶν,* σὺ εἶ μόνος· βοήθησόν μοι *τῇ μόνῃ* καὶ μὴ ἐχούσῃ βοηθὸν *εἰ μὴ σέ.*　　3

And she prayed to the Lord, the God of Israel, and said, 'My Lord, our king, there is only you. Come help me who am alone and not having a helper other than you.

ὅτι κίνδυνός μου ἐν τῇ χειρί μου.

For my danger is in my hand.

ἐγὼ *δὲ* ἤκουσα πατρικῆς μου *βίβλου* ὅτι *ἐλυτρώσω* τὸν Ισραηλ ἐκ πάντων τῶν ἐθνῶν καὶ τοὺς πατέρας *αὐτῶν* ἐκ τῶν προγόνων αὐτῶν *ἐπιθέμενος αὐτοῖς Ισραηλ* κληρονομίαν αἰώνιον καὶ ἐποίησας αὐτοῖς ἃ ἐλάλησας *αὐτοῖς καὶ παρέσχου ὅσα ᾔτησαν.*

And I have heard from the book of my ancestors that you delivered Israel out of all the nations and their ancestors out of their progenitors, imposing to them, Israel, an eternal inheritance. And you did for them that which you had said to them and rendered as much as they had requested.

ἡμάρτομεν ἐναντίον σου, καὶ παρέδωκας ἡμᾶς εἰς χεῖρας τῶν ἐχθρῶν ἡμῶν,

We have done wrong before you, and you have given us over into the hands of our adversaries,

εἰ ἐδοξάσαμεν τοὺς θεοὺς αὐτῶν· δίκαιος εἶ, κύριε.

since we glorified their gods. You are righteous, Lord.

καὶ νῦν οὐχ ἱκανώθησαν ἐν πικρασμῷ δουλείας ἡμῶν, ἀλλ' ἐπέθηκαν τὰς χεῖρας αὐτῶν ἐπὶ τὰς χεῖρας τῶν εἰδώλων αὐτῶν

And now they are not satisfied by our bitter servitude, but they have placed their hands upon the hands of their idols,

ἐξᾶραι ὁρισμον στόματός σου, ἀφανίσαι κληρονομίαν σου καὶ ἐμφράξαι στόμα αἰνούντων σε καὶ σβέσαι δόξαν οἴκου σου καὶ θυσιαστηρίου σου

to tear out the decree of your mouth, to destroy your inheritance, and to stop up the mouth of those who praise you, and to extinguish the glory of your house and your altar,

ὅτι κίνδυνός μου ἐν χειρί μου. 4

For my danger is in my hand.

ἐγὼ ἤκουον *ἐκ γενετῆς* μου *ἐν φυλῇ* 5 *πατριᾶς* μου ὅτι σύ, *κύριε, ἔλαβες* τὸν Ισραηλ ἐκ πάντων τῶν ἐθνῶν καὶ τοὺς πατέρας *ἡμῶν* ἐκ *πάντων* τῶν προγόνων αὐτῶν εἰς κληρονομίαν αἰώνιον καὶ ἐποίησας αὐτοῖς *ὅσα* ἐλάλησας.

I heard from my birth in the tribe of my ancestors that you, Lord, took Israel out of all the nations and our ancestors out of all their progenitors for an eternal inheritance, and you did for them as much as you had said.

καὶ νῦν ἡμάρτομεν ἐνώπιόν σου, καὶ 6 παρέδωκας ἡμᾶς εἰς χεῖρας τῶν ἐχθρῶν ἡμῶν,

But yet now we have done wrong before you, and you have given us over into the hands of our adversaries,

ἀνθ' ὧν ἐδοξάσαμεν τοὺς θεοὺς αὐτῶν· 7 δίκαιος εἶ, κύριε.

because we glorified their gods. You are righteous, Lord.

καὶ νῦν οὐχ ἱκανώθησαν ἐν πικρασμῷ 8 δουλείας ἡμῶν, ἀλλὰ ἔθηκαν τὰς χεῖρας αὐτῶν ἐπὶ τὰς χεῖρας τῶν εἰδώλων αὐτῶν

And now they are not satisfied by our bitter servitude, but they have placed their hands upon the hands of their idols,

ἐξᾶραι ὁρισμὸν στόματός σου *καὶ* 9 ἀφανίσαι κληρονομίαν σου καὶ ἐμφράξαι στόμα αἰνούντων σοι καὶ σβέσαι δόξαν οἴκου σου καὶ θυσιαστήριόν σου

to tear out the decree of your mouth, and to destroy your inheritance, and to stop up the mouth of those who praise you, and to extinguish the glory of your house and your altar,

καὶ ἀνοῖξαι στόματα ἐχθρῶν εἰς
ἀρετὰς ματαίων καὶ θαυμασθῆναι
βασιλέα σάρκινον εἰς τὸν αἰῶνα.

and to open the mouths of adversaries for
the praise of deceptive things, and to revere
a mortal king forever.

μὴ δὴ παραδῷς, κύριε, τὸ σκῆπτρόν σου
τοῖς μισοῦσί σε ἐχθροῖς, καὶ μὴ
χαρείησαν ἐπὶ τῇ πτώσει ἡμῶν· στρέψον
τὰς βουλὰς αὐτῶν ἐπ' αὐτούς, τὸν δὲ
ἀρξάμενον ἐφ' ἡμᾶς εἰς κακὰ
παραδειγμάτισον.

Indeed, do not give over, Lord, your sceptre
to adversaries who hate you, that they do
not rejoice at our calamity. Turn their
intentions against them, and make example
of the one who governed over us for evil.

ἐπιφάνηθι ἡμῖν, κύριε, καὶ γνώσθητι
ἡμῖν ἐν καιρῷ θλίψεως ἡμῶν καὶ μὴ
θραύσῃς ἡμᾶς.

Show forth to us, Lord, and be known to us
in this time of our affliction, and do not
shatter us.

δὸς λόγον εὔρυθμον εἰς τὸ στόμα μου καὶ
χαρίτωσον τὰ ῥήματά μου ἐνώπιον τοῦ
βασιλέως καὶ μετάστρεψον τὴν
καρδίαν αὐτοῦ εἰς μῖσος τοῦ
πολεμοῦντος ἡμᾶς εἰς συντέλειαν αὐτοῦ
καὶ τῶν ὁμονοούντων αὐτῷ·

Put eloquent speech into my mouth and
make favorable my speeches before the king,
and turn around his heart to hatred of the
one who is fighting us, for the destruction
of him and those who agree with him.

ἡμᾶς δὲ ῥῦσαι ἐν τῇ χειρί σου τῇ
κραταιᾷ καὶ βοήθησόν μοι, ὅτι σὺ
πάντων γνῶσιν ἔχεις

But rescue us in your powerful hand, and
come help me. For you have knowledge of
all things,

καὶ οἶδας ὅτι βδελύσσομαι κοίτην
ἀπεριτμητου καὶ ἐμίσημα δόξαν ἀνόμου
καὶ παντὸς ἀλλογενοῦς.

καὶ ἀνοῖξαι στόμα ἐθνῶν εἰς ἀρετὰς   10
ματαίων καὶ θαυμασθῆναι βασιλέα
σάρκινον εἰς αἰῶνα.

and to open the mouth of nations for the
praise of deceptive things, and to revere a
mortal king forever.

μὴ παραδῷς, κύριε, τὸ σκῆπτρόν σου τοῖς   11
μὴ οὖσιν, καὶ μὴ καταγελασάτωσαν εν
τῇ πτώσει ἡμῶν, ἀλλὰ στρέψον τὴν
βουλὴν αὐτῶν ἐπ' αὐτούς, τὸν δὲ
ἀρξάμενον ἐφ' ἡμᾶς παραδειγμάτισον.

Do not give over, Lord, your sceptre to that
which is not, that they do not deride our
calamity. But turn their intention against
them, and make example of the one who
governed over us.

μνήσθητι, κύριε, γνώσθητι ἐν καιρῷ   12
θλίψεως ἡμῶν καὶ ἐμὲ θάρσυνον,
βασιλεῦ τῶν θεῶν καὶ πάσης ἀρχῆς
ἐπικρατῶν.

Remember, Lord; be known in this time of
our affliction. And make me courageous, king
of the gods and ruler over all authority.

δὸς λόγον εὔρυθμον εἰς τὸ στόμα μου   13
ἐνώπιον τοῦ λέοντος καὶ μετάθες τὴν
καρδίαν αὐτοῦ εἰς μῖσος τοῦ πολεμοῦντος
ἡμᾶς εἰς συντέλειαν αὐτοῦ καὶ τῶν
ὁμονοούντων αὐτῷ·

Put eloquent speech into my mouth before
the lion, and change over his heart to hatred
of the one who is fighting us, for the
destruction of him and of those who agree
with him.

ἡμᾶς δὲ ῥῦσαι ἐν χειρί σου καὶ βοήθησόν   14
μοι τῇ μόνῃ καὶ μὴ ἐχούσῃ εἰ μὴ σέ, κύριε.
πάντων γνῶσιν ἔχεις

But rescue us in your hand, and come help
me who am alone and do not have (anyone)
other than you, Lord. You have knowledge
of all things,

καὶ οἶδας ὅτι ἐμίσησα δόξαν ἀνόμων καὶ   15
βδελύσσομαι κοίτην ἀπεριτμήτων καὶ
παντὸς ἀλλοτρίου.

and you know that I detest the bed of the uncircumcised and I hate the glory of the lawless and all foreigners.

σύ, <u>κύριε</u>, οἶδας τὴν ἀνάγκην μου, ὅτι βδελύσσομαι τὸ σημεῖον τῆς ὑπερηφανίας, ὅ ἐστιν ἐπὶ τῆς κεφαλῆς μου, καὶ οὐ φορῶ εἰ μὴ ἐν ἡμέρᾳ ὀπτασίας μου καὶ βδελύσσομαι αὐτὸ ὡς ῥάκος <u>ἀποκαθημένης</u>.

You, Lord, know my obligation, that I detest the mark of high position, which is upon my head, and I do not wear it except during the day of my appearance, and I detest it like the rag of one who sits apart.

καὶ οὐκ ἔφαγεν ἡ δούλη σου ἐπὶ τῶν τραπεζῶν <u>αὐτῶν ἅμα</u>, καὶ οὐκ ἐδόξασα βασιλέως συμπόσια <u>καὶ οὐκ</u> ἔπιον σπονδῆς οἶνον·

And your servant has not eaten upon their tables at the same time, and I have not honored the drinking festivities of the king and I have not drunk the wine of the drink-offerings.

καὶ οὐκ εὐφράνθη ἡ δούλη σου ἐφ' ἡμέραις μεταβολῆς <u>μου εἰ μὴ</u> ἐπὶ σοί, <u>δέσποτα</u>.

And your servant has not been joyful since the days of my moving, except in you, master.

<u>καὶ νῦν</u>, <u>δυνατὸς ὢν</u> ἐπὶ πάντας, εἰσάκουσον φωνῆς ἀπηλπισμένων καὶ ῥῦσαι ἡμᾶς ἐκ χειρὸς τῶν πονηρευομένων <u>ἐφ' ἡμᾶς</u> καὶ <u>ἐξελοῦ</u> με, <u>κύριε</u>, ἐκ <u>χειρὸς</u> τοῦ φόβου μου.

And now, being powerful over everything, listen to the voice of those who are despairing, and rescue us from the hands of the wrongdoers against us, and take me away, Lord, from the hand of my fear.'

and you know that I hate the glory of the lawless and I detest the bed of the uncircumcised and every foreigner.

σὺ οἶδας τὴν ἀνάγκην μου, ὅτι 16 βδελύσσομαι τὸ σημεῖον τῆς ὑπερηφανίας <u>μου</u>, ὅ ἐστιν ἐπὶ τῆς κεφαλῆς μου ἐν ἡμέρ<u>αις</u> σπτασίας μου· βδελύσσομαι αὐτὸ ὡς ῥάκος <u>καταμηνίων</u> καὶ οὐ φορῶ <u>αὐτὸ</u> <u>ἐν ἡμέραις ἡσυχίας μου</u>.

You know my obligation, that I detest the mark of my high position, which is upon my head during my visible days. I detest it like a menstrual rag and I do not wear it during my resting days.

καὶ οὐκ ἔφαγεν ἡ δούλη σου τράπεζαν 17 <u>Αμαν</u>, καὶ οὐκ ἐδόξασα συμπόσι<u>ον</u> βασιλέως <u>οὐδὲ</u> ἔπιον οἶνον σπονδῶν·

And your servant has not eaten (at) Haman's table, and I have not honored the drinking festivity of the king nor have I drunk the wine of drink-offerings.

καὶ οὐκ ηὐφράνθη ἡ δούλη σου ἀφ' ἡμέρας 18 μεταβολῆς μου <u>μέχρι νῦν πλὴν</u> ἐπὶ σοί, <u>κύριε ὁ θεὸς Αβρααμ</u>.

And your servant has not been joyful since the days of moving until now, except in you, Lord, the God of Abraham.

<u>ὁ θεὸς ὁ ἰσχύων</u> ἐπὶ πάντας, εἰσάκουσον 19 φωνὴν ἀπηλπισμένων καὶ ῥῦσαι ἡμᾶς ἐκ χειρὸς τῶν πονηρευομένων καὶ <u>ῥῦσαί</u> με ἐκ τοῦ φόβου μου.

God, who is strong over everything, listen to the voice of those who are despairing, and rescue us from the hands of wrongdoers, and rescue me from my fear.'

Notes

Verse 2. B's use of a personal pronoun with regard to Esther's glory, in the first phrase of this verse, functions to connect the honor, magnificence, or glory more closely to her. As 'her glory' (τῆς δόξης αὐτῆς), it is expressly her position or attitude. A's differing use of the δόξης and pronoun instead stresses the distancing of Esther from such glory, as she is said to take the glorious clothing off 'from herself' (ἀφ' ἑαυτῆς).

The phrase πᾶν σημεῖον ἐπιφανείας αὐτῆς, unique to A, is difficult to translate. The noun ἐπιφάνεια, an 'appearance' or a 'coming into view', can be used in a variety of ways. With regard to human beings, in distinction from deities or objects, the word is often used to express the appearance or visible outward distinction shown by a person of high rank. This is the meaning conveyed in this context. It thus reflects Esther's honor and her position in the kingdom as queen, which is manifested by her outward appearance.

A, with its two phrases about Esther's appearance ('the garments of glory', τὰ ἱμάτια τῆς δόξης, and 'every mark of her manifested rank', πᾶν σημεῖον ἐπιφαναίας αὐτῆς), shows a portrait of her as wearing more magnificent finery. However, this emphasis upon her glorious appearance and position also works to show Esther as going to a greater length to humble herself, when removing all of this indicative clothing for prayer. Likewise, two expressions are used at the end of this verse to describe two aspects which she acts to remove, 'every mark of her ornamentation' (πᾶν σημεῖον κόσμου αὐτῆς) and 'exultation of pleasing hair' (ἀγαλλιάματος τερπνῶν τριχῶν). Her overall transformation appears greater, covering and/or removing four visible aspects of her regal position. B, correspondingly, states only two aspects at these points, 'the garments of her glory' (τὰ ἱμάτια τῆς δόξης αὐτῆς) at the beginning of the verse, and 'every area of her exultant ornamentation' (πάντα τόπον κόσμου ἀγαλλιάματος αὐτῆς) at the end of the verse.

B provides only an outward view of Esther's changed appearance. It notes that she puts on clothing of mourning ('garments of anguish and sorrow', ἱμάτια στενοχωρίας καὶ πένθους), but not whether she herself actually feels distress or sadness. Then it describes only the hair with which she covers herself, 'she covered (with) her tangled hair' (ἔπλησεν στρεπτῶν τριχῶν αὐτῆς).

A provides a view of Esther's inner emotions as well as her physical appearance. She does not, as expressed in a sort of odd expression, put on the proper clothing for mourning, but the actual emotions themselves ('she put on anguish and sorrow', ἐνεδύσατο στενοχωρίαν καὶ πένθος). Then it suggests that she feels her lowness or humiliation (ταπεινώσεως) as well as visibly demonstrating her lowness of condition.

In A, Esther's hair is described as beautiful or delightful, and hence one of the items that she covers ('pleasing hair', τερπνῶν τριχῶν). It is not entirely clear whether Esther herself delights in her hair or whether it is judged that way by others, but the ἀγαλλιάματος ('transport of joy, exultation') would tend to suggest that it is a source of happiness to her. In contrast, in B Esther's hair must not be attractive or pleasant, for it is one of the items she instead uses to debase her appearance. And its wording (κόσμου ἀγαλλιάματος αὐτῆς) suggests that she rejoices at her items of decoration or ornamentation instead. (Dorothy states that in B Esther actually cuts her hair, but he does not explain how he comes to such a reading from the text ['Books', p. 148].)

Verse 3. In B, Esther expresses a sense of connection with the Jews. She qualifies her address to God ('the Lord', κυρίου) with the phrase 'God of Israel' (θεοῦ Ισραηλ). B also accentuates the personal aspect of Esther's relationship with God. Though she uses the same terminology to refer to God as in A, in B Esther adds personal possessive pronouns ('my lord', κύριε μου; 'our king', ὁ βασιλεὺς ἡμῶν).

In A, Esther sees God's character as being one who hastens to rescue or to help (βοηθός). As she finds herself without anyone to help besides God, it appears that she calls upon God not foremost because of any relationship with God but because she knows that God has a reputation for helping human beings in distress. Dorothy is correct in noting that A focuses upon God as a helper at this point in Esther's prayer ('Books', p. 148).

A represents Esther as acknowledging her humble position, for she claims that she is low or debased when asking for God's help ('help me, the debased one', βοήθησόν μοι τῇ ταπεινῇ).

B portrays Esther as feeling alone. Her reason for seeking God's help is that she is alone in being without any other help ('help me, the one alone', βοήθησόν μοι τῇ μόνῃ). Thus, God's singularity or aloneness here parallels her own aloneness. The phrase σὺ εἶ μόνος is ambiguous. It is uncertain whether Esther is here speaking of God's character (for instance, as unified in being, the sole god, or the sovereign in control of all other beings) or if she is here stating obliquely what in A she does directly, that God is the only helper of which she knows for the present circumstances.

Verse 5. A's Esther is possibly educated, or intellectual to some degree, as she receives understanding from a book or some version of a written form of the story of Israel's traditions ('I have heard from the book of my ancestors', ἐγὼ ... ἤκουσα πατρικῆς μου βίβλου). In A, it is not clear whether Esther herself actually read this book or only heard it read by others, but the former cannot be ruled out. Though the verb ἀκούω has the simple meaning of 'to hear', it also signifies more generally to learn or to understand. It can refer to the readers of a written work (in the substantive), to the situation of being informed about something, or to how one learns religious teachings. This expression is quite under-standable in this context, not the odd expression that Dorothy has suggested ('Books', p. 149). As Moore notes, B is more ambiguous as to whether her learning is formal biblical teaching or that of informal daily living (*Additions,* p. 210).

B gives the impression that Esther has lived her whole life within the Jewish community, for she asserts that she learned of God's actions 'from my birth in the tribe of my ancestors' (ἐκ γενετῆς μου ἐν φυλῇ πατριᾶς μου). Her reference to the tribes (φυλῇ) shows that she thinks of the Jews in a communal and familial sense. It also suggests that she knows something of the previous history of Israel, as during this present time of the exile and diaspora, the Jews would no longer have been living according to their tribal connections.

In B, Esther's reference to the forefathers as 'our ancestors' (τοὺς πατέρας ἡμῶν) suggests that she feels a part of these people and God's actions toward them. She sees them as her ancestors as well. In contrast, Esther in A expresses distance by referring to them as 'their [Israel's] ancestors' (τοὺς πατέρας αὐτῶν), placing them in the realm of Israel's ancient history and not a part of her own situation.

In B, Esther addresses God directly (as 'Lord', κύριε), which makes her speaking to God more conversational and her knowledge of God more relational.

A presents God's past action for the Israelites particularly as being liberating or salvific. When setting aside the nation for an inheritance, the verb λυτρόω, 'to release for a ransom, redeem, or liberate' is used. B uses the more general verb λαμβάων (ἔλαβες), 'to take, seize upon'.

The final phrase, unique to A, adds two dimensions to this verse. First, it makes it clear that, in this instance of God's past action on behalf of Israel, the people took the initiative in asking for God's deliverance; God gave them what they had first requested (ὅσα ᾔτησαν). The pronoun αὐτοῖς, 'to them', likewise suggests that there had been some type of communication between God and Israel before deciding to act for them.

Secondly, this phrase shows Esther as recognizing God as having the characteristic of granting humans' requests, particularly for deliverance or rescue.

Verse 6. The conjunctions used by A and B at the beginnings of vv. 5 and 6 cause differing progressions in the narratives. A's δὲ at the beginning of v. 5 links it with the preceding statement of v. 4. Esther first notes her very present danger (v. 4) and connects this realization with her next thought, in which she reminds herself that God saves persons in dangerous situations (v. 5). B's καὶ νῦν at the beginning of this verse connects it with B's own previous statement, the recognition that God had been faithful in promising and acting on behalf of Israel (v. 5). Unlike in A, B's v. 5 does not mention any part that Israel played in this action. But this verse does suggest Israel's action, except that it is here Israel's recent wrongdoing. Perhaps the καὶ should here be understood in the contrastive sense, linking two clauses in which the latter states a surprising or unexpected result of the former.

Verse 8. A's ἐπέθηκαν and B's ἔθηκαν (from ἐπιτίθημι and τίθημι, respectively) are essentially synonomous ('to lay, place, put (upon)'). Dorothy is incorrect to read them differently, when he states that A alone reflects a covenant made with idols ('Books', pp. 149-50).

Verse 10. In A, it is enemies or adversaries (ἐχθρῶν) who are charged with honoring deception. It is not clear whether this designation refers to God's enemies or the Jews' enemies, though if speaking of the same group as mentioned in v. 6, 'our adversaries' (τῶν ἐχθρῶν ἡμῶν) it would be specifically the people's enemies. In any case, it is a more recognizable and expected group who are deceitful.

In B, it is the nations in general (ἐθνῶν) who are accused of honoring deceptive things, charging all non-Jews, without distinction, of lying. The idea expressed here hearkens back to the similar terminology of v. 5, which describes how God made Israel separate from the other nations (πάντων τῶν ἐθνῶν) and how this was a very positive action.

Verse 11. In A, it is adversaries or enemies ('adversaries who hate you', τοῖς μισοῦσί σε ἐχθροῖς) about whom Esther is concerned. Another trait is here added to their character: they hate God. Thus these persons are not just those who hate the Jews and work against them, as suggested by the references to them in vv. 6 and 10, but also those who also hold God in contempt.

In B, Esther fears that God's sovereignty will go to something that has no being, or is not. It is unclear exactly to what the phrase μὴ οὖσιν refers. Is Esther here considering divine power in a cosmic realm? Is she equating evil with nothingness? Is she suggesting that only the God of the Jews has true existence? (Three manuscripts in the B textual tradition here read μισοῦσι σε, 'those who hate you', in place of μὴ οὖσιν, which would bring it more into conformity with A.)

In B, as μὴ οὖσιν is in the singular, it cannot be who is referred to as mocking or jeering (καταγελασάτωσαν) and whose purpose is to be turned against themselves ('their intention against them', τὴν βουλὴν αὐτῶν ἐπ' αὐτούς), which are plural. The last plural noun before this is ἐθνῶν, 'the nations', in v. 10. It is not clear whether the subject of these actions is the nations or still the adversaries spoken of first in v. 6.

A anticipates that the adversaries would rejoice or be glad (χαρείησαν) at the Jews' misfortune; B instead anticipates that such persons, in the form of the nations, would deride or jeer (καταγελασάτωσαν). In A, Esther's fear primarily reflects the adversaries' emotional state, that they would have joy and happiness if the Jews were defeated. In B, her fear is more interpersonal, that the Jews may become a laughing-stock for all these among whom they live.

Verse 12. A presents Esther as first either desiring revelation from God in general or appealing to God to become manifest to the people (as in an epiphany) (ἐπιφάνηθι ἡμῖν κυριε). B has Esther instead first requesting that God bear something in mind ('remember, Lord', μνήσθητι, κύριε). What exactly God is to remember is not explicitly stated here, but in context it is most likely that God took Israel out of the nations and made it an eternal inheritance, as previously stated in v. 5.

In B, Esther asks God for courage ('make me courageous', ἐμὲ θάρσυνον). Esther's hope for her own boldness in this situation is linked with God's taking action on behalf of the people, when God remembers and makes God's self known.

B presents Esther's desire that God be known generally to all people (γνώσθητι), rather than to just the Jewish people as in A ('be known to us', γνώσθητι ἡμῖν).

In A, God is seen to be, at least partially, responsible for the Jews' defeat. Esther asks God not to break them apart ('do not shatter us', μὴ θραύσῃς ἡμᾶς), and thus intimates that it is God's intentionality behind their present danger. This idea of God's causality echoes that of v. 6, in which she declares that God actually gave the people over to their enemies.

In B alone, Esther views God as exalted, as a 'king of the gods and ruler over all authority' (βασιλεῦ τῶν θεῶν καὶ πάσης ἀρχῆς ἐπικρατῶν). God is cast in a universal sovereign role, over both the divine realm (other gods) and the human realm (human authority).

A shows Esther as speaking for the Jewish people and not only for herself, in asking for God's action toward them all. In this verse, there are four references to them (ἡμῖν, ἡμῖν, ἡμῶν, ἡμᾶς), in contrast to only one in B (ἡμῶν).

Verse 13. A emphasizes Esther's speaking. She desires an ordered, aesthetic message ('eloquent speech', λόγον εὔρυθμον) as in B. But she also desires that her words might be pleasing ('make favorable my speeches', χαρίτωσον τὰ ῥήματά μου). She is more strongly portrayed as eloquent and rhetorical. At the same time, she is dependent upon God to find the right things to say to the king. The plural ῥήματά, denoting more than one speech, here suggests that Esther already has a plan of having the two speaking occasions with the king and is anticipating the arguments she will need to bring forward to him. As B includes only one reference to Esther's speaking, it tends to place less emphasis on her own actions of persuasion and thus to stress more God's action in changing the king's heart.

In B, Esther describes the king as a lion (τοῦ λέοντος). The significance of this term may be that Esther finds the king to be a terrifying beast, or that he acts more like an animal than a rational human being.

Verse 14. A views God not only as able to rescue but as also especially exhibiting God's strength in doing so, by noting God's 'powerful hand' (τῇ χειρί σου τῇ κραταιᾷ).

In B, Esther finds herself to be very much alone, a fact that she emphasizes for the second time during the prayer (cf. v. 3). It includes two significant phrases of Esther not in A: '(I) who am alone' (τῇ μόνῃ) and 'do not have (anyone) other than you' (μὴ ἐχούσῃ εἰ μὴ σέ). She requests God's help expressly because she sees no one else to whom to turn for help. B gives the impression that Esther is here asking for two distinct things from God, to rescue the Jewish people and to alleviate her own loneliness, more than does A, in which the two requests (to rescue and to help) appear more necessary to each other.

A's Esther does not provide an explicit reason for why God should help her, in contrast to B's reason of her aloneness. If linking this phrase with what was last expressed (v. 13b), as the context might suggest, God's help is necessary to turn around the king's intentions. If linking it with the following sentences, as the ὅτι (v. 15) might suggest, Esther is asking for help on the basis of her own abhorrence of things foreign and honored.

In B, Esther's addressing God by title ('Lord', κύριε) renders her either as more conversational and relational or as further stressing her state of aloneness.

Verse 15. The two items which merit Esther's distaste ('I detest the bed of the uncircumcised', βδελύσσομαι κοίτην ἀπεριτμήτου/ ἀπεριτμήτων; 'I hate the glory of the lawless', ἐμίσημα δόξαν ἀνόμου/ἀνόμων) are almost exactly the same in A and B, but in reversed order. However, this difference in placement does not significantly affect the meaning of the verse.

Verse 16. In A, Esther addresses God directly ('Lord', κύριε), either to stress the message that she does not like her royal position or to emphasize the relational aspect of her prayer.

B portrays Esther as acknowledging her high or arrogant position more, for she refers to it as specifically her own ('my high position', τῆς ὑπερηφανίας μου).

A speaks of the rag or cloth of 'one whe sits apart' (ἀποκαθημένης), in contrast to B's more explicit 'menstrual' or 'monthly' (καταμηνίων) rag. Esther chooses euphemistic language rather than B's literally descriptive term for the biological process of menstruation. Though the difference in terminology at this point may be a result of the types of communities who formed each of these texts, as Dorothy has suggested ('Books', p. 151), the effect of A's more euphemistic language upon the characterization of Esther is to make her appear to be a person who chooses her words with care.

According to B, Esther appears to have two types of activities in her role as queen. She speaks of 'my visible days' (ἡμέραις ὀπτασίας μου), distinguishing them from 'my resting days' (ἡμέραις ἡσυχίας μου). And she wears different attire for each type of day. It is more clear here than in A, which exhibits only the first type, that Esther has times when she has official responsibilities to represent the Persian government in public, but also is allowed a private life of time to herself.

Verse 17. In B, Esther is careful to avoid Haman's table (τράπεζαν Αμαν) in particular. In A, Esther is portrayed as not eating at the same table as certain people, but the referent of the pronoun αὐτῶν is ambiguous ('their tables', τῶν τραπεζῶν αὐτῶν). It can most likely be understood as reference to the Persians in general or to the uncircumcised, lawless, and foreign peoples previously mentioned in v. 15. The entire phrase ἐπὶ τῶν τραπεζῶν αὐτῶν can be understood either as 'upon the tables together with them' or 'upon their tables at the same time'; the difference would lie in whether Esther is primarily opposed to the people themselves or to their tables (and the food on them).

Verse 18. In A, Esther views God as her leader or master (δέσποτα). As the term δέσποτης, of which δέσποτα is the vocative form, is used by slaves to refer to their masters as well as to denote one's possession by a supreme deity or divine authority, it is suggested here that Esther feels herself to be speaking to one at a much higher, or even possessive, level than she.

B exhibits Esther as recalling her ancestors when addressing God ('Lord, God of Abraham', κύριε ὁ θεὸς Αβρααμ). She sees her present situation here in light of that of her forebear Abraham.

Verse 19. A uses the term δυνατὸς ὤν to describe God's strength, and B uses the term ὁ ἰσχύων. However, both of these words, the adjective δυνατός and the verb ἰσχύω, carry a very similar range of meanings ('mighty, powerful, strong, able'), and hence do not indicate a significant difference between how God is seen here in A and B.

A stresses that the wicked or evil ones ('the wrongdoers against us', τῶν πονηρευομένων ἐφ' ἡμᾶς) are deliberately working against the Jewish people and not just practicing evil in general. Esther also includes herself with those so threatened.

In B, Esther requests that God rescue or deliver two things, the people from wrongdoers and Esther herself from fear, using the same verb for each action (ῥῦσαι, from ἐρύω). A uses ῥῦσαι only in reference to the people. For Esther herself it uses ἐξελοῦ, 'to take away, make come to an end' (from ἐξέρομαι), which suggests less of a salvatory aspect in God's help for herself.

Analysis
A Text. We see Esther's inner emotional state more completely, and not only her outer appearance, in this narrative. When first preparing to approach God in prayer, Esther is troubled, full of grief, and sorrowful. Though she finds joy and pleasure in her hair, she even covers that up. Esther also feels a sense of lowness or humiliation during the time of prayer, as well as fear.

Esther is an intelligent and thinking person. In the situation with which she is now faced, to go before the king, she asks God more particularly to make the matter intelligible as well as to reveal God's self or to be present with the people. It is revelation or insight of some type that she finds of crucial importance to help her deal effectively with this problem. This narrative also emphasizes Esther's actions of speaking well; she is shown to possess rhetorical and persuasive abilities. She is concerned with finding just the right things to say to the king, and is even now preparing her plan for the speeches she will present to him. It is more clear that it will be as much Esther's persuasive speaking as God's own action that will turn around Ahasuerus's heart and save the Jews. And it is also likely that she is educated or literate, for she learns of Israel's traditions from a written book.

At the beginning of this episode, Esther conveys a very regal presence; her rank as queen is immediately obvious in her magnificent appearance. However, she immediately removes or covers all her ornamentation. Esther's transformation in this text is greater, from nobly bedecked queen to humble suppliant, and her actions to humble herself from her royal position are more deliberate. Later in her prayer she stresses before God that she dislikes her crown as the symbol of her high position. With regard to her presence within the court, Esther is somewhat alienated, in that she does not eat with the Persians. Though this practice may be an indication of her piety, such is not directly stated by the narrative.

Esther bears a mixed relationship with her people. On the one hand, she very much sees herself as speaking for the Jews in this present situation. She prays explicitly on their behalf that God would make God's self known and not break them apart, and she sees their trouble and afflictions as her own. However, Esther also appears, to a degree, alienated from the Jewish historical tradition. She does not so much claim Israel's ancestors as her ancestors as well. And she learns of its history in an academic manner, only from the written records and not through being taught the traditions personally.

In her prayer, Esther uses expressions for God and her feelings of need for God common to the language used in biblical prayers in general. Yet certain of the themes she introduces in her prayer still reflect her unique character. In the words of Esther's prayer, God appears far above Esther and not so much in relationship with her. For instance, she does not necessarily call on God because she thinks of God as her God or her people's God. Esther highlights her own feelings of humility when appealing to God's care for the weak The particular manner in which she desires God's assistance is by guiding her, helping her to speak persuasively to the king. Oddly enough, though, she also credits God with being responsible for the Jews' present predicament. Esther, in this narrative, also recognizes human beings as taking initiative when asking things from God, and God as the one who answers such prayer. She recalls, from the history of Israel, how God did what the people had first requested. And her knowledge of how God has acted in the past in responding to people's needs leads her to believe that God will do so again with regard to her present request.

Esther is quite concerned with the actions of adversaries, whom she depicts as a distinct group of people. She sees this group as those who were given control over the Jews, but also, in this narrative, as the people who praise deception, who hate God, and who are intentionally working against the Jews. Esther's fear is that God will give over control to these adversaries, and she imagines their happiness at the Jews' defeat.

B Text. In this narrative, we almost immediately see Esther's concern with being properly attired for addressing God. She takes care to humble her appearance by changing her clothing, and she even goes as far as to tangle up her own hair. Esther's physical preparations for addressing God in prayer are more apparent than her mental preparations. Indeed, she seems to reflect her distraught emotions not directly but through her choice of garments and physical adornments.

We are also given certain information about Esther's role in the Persian court. First of all, Esther recognizes her glory and her high position as particularly her own, and she even takes joy from the decoration that she wears as queen. However, Esther has a disjointed life in her new position. She tries to hold together her two identities during day-to-day court life, one in which she is available for public appearances and the other in which she is allowed to pursue her own leisure by herself. In the court environment, Esther had already recognized Haman as an enemy of significance, for she has been refusing to dine with him. She has evidently found him to be a particular menace, since she keeps away from him, but not necessarily from the rest of the Persians in the court.

The language Esther utilizes in her prayer accentuates her alienation. When speaking of her need for God's help, she describes this need particularly in terms of her aloneness. It is this aspect of alienation that Esther emphasizes when requesting God's help for the weak. At first she feels alone particularly because she sees no one else to help her in this situation; it is this lack of assistance in the present situation which prompts her to call upon God. But by the end of the prayer she is pleading with God to alleviate her own feelings of loneliness in addition to rescuing the people. In having no one else around, Esther's primary relationship must be with God. Also, in this narrative, Esther exhibits a mixture of courage and fear. On the one hand, she visualizes her encounter with Artaxerxes in terms of facing a violent beast instead of the man she has known. And she requests God to remove this fear. But on the other hand, she confidently hopes that God will provide her with courage when God begins to act to deliver the Jews.

In this narrative, the connection between Esther and the Jewish people is strong. She sees herself as being part of the Jews and as sharing the same God. Esther has lived her whole life within the community and has been taught its traditions and history from her birth. She claims Israel's ancestors as also her own, and even sees her present situation in light of how God once acted towards the patriarch Abraham. And she herself shares the Jews' relationship with God. God is not just a god, or only her god, but also a national deity. Esther views herself as part of the people and the heritage of Israel, and hence she feels that she can call upon their God.[1]

---

1. In consideration of this scene, Dorothy's assertion that the author of the A text emphasizes the glory of being the covenant people at every opportunity is inaccurate ('Books', p. 148). In Esther's prayer, it is the B text, not the A text, which most stresses Israel's covenant relationship with God.

Esther is concerned with the role and actions of Gentiles as a whole, whom she terms as the nations, as well as specific enemies of the Jews. In her prayer, she differentiates between two types of people, the nations and those who praise God. She has a low regard of these peoples, describing them as praising deception, holding negative intentions towards the Jews, and waiting to jeer at their misfortune. Esther is concerned about international relations and how the Jewish people are able to live and function with others in their foreign communities. One of the things she asks God to remember is how God removed Israel from out of the nations. In general, this narrative exhibits a lower tolerance of Gentiles throughout this episode.

With regard to Esther's view of God, she considers God's very being. She finds God as the sole, unique God, and the only thing that is, in contrast with that which does not have existence. Her God is sovereign over everything, ruling over all in the divine and human realms. She highlights the universal aspect of God, but also God as having a particular character as Israel's God. Though Esther speaks often of what God has done for the Jews as a people, the tone of her prayer is rather more conversational in general and suggests that Esther herself has a close and personal relationship with God. She stresses God's listening to despairing persons, a category into which she places herself. And Esther believes that God is generous and faithful to do what God says, even in contrast to Israel's wrongdoing.

Esther, in this narrative, knows God particularly as one who rescues and delivers. She emphasizes God's taking Israel out of other nations, and later asks God to remember this action of liberation. As a deliverer, she finds God equally able to rescue on the communal (Israel from its coming disaster) and the individual (Esther herself from her own fear) levels. And Esther speaks as though it is God's action itself which is most crucial in changing a situation around; she tends to place less emphasis upon human initiative and action.

Relationship of Esther's Prayer to Mordecai's Prayer

There are basic similarities between the prayers of Mordecai and Esther.[1] These similarities run along the lines of how each views God's

---

1. Mordecai's prayer is represented by the versification C.1-11 in the Göttingen edition and by 13.8-17 in the numerical system of nomenclature. As it is sufficiently brief in length, I have not indicated particular verse references in this discussion of similarities and differences. As with Esther's prayer, Mordecai's prayer also varies to

character, how each uses details from Israel's history, and for what each asks. First, both Esther's and Mordecai's prayers highlight several attributes of the character of God. Both address God as 'lord' and 'king'. They agree in viewing God as having strength and power, and as ruling over all things. Moreover, both stress that God knows all things, and that God listens to the voices of people. Secondly, Esther and Mordecai both bring up the fact that God acted in the past to establish Israel as God's eternal inheritance. They refer to Israel's tradition, and to the ancestral tradition in particular. Esther (in the B text) and Mordecai (in both the A and B texts) each make explicit reference to Abraham, viewing their situations in light of God's past action through Abraham. And both speak of their own choices and actions in a similar fashion. Each expresses how God knows everything, and then explains what in particular God knows about him or her—Mordecai, his reasons for not bowing to Haman, and Esther, her feelings about her royal position and duties. Both, in their prayers, also see God as having been responsible (Esther) or having the possibility of being responsible (Mordecai) for the downfall of the Jews, and thus both similarly ask that God would choose not to destroy them.

However, when compared with Mordecai's prayer, Esther's prayer exhibits numerous differences which affect the portrayal of Esther as a whole in the two Greek narratives. First, Esther differs from Mordecai in her reason for praying and the attitude she exhibits throughout her prayer. Mordecai prays in order to call to remembrance the works of God. He speaks at length of God's character and his own actions, and only towards the end asks that God would act in the present situation. Esther, on the other hand, runs to prayer because she is distraught and agonized. Her first words are to ask God for help, and throughout the rest of the prayer Esther has a sense of the danger at hand.[1] Furthermore, Mordecai does not change his appearance or humble his attitude in preparation for praying, though Esther goes through an elaborate process. While we might assume that Mordecai is still in his sackcloth, later on in the story, when he himself is given fine regal clothing and an honored position, he has no problem with accepting

a degree between the A text and B text versions. I have only included for comparison those details which are shared by both versions for each respective prayer.

1. Though Esther requests God's assistance, her prayer is not self-centered, as Moore has pointed out. He finds her primary concern for the safety of her people to be admirable (*Additions*, p. 213).

them. Esther, in contrast, emphasizes instead how much she dislikes her royal ornamentation and prestigious position. He speaks of the joy he hopes to have and how he desires to celebrate, and particularly to join the feasting and praising of the community. She instead speaks of how she has not felt joy for years, has declined to participate in feasts, and feels very much alone. How both of them express their own wrongdoing also differs. Mordecai strongly defends his decision not to bow down to Haman, arguing that he would have exhibited pride and ignored God's glory if he had done so. Esther, though, takes responsibility for wrongdoing and confesses to not just her own sin but that of all the people. For the present threat to the Jews, Mordecai denies responsibility, although it was his very actions which precipitated the decree against them. Esther, on the other hand, takes on the guilt of the nation, when she herself actually did nothing to bring about these events.

Esther and Mordecai also view God differently. Mordecai envisions God in a creative role and stresses how God is undefeatable, even suggesting that God acts as a warrior in resisting anything which tries to act contrary to God's will. He holds a greater concern for God's glory, and sees the role of human beings to acknowledge this divine glory above all. Esther does not stress these qualities as much, but she views God primarily as a helper and consoler to those who feel afraid, alone, or distressed.

In their prayers, Mordecai and Esther ask for different things from God and put forth different reasons for why God should act on their behalf, within the general context of saving the people. Mordecai asks for God's mercy so that the people may continue to praise God. He desires an outcome in which the Jews no longer mourn but have festival. Esther instead asks God to reveal God's self, to work by means of rescue, and imagines an outcome not of jubilation but merely one in which the people are saved and she is no longer afraid. She, furthermore, sees herself as an instrument of the people's salvation, which Mordecai does not. Each asks God to listen, but Mordecai asks this because of God's mercy towards God's chosen ones and Esther asks it because people are in despair.

In presenting an argument for why God should act, both Mordecai and Esther refer to the tradition of God making Israel an inheritance, but they use this concept in different ways. Mordecai's reasoning highlights the special nature of Israel, whereas Esther's reasoning trusts that God is faithful to do as God promises. In addition, he refers to the people being

delivered from Egypt and hints at the theological themes of exodus and
liberation, themes which are not as explicitly present in her prayer. In all,
Mordecai more readily views himself as one of God's chosen inheritance
than does Esther, who tends to view herself as one who is oppressed.
Mordecai argues that God should act for the people primarily because of
God's character and interests; God's special inheritance, or portion, is in
danger. Esther's argument is instead centered around people's needs.
She reasons that God should act because people are in trouble and see
no other means of escape.

Mordecai and Esther express divergent ideas with regard to attitudes
towards the Persians or other non-Jews. Mordecai here notes only the
destruction of the Jews as the primary disagreeable action of these
enemies, whereas Esther lists several other of their activities as well. She
asks that these enemies be defeated or somehow harmed in addition to
the Jews being saved, whereas he asks only that the Jews not be hurt. In
sum, Mordecai desires things to happen to only the Jews, but Esther
desires God to act both for the Jews and against the Persians.

Effects of This Episode on the Esther Story
Numerous details of the story or aspects of Esther's character which are
not in the M text are provided either solely or principally by this Greek
section. These additional details fall within the general categories of
Esther's religiosity, her response to the recent events, her sexual and
dramatic abilities, her relationship with the Persians, and her role in
future events.

Esther is a pious person. Her character includes a religious dimension.
She appears accustomed to praying, as she enters readily into lengthy
and articulate prayer. We know Esther as one who recognizes the God
of Israel, is in a relationship with God, and is dependent upon God for
guidance and wisdom. She is concerned with doing the things of which
God approves and with having a proper attitude before God. She,
correspondingly, disapproves of idolatry and refuses to participate in
worship of other gods, particularly the god(s) of the Persians. Esther is
familiar with Israel's historical and religious traditions, and she uses them
to interpret her own situation. In her prayer, she includes many of the
fundamental theological themes found in biblical literature, including
God as omnipotent and omniscient, God as hearing and answering
prayers, worship of God alone, God's choosing Israel as distinct from all
other nations, concern for the temple, God as punishing sin, God as one

who liberates, and God's special concern for the oppressed.

Esther further recognizes the import of Haman's actions and responds emotionally to the present situation. The recent events have upset her and caused her to be filled with anxiety and sorrow. She is concerned for and worried about the fate of her people. And she is afraid, sensing herself in as much danger as the Jews outside the court. Esther's recognition of the risk of approaching the king makes her apprehensive about doing so. She needs help in dealing with this situation, but only God's help will do. Moreover, Esther feels herself to be alienated from others, particularly those on whom she might rely. She can only rely on God.

We also learn, in this section, more about Esther's life in the Persian court. For instance, she has been unhappy since going there and she does not enjoy some of the obligations of being queen. She hates sleeping with the king. Esther does not eat with the Persians, perhaps because of Jewish dietary regulations (although this is never stated), nor does she worship with them. Esther appears alienated within the court, different from the rest. In this episode there is not even evidence of the female servants and eunuchs who have been ever present throughout the earlier events of the story. Moreover, Esther holds real animosity towards Gentiles as a whole. She detests those who are uncircumcised or whom she considers lawless or foreign because they neglect to worship God and attempt to destroy that which is of God, including the Jewish people. Esther views such persons as enemies both of the Jews and of God.

Esther's disclosure of her discomfort in the life of the court highlights her ability as a lover and reveals her talent for acting. Though Esther herself finds sex with the king to be detestable, he apparently has had no inkling of her displeasure. He thinks that she is the best in bed of all the young Persian women he tries. Esther must be a great lover. But she also must be a phenomenal actor to fool one as experienced as he. Esther's ability to feign enjoyment extends to her life as a whole. Though she reveals in her prayer that she dislikes much of what occurs in Persian court life, she has still been able to win the favor and obedience of the court servants. They perceive her as an excellent choice for the queenship. Esther plays the part of a Persian monarch, and she does so very well. But we, and God, know that she finds her new position personally distasteful.

Finally, this Greek section portrays more clearly Esther's role in the salvation of the Jews. She expresses strong feeling about the Jews' welfare and sees her own action as instrumental in maintaining Israel's tradition. It is important to her that she present her arguments before the king as best she can. And we also know that it will be not just Esther but God working through Esther that brings reversal to the situation.

Episode 4 (15.1-16)

This episode occurs immediately after Esther concludes her prayer in the Greek narratives, the A and B texts. In the M text, it directly follows the conversation between Esther and Mordecai. In the two longer Greek texts, Esther begins to carry out her decision to go to the king and to request that he override the edict requiring the destruction of the Jewish people. She takes care to prepare her appearance, offers a brief prayer, and sets out accompanied by servants. Though her beauty is evident, she is anxious. Esther enters the throne room of the king, he expresses a great anger, and she feels weakened. The king becomes gentle and encourages her, and he touches her with his sceptre. Esther relates her vision of him, which affects her adversely, so the king again encourages her.

The portion of the M text which relates the events of this episode, Esther's approach to the king, is much shorter. It comprises only two verses in contrast to the fifteen and sixteen verses of the Greek narratives. The M text is much abbreviated in content as well, exhibiting only some of the actions and details of the Greek versions. In it, Esther comes to the proper place in the palace before the king. When the king sees her, she wins his favor. He stretches forth his sceptre towards her, and she touches it.

This episode is represented by the versification D.1-16 in the Göttingen edition of the Greek texts, and by the versification 5.1-2 in BHS for the Hebrew text. As with the last episode, the analysis of this episode will again vary from the standard pattern. In the Text section, the two verses of the M text will be placed as they best correspond to the Greek texts and considered along with them where appropriate. Each of the three narratives will be analyzed with regard to their unique characterization of Esther, as usual. In addition, the manner in which the details shared by the A and B texts but not by the M text affect the general portrayal of Esther's character will be noted.

Text

Καὶ ἐγενήθη ἐν τῇ ἡμέρᾳ τῇ τρίτῃ, ὡς ἐπαύσατο Εσθηρ προσευχομένη, ἐξεδύσατο τὰ ἱμάτια τῆς θεραπείας καὶ περιεβάλετο *τὰ ἱμάτια* τῆς δόξης	Καὶ ἐγενήθη ἐν τῇ ἡμέρᾳ τῇ τρίτῃ, ὡς ἐπαύσατο προσευχομένη, ἐξεδύσατο τὰ ἱμάτια τῆς θεραπείας καὶ περιεβάλετο τὴν δόξαν *αὐτῆς*	ויהי ביום השלישי ותלבש אסתר <u>מלכות</u> 1

And when it came to be the third day, when Esther ceased praying, she took off the garments of worship and clothed herself (with) the garments of glory.

And when it came to be the third day, when she ceased praying, she took off the garments of worship and clothed herself (with) her glory.

And it was on the third day, and Esther was clothed (in) royal aspect.

καὶ *γενομένη* ἐπιφανὴς *καὶ* ἐπικαλεσαμένη τὸν πάντων *γνώστην* καὶ σωτῆρα θεὸν παρέλαβε *μεθ' ἑαυτῆς* δύο ἅβρας	καὶ *γενηθεῖσα* ἐπιφανὴς ἐπικαλεσαμένη τὸν πάντων *ἐπόπτην* θεὸν καὶ σωτῆρα παρέλαβεν τὰς δύο ἅβρας	2

And she became manifestly splendid, also calling upon the one knowledgeable of all things and savior, God. She took along with her two servants.

And she was made manifestly splendid, calling upon the eyewitness of all things, God, and savior. She took along two servants.

καὶ τῇ μὲν μιᾷ ἐπηρείδετο ὡς τρυφερευομένη,	καὶ τῇ μὲν μιᾷ ἐπηρείδετο ὡς τρυφερευομένη,	3

And upon one she leaned as if being delicate,

And upon one she leaned as if being delicate,

ἡ δὲ ἑτέρα ἐπηκολούθει *ἐπι*κουφίζουσα *τὸ ἔνδυμα* αὐτῆς,	ἡ δὲ ἑτέρα ἐπηκολούθει κουφίζουσα *τὴν ἔνδυσιν* αὐτῆς,	4

and the other one followed along, supporting the burden of her cloak.

and the other one followed along, supporting the burden of her clothing.

καὶ αὐτὴ ἐρυθριῶσα *ἐν* ἀκμῇ κάλλους αὐτῆς, καὶ τὸ προσωπον αὐτῆς ὡς προσφιλές, ἡ δὲ καρδία αὐτῆς ἀπεστενωμένη.	καὶ αὐτὴ ἐρυθριῶσα ἀκμῇ κάλλους αὐτῆς, καὶ τὸ πρόσωπον αὐτῆς *ἱλαρὸν* ὡς προσφιλές, ἡ δὲ καρδία αὐτῆς ἀπεστενωμένη *ἀπὸ τοῦ φόβου*.	5

And she was blushing in the height of her beauties, and her face was as though amicable. But her heart was cramped up.

And she was blushing to the height of her beauties, and her face was cheerful, as though amicable. But her heart was cramped up by fear.

καὶ εἰσελθοῦσα τὰς θύρας ἔστη ἐνώπιον τοῦ βασιλέως, καὶ ὁ βασιλεὺς ἐκάθητο ἐπὶ τοῦ θρόνου τῆς βασιλείας αὐτοῦ καὶ πᾶσαν στολὴν ἐπιφανείας ἐνδεδύκει, ὅλος _διάχρυσος_, καὶ λίθοι πολυτελεῖς _ἐπ' αὐτῷ_, καὶ φοβερὸς σφόδρα.

καὶ εἰσελθοῦσα _πάσας_ τὰς θύρας _κατέστη_ ἐνώπιον τοῦ βασιλέως, καὶ _αὐτὸς_ ἐκάθητο ἐπὶ τοῦ θρόνου τῆς βασιλείας αὐτοῦ καὶ πᾶσαν στολὴν τῆς ἐπιφανείας _αὐτοῦ_ ἐνδεδύκει, ὅλος _διὰ χρυσοῦ_ καὶ λίθων πολυτελῶν, καὶ _ἦν_ φοβερὸς σφόδρα.

ותעמד _בחצר בית־המלך הפנימית_ 6
נכח _בית המלך_ והמלך יושב על־כסא
מלכותו _בבית המלכות נכח פתח הבית_

And, going through the doors, she stood before the king. And the king was sitting upon the throne of his royalty, and he had been clothed in an entire robe of manifested rank, wholly interwoven with gold, and expensive stones upon it. And he was extremely fear-inspiring.

And, going through all the doors, she stood there before the king. And he was sitting upon the throne of his royalty, and he had been clothed in an entire robe of his manifested rank, gold all throughout and expensive stones. And he was extremely fear-inspiring.

And she stood in the inner court of the house of the king, opposite to the house of king. And the king was sitting upon the throne of his royalty, in the house of the kingdom, opposite to the door of the house.

καὶ ἄρας τὸ πρόσωπον αὐτοῦ πεπυρωμένον _ἐν_ δόξῃ _ἐνέβλεψεν αὐτῇ ὡς ταῦρος_ ἐν ἀκμῇ θυμοῦ _αὐτοῦ_, καὶ _ἐφοβήθη_ ἡ βασίλισσα καὶ μετέβαλε τὸ _πρόσωπον_ αὐτῆς ἐν ἐκλύσει καὶ ἐπέκυψεν ἐπὶ τὴν κεφαλὴν τῆς ἄβρας τῆς προπορευομένης.

καὶ ἄρας τὸ πρόσωπον αὐτοῦ πεπυρωμένον δόξῃ ἐν ἀκμῇ θυμοῦ ἔβλεψεν, καὶ _ἔπεσεν_ ἡ βασίλισσα καὶ μετέβαλεν τὸ _χρῶμα_ αὐτῆς ἐν ἐκλύσει καὶ _κατ_επέκυψεν ἐπὶ τὴν κεφαλὴν τῆς ἄβρας τῆς προπορευομένης.

ויהי _כראות המלך את־אסתר_ המלכה 7
עמדת בחצר נשאה חן בעיניו

And lifting his face which had been set afire in glory, he gazed directly at her like a bull in the height of its anger. And the queen was afraid, and her face changed over in faintness, and she bent over upon the head of the servant who was going in front.

And lifting his face which had been set afire (with) glory, he looked out in the height of anger. And the queen fell and her complexion changed over in faintness, and she bent down over upon the head of the servant who was going in front.

And it was that as the king saw Esther the queen standing in the courtyard, she bore favor in his eyes.

		8
καὶ μετέβαλεν ὁ θεὸς τὸ πνεῦμα τοῦ βασιλέως <u>καὶ μετέθηκε τὸν θυμὸν αὐτοῦ</u> εἰς πραότητα, καὶ ἀγωνιάσας <u>ὁ βασιλεὺς κατε</u>πήδησεν ἀπὸ τοῦ θρόνου αὐτοῦ καὶ ἀνέλαβεν αὐτὴν ἐπὶ τὰς ἀγκάλας αὐτοῦ καὶ παρεκάλεσεν αὐτὴν	καὶ μετέβαλεν ὁ θεὸς τὸ πνεῦμα τοῦ βασιλέως εἰς πραύτητα, καὶ ἀγωνιάσας <u>ἀνε</u>πήδησεν ἀπὸ τοῦ θρόνου αὐτοῦ καὶ ἀνέλαβεν αὐτὴν ἐπὶ τὰς ἀγκάλας αὐτοῦ, <u>μέχρις οὗ κατέστη</u>, καὶ παρεκάλει αὐτὴν <u>λόγοις εἰρηνικοῖς</u>	
And God changed the spirit of the king, and transferred his anger to mildness. And in anguish the king leaped down from his throne and he took her up in his arms, and he encouraged her.	And God changed the spirit of the king to mildness, and in anguish he leaped up from his throne and he took her up in his arms, until she stood there. And he encouraged her with peaceful words.	

		9
καὶ εἶπεν Τί ἐστιν, Εσθηρ; ἐγώ <u>εἰμι</u> ἀδελφός σου, θάρσει,	καὶ εἶπεν <u>αὐτῇ</u> Τί ἐστιν, Εσθηρ; ἐγὼ ὁ ἀδελφός σου, θάρσει,	
And he said, 'What is it, Esther? I am your brother. Be confident.	And he said to her, 'What is it, Esther? I am your brother. Be confident.	

		10
οὐ μὴ ἀποθάνῃς, ὅτι κοινόν ἐστι τὸ <u>πρᾶγμα</u> ἡμῶν,	οὐ μὴ ἀποθάνῃς, ὅτι κοινὸν τὸ <u>πρόσταγμα</u> ἡμῶν ἐστιν·	
You will not die, for our transaction is for the general public,	You will not die, for our command is for the general public.	

		11
<u>καὶ οὐ πρὸς σὲ ἡ ἀπειλή· ἰδοὺ τὸ σκῆπτρον ἐν τῇ χειρί σου·</u>	<u>πρόσελθε.</u>	
and the threat is not against you. Indeed, the sceptre is in your hand.'	Come near.'	

			12
καὶ ἄρας τὸ σκῆπτρον ἐπέθηκεν ἐπὶ τὸν τράχηλον αὐτῆς καὶ ἠσπάσατο αὐτὴν καὶ εἶπεν Λάλησόν μοι.	καὶ ἄρας τὴν χρυσῆν <u>ῥάβδον</u> ἐπέθηκεν ἐπὶ τὸν τράχηλον αὐτῆς καὶ ἠσπάσατο αὐτὴν καὶ εἶπεν Λάλησόν μοι.	<u>ויושׁט המלך לאסתר</u> את־שׁרביט <u>הזהב אשׁר בידו ותקרב אסתר ותגע</u> <u>בראשׁ השׁרביט</u>	
And he raised the sceptre; he laid (it) upon her neck and greeted her affectionately. And he said, 'Speak to me.'	And he raised the golden rod; he laid (it) upon her neck and greeted her affectionately. And he said, 'Speak to me.'	And the king extended to Esther the golden sceptre which was in his hand, and Esther drew near and touched the top of the sceptre.	

καὶ εἶπεν αὐτῷ Εἶδον σε
ὡς ἄγγελον θεοῦ, καὶ
<u>ἐτάκη</u> ἡ καρδία μου ἀπὸ
<u>τῆς δόξης τοῦ θυμοῦ</u> σου,
κύριε.

καὶ εἶπεν αὐτῷ Εἶδόν σε,　　　13
κύριε, ὡς ἄγγελον θεοῦ,
καὶ <u>ἐταράχθη</u> ἡ καρδία μου
ἀπὸ <u>φόβου τῆς δόξης</u> σου·

And she said to him, 'I saw
you like an angel of God,
and my heart was melted by
the glory of your anger, lord.'

And she said to him, 'I saw
you, lord, like an angel of
God, and my heart was
troubled by fear of your glory.

ὅτι θαυμαστὸς εἶ, κύριε, καὶ　　　14
τὸ πρόσωπόν σου χαρίτων
μεστόν.

For you are wonderful, lord,
and your face is full of
graciousness.'

<u>καὶ ἐπὶ τὸ πρόσωπον
αὐτῆς μέτρον ἰδοῶτος·</u>

<u>ἐν δὲ τῷ διαλέγεσθαι</u>　　　15
<u>αὐτὴν ἔπεσεν ἀπὸ</u>
<u>ἐκλύσεως·</u>

And upon her face was a
measure of perspiration.

But during her discourse she
fell from faintness.

καὶ ἐταράσσετο ὁ
βασιλεὺς καὶ πᾶσα ἡ
θεραπεία αὐτοῦ, <u>καὶ</u>
παρεκάλ<u>ουν</u> αὐτήν.

καὶ ὁ βασιλεὺς　　　16
ἐταράσσετο, καὶ πᾶσα ἡ
θεραπεία αὐτοῦ
παρεκάλ<u>ει</u> αὐτήν.

And the king was troubled,
and each servant of his, and
they encouraged her.

And the king was troubled,
and each servant of his; (so)
he encouraged her.

Notes

Verse 1. M lacks a reference to Esther's stopping her prayer. Such an omission is not surprising, of course, as M does not include her praying as part of its plot. This narrative, however, might have noted that Esther ceased her fasting, the religious action of which she *does* partake (cf. 4.16), which would have been consonant with its overall plot. As M has this episode begin three days later ('and it was on the third day', ויהי ביום השלישי), the reader may be expected to assume that Esther has concluded her three-day fast, but such is not made explicit in the text. We can compare A's mention here of Esther ceasing her praying, when it had earlier noted her intention to pray earnestly to God instead of to fast (4.16, in variance with M and B). As in general, M does not here give Esther a religious character to the extent of the Greek narratives. The lack of mention of her ceasing to fast makes Esther's action of fasting appear less necessary for her subsequent success with the king than her action of praying does in A and B.

A places the most emphasis upon Esther's actual changing of clothing. Two parallel sets of clothing are involved in her change, the garments or clothing of worship (τὰ ἱμάτια τῆς θεραπείας) and the garments of glory and magnificence (τὰ ἱμάτια τῆς δόξης). B includes only one set of clothing ('the garments of worship', τὰ ἱμάτια τῆς θεραπείας), and M lacks any reference to particular clothing at all.

M does not state that Esther had to change out of certain clothing or to put special clothing on for her meeting with the king. It notes only that she is wearing 'royalty' or 'royal power'. The מלכות can refer to a variety of things based upon one's royal power or reign; apparel is a less frequent type of its usage. Thus, although this verse may be read to suggest clothing, it does not stress particular garments. The verb לבש ('and she was clothed in', ותלבש) can signify either that Esther was already wearing her aspect of royalty or that she puts it on now for the occasion.

B alone, with its inclusion of the possessive pronoun αὐτῆς, suggests that Esther's glory or honor is her possession or somehow essentially connected to her ('her glory', τὴν δόξαν αὐτῆς). The singular δόξαν could be understood as a collective here, as 'her glorious things', but it still would remain unclear exactly from what she obtains such an appearance of glory.

In M, the primary characteristic of Esther's persona at this point in the story is her impression of royalty. She is a royal figure. Esther is not just magnificent, glorious, or attractive in some fashion. Rather, she is presented in terms of her queenly position and authority.

Verse 2. B's passive participle γενηθεῖσα ('she was made to be'), in contrast to A's middle form (which is used in the active sense for γίνομαι) γενομένη ('she became'), suggests that Esther is herself less responsible for her transformation of appearance and makes it seem less her own intentional action.

In A, the ἐπιφανὴς recalls 14.2, in which Esther is also described by a form of ἐπιφαίνω (ἐπιφανείας). (B uses this term here but not in 14.2.) There it describes her appearance before she changes clothes in preparation to pray. This dual usage creates an inclusio, suggesting that Esther is now returning to the same type of appearance that she had before beginning her prayer.

M's lack of these events portrays two divergent impressions about Esther's approach to the king. She goes by herself, without either servants or God. And we have no intimation that Esther is relying upon God to help her through the present ordeal.

Verse 3. The ὡς of A and B draws into question how weak Esther feels at this point in her approach. Esther does not lean upon her servants or have them help carry her clothing (v. 4) because she is unable to support herself but because she wants to convey the impression of one who is dainty and gentle when the king first lays eyes upon her. She desires to appear as if she is soft and delicate ('as if being delicate', ὡς τρυφευομένη). Moore's suggestion that Esther's need of support at this point is a result of her three-day fast could apply only to B, for in A she does not fast but holds a worship service (cf. 4.16) (*Additions*, pp. 217-18).

Verse 4. M's lack of the information in A's and B's vv. 3-4 leads the king, as well as the reader, not to question that Esther is anything but strong. It certainly conveys no portrait of her as weak enough to need assistance in carrying her own body or her clothing.

Verse 5. The phrase (ἐν) ἀκμῇ κάλλους αὐτῆς is troublesome to understand and render with precision. The accusative sense of κάλλους is difficult to reflect in translation. Its plural aspect is also problematic, for if one wanted to refer to Esther's goodness or beauty in general, a singular form of καλός would more likely be used. What is meant by the κάλλους in each narrative is not entirely clear. It may refer to Esther's beautiful objects (clothing, jewels, and the like) or to her own beautiful features.

In A and B, Esther is again feigning a certain type of appearance (cf. v. 3). The phrase ὡς προσφιλές ('as though amicable') suggests that she is deliberately putting forward a pleasing, cheerful face before the king, regardless of what she actually feels in his presence.

In B, Esther's face is described as appearing happy or cheerful (ἱλαρὸν) as well as exhibiting a friendly expression before the king. She makes her outward impression more calm and unruffled, though her anxiety is actually greater here than in A.

B is more emphatic than is A in describing Esther's feelings of fear. Whereas the expression καρδία αὐτῆς ἀπεστενωμένη ('her heart was cramped up'), which is shared by both A and B, suggests Esther's dread and anxiety, B includes the more specific mention of fear (ἀπὸ τοῦ φόβου) in addition.

M provides a different perspective on Esther. She makes no calculated appearance out of the ordinary, emphasizing either special clothing or her own beautiful features. Nor do we know Esther to be playing a role, appearing calm when she has great anxiety or fear.

Verse 6. The three narratives represent a progression of difficulty in getting to the king's presence. In M, Esther has the easiest time of it; she merely goes into the courtyard. A notes that Esther has to go through doors or gates (τὰς θύρας) before being able to stand in front of him. And B portrays the king as most protected and inaccessible, and the furthest away from Esther and the others. It states that Esther has to travel through 'all' the doors (πάσας τὰς θύρας).

M stresses that this meeting takes place in the palace, a detail not even mentioned by A or B. Three times in this short verse it refers to the house of the king, twice using the phrase בֵּית־הַמֶּלֶךְ ('the house of the king') and once using בֵּית הַמַּלְכוּת ('the house of the kingdom').

M does not describe the king's clothing. It provides no idea of any magnificence of his physical appearance.

B's inclusion of the possessive pronoun αὐτοῦ makes it explicit that it is the king's own visible or glorious appearance which affects Esther ('his manifested rank', τῆς ἐπιφανείας αὐτοῦ).

M exhibits an extreme interest in precision of location. First, it tells exactly where Esther stands ('in the inner court of the house of the king, opposite to the house of the king', בַּחֲצַר בֵּית־הַמֶּלֶךְ הַפְּנִימִית נֹכַח בֵּית הַמֶּלֶךְ), and then exactly where the king is sitting ('in the house of the kingdom, opposite to the door of the house', בְּבֵית הַמַּלְכוּת נֹכַח פֶּתַח הַבָּיִת).

The language of A and B's final phrases is imprecise regarding exactly what is fearful about this scene. In B's ἦν φοβερὸς σφόδρα, the ἦν could refer back to any singular noun before it: the king (τοῦ βασιλέως), the throne (τοῦ θρόνου), the royal aspect (τῆς βασιλείας), the robe (στολὴν), the manifestation (τῆς ἐπιφανείας), or the gold (χρυσοῦ). However, it is most likely, within context, to refer to the king. Thus, it is the king himself who is the object of terror. M provides no indication of how the king or this entire scene appears to others, nor any emotional reaction which these things engender.

Verse 7. A shows the king as expressing greater anger towards Esther than does B. First, his manner of looking out is described by a verb (ἐμβλέπω) which suggests greater intensity of his gaze and her as its object (ἐνέβλεψεν, 'he directed a gaze, looked at'). Secondly, Esther, as referred to by the pronoun αὐτῇ only in A, is the particular object of his intense stare. And thirdly, the king is acting here as an animal, a bull (ταῦρος); indeed, as a strong animal who can do a great deal of damage when aroused. The anger he expresses is, furthermore, not only the acme or extreme of human anger or of wrath in general, as in B, but of a bull's anger ('a bull in the height of its anger', ταῦρος ἐν ἀκμῇ θομοῦ αὐτοῦ), which one would assume could be quite extreme indeed. (Dorothy's suggestion of A's 'bull' as a reference to Gentiles is tenuous, at least within this context ['Books', pp. 158-59].)

M includes no hint that the king visibly appears, or is, in a mood any different than typical. He displays no anger or animal-like behavior.

M states again (cf. v. 6) with precision where this encounter occurs—in the courtyard or enclosed area (בחצר).

M refers to Esther by personal name as well as by title ('Esther the queen', אסתר המלכה).

The three narratives present variant responses of Esther to the king. A shows Esther's initial response to be emotional: she is afraid ('and the queen was afraid', καὶ ἐφοβήθη ἡ βασίλισσα). Such is the anticipated response, as the vision of the king sitting in majesty has been previously described as inspiring fear (v. 6), and his anger towards her is greater. B, in contrast, portrays Esther's response as physical: she falls down ('and the queen fell', και ἔπεσεν ἡ βασίλισσα). And in M, her response affects the king as well, for she wins over his good pleasure ('she bore favor in his eyes', ונשאה חן בעיניו). However, we are not told in what manner she pleases him.

Esther's action of falling over upon her servant is more pronounced in B than in A. B uses the verb καταπέκυψεν, in contrast to A's ἐπέκυψεν. The κατά prefix emphasizes the downward essence of her bowing or bending action. (The verb κατεπικύπτω is a fairly uncommon form. For instance, Liddell and Scott's lexicon, which in general does not tend to list biblical citations with frequency, cites its occurrence only here when giving its definition (Henry George Liddell and Robert Scott, *A Greek-English Lexicon* [Oxford: Clarendon Press, 9th edn, 1954], p. 924). With both her first fall and then her bending over further and relying more heavily upon the support of her servant,

Esther exhibits greater physical weakness in B than in A.

In M, this verse as a whole presents a portrayal of Esther as strong and confident. She is not afraid, does not feel weak, and does not fall down. Her action of standing (עמדת) is in direct contrast with her falling (ἔπεσεν) in B.

Verse 8. A's repetition of the king's anger from the previous verse (τὸν θυμὸν αὐτοῦ) makes his emotional transformation now appear greater. His outlook has shifted across the extremes of an emotional spectrum, from intense rage to meekness and concern for Esther.

B provides a motive for the king's action of embracing Esther. His goal is to make her stand up ('until she stood there', μέχρις οὗ κατέστη). The κατέστη here recalls the κατέστη of v. 6, where Esther first stands before the king. She undergoes a progression throughout these three verses—she stands, then falls, her complexion shows her faintness, she leans upon her servant, and now is made to stand again—and the king brings her back again to exactly the same place at which she was when first coming in to speak with him. Perhaps his goal is to try to undo her falling, so they might start over again.

In B alone the king speaks particularly for peace. The noun εἰρήνη, from which this adjective εἰρηνικοῖς is derived, carries a fairly narrow range of meaning. It signifies just what pertains to peace, which hints that there was some sort of violence or argument for which the king is trying to make amends. The use of peaceful speech intimates that the previous brief encounter was to some degree conflictual, and that the king desires a truce to be called and they be again in accord.

Each of these two narratives presents certain ideas not found in the other. A specifies that the king's mood is transferred by God out of an angry state, and B notes that the king's embracing of Esther is to cause her to stand and that he speaks a peaceful message to her. In their overall effect upon the verse, A's extra details provide us with a clearer picture of the emotions of the king. B's details instead highlight the king as especially affectionate to Esther and provide a general sense of more action occurring at this point in the story.

M's lack of these actions leaves us without any indication that the king exhibits the same anger, mildness, and explicit concern for Esther as do the other two texts at this point in the plot.

Verse 9. The king in B is more relational, for he speaks directly to Esther ('and he said to her', καὶ εἶπεν αὐτῇ).

In A, within the context of these three verses, the king's instructions to Esther take on a fuller meaning. In v. 7 we were told that Esther is afraid. Now, the king's encouragement to her to be hopeful, of good cheer, or confident (θάρσει), suggests two things. First, she is specifically being asked to banish her fear and be courageous. Secondly, the king had insight into her inner feelings at that time, sensing that she was actually afraid. B's first reference to Esther's fear comes earlier in this episode (v. 5), before the king even sees her. Thus it has less effect on the understanding of his present instructions to her.

Verse 10. This verse includes a puzzling phrase: ὅτι κοινόν ἐστι τὸ πρᾶγμα ἡμῶν in A, ὅτι κοινὸν τὸ πρόσταγμα ἡμῶν ἐστιν in B. There are two issues at stake: how one understands the τὸ πρᾶγμα/τὸ πρόσταγμα, and how one understands the κοινόν. First, the noun πρᾶγμα (used in A and in four manuscripts of the B textual tradition) refers generally to something that is done, a deed, fact, affair, transaction, or work. The term πρόσταγμα (used in B) is more narrowly defined as a command or ordinance. The distinction in the definitions of these two terms is also noted by Dorothy, though he only addresses the differences in these verses in light of textual dependence ('Books', pp. 159-60). These terms might, within the plot of the story, be referring to any of three things: Haman's edict against the Jews, the king's rule about anyone coming to him unsummoned, or the overall affairs and rulership of the kingdom. Accordingly, with these three options, the pronoun ἡμῶν would also refer to different individuals: if the decree against the Jews, the ἡμῶν would stand for Haman and the king; if the king's rule, it would refer to the persons and customs of the Persians in general; if the rulership of the kingdom, it would refer to the king and Esther. Secondly, the κοινόν could also signify a variety of things. Much like our English term 'common', κοινός can signify that which is ordinary, everyday, or profane, or that which is shared by more than one individual. It can also be used, in the singular, as a collective to refer to the general public or the masses. Either understanding of κοινόν is logical within the context of the story. It may signify that Esther and the king mutually share the commanding of the kingdom or that Esther is exempted from harm because she is not one of the common folk.

Verse 11. In B, this verse concludes a series of three verses which emphasize Esther's closeness with the king. In v. 9, he tells her that he is like a brother to her. In his next statement (v. 10), he hints again at their familial type of relationship, as κοινός can be used to refer to relatives and particularly to brother and sister. Now, in this verse, he is requesting that Esther come near to him, in physical proximity as well as the emotional closeness he has just expressed between them.

In A, the king further emphasizes Esther's exemption from the threat (ἡ ἀπειλή). He gives her more information and encouragement.

A's notation of the 'sceptre in your hand' (τὸ σκῆπρον ἐν τῇ χειρί σου) has two effects upon our view of Esther's power. It recalls that she has power in general in her role as queen. And it suggests a certain degree of power in this particular situation. This reference to Esther's relationship to the sceptre before being touched by it makes her appear more in control of the present events than in B.

M's lack of the king's statements to Esther throughout these three verses (vv. 9-11) has an effect upon the portrayal of Esther. First, Esther goes ahead with her request to the king without being encouraged by him nor assured that she will not be killed. And secondly, M does not here reflect statements of closeness between Esther and the king, as brother (in A and B) and in physical distance (in B).

Verse 12. M represents a compilation of details in A's and B's texts of v. 11. Esther first approaches the king ('and Esther drew near', ותקרב אסתר), which mirrors the king's command for her to approach him in B ('come near', πρόσελθε). M, though, portrays her as performing this action of her own initiative. Esther then reaches for the sceptre ('and she touched the top of the sceptre', ותגע בראש השרבים), which is similar to the king's statement in A that she holds the sceptre ('the sceptre is in your hand', τὸ σκῆπτρον ἐν τῇ χειρί σου). However, there is a degree of contrast. A speaks of the sceptre actually being in Esther's hand, whereas in M it is the king who has it in hand ('the golden sceptre which was in his hand', את־שרבים הזהב אשר בידו).

In A and B, the king just lifts up the sceptre ('he raised the sceptre/ golden rod', ἄρας τὸ σκῆπτρον/τήν χρυσῆν ῥάβδον); in M, he actually holds it out towards her, in a gesture suggesting greater acceptance to whatever her petition might be ('and the king extended to Esther the golden sceptre', ויושט המלך לאסתר את־שרבים הזהב).

A and B use different terminology to refer to what the king raises; A names it more particularly as a sceptre or staff used for command (σκῆπτρον), while B speaks of it more generally as a rod, wand, or stick (ῥάβδον). It is ambiguous with what description M agrees, for the word it uses here (שרביט) may refer to either. The term שרביט is unique to the book of Esther, as a variant form of the more common שבט, a rod used for any variety of activities, one of which is ruling. שבט specifically denotes a sceptre at several places in the biblical literature, some of which use the term with forms of משל and מלך (for instance, Ps. 45.6, Isa. 14.5, Ezek. 19.14). As M uses שרביט in reference to kingship, it most likely carries the more specific meaning of 'sceptre' here as well, as a rod used particularly for ruling. Thus, A and M both exhibit a more pronounced view of the king as a royal and/or authority figure.

A, B, and M display an intermingling of details with regard to the stick. A and M present it as a sceptre (τό σκῆπτρον, שרביט), and B and M describe it as being gold (χρυσῆν, הזהב). That the king is described with both of the more royal details ('golden sceptre') in M alone makes him appear the most regal and authoritative there.

A and B present the king as more affectionate to Esther and concerned about her. He welcomes her to him ('he greeted her affectionately', ἡσπάσατοα αὐτὴν), probably with at least a degree of warmth. And then he wants her voice and her perspective, in requesting that she speak her mind ('and he said, "Speak to me,"' καὶ εἶπεν Λάλησόν μοι).

In M, Esther herself does the action necessary to come into contact with the sceptre, in coming near to it (תקרב) and touching it (תגע). In A and B, though, the king performs the action, by touching Esther with it ('he laid it upon her neck', ἐπέθηκεν ἐπὶ τὸν τράχηλον αὐτῆς).

M gives the overall impression of these events having a more solemn and restrained quality. They occur without speech, whereas in A and B they appear as more spontaneous, emotional, and vocal.

Verse 13. The term ἄγγελον θεοῦ in this verse can be understood generally as a messenger of God or more specifically as an angel of God in this context. By speaking of the king in this manner, Esther is beginning to flatter and honor him.

That which affects Esther's heart in A is the magnificence of the king's wrath ('the glory of your anger', τῆς δόξης τοῦ θυμοῦ). Honor, glory, or majesty moves her, but she also sees this glory as being somehow connected to his anger in a way which is not obvious. The reference to anger (θυμοῦ) here recalls the same term when used earlier to speak of the king's emotional state (cf. vv. 7, 8). In B, Esther's heart is explicitly affected by fear, especially fear of the king's magnificence ('fear of your glory', φόβου τῆς δόξης σου). It also refers to his δόξης, but towards more negative ends. Esther's response here reflects her heart's response of v. 5, before she sees the king, when it was likewise troubled by some sort of fear (φόβου).

Verse 14. This verse, which is represented only by B, demonstrates that Esther holds the king in high regard. She finds him to be wonderful and glorious (θαυμαστὸς), as well as charming or generous (χαρίτων). She has apparently interpreted his recent actions towards her as benevolent.

Esther notes the outward expression of the king's face, telling him that he appears extremely kind and gracious ('your face is full of graciousness', τὸ πρόσωπόν σου χαρίτων μεστόν). This phrase signals a change from the events of v. 7, when the expression on that same face was flaming anger. The transformation of his disposition, from rage to grace, has been quite rapid, and we have seen it through Esther's eyes.

The existence of this verse makes Esther appear more deferential to the king, as the content of her statement is only to tell him how great he is.

The effect of M's lack of these two verses, vv. 13-14, is that we do not know how Esther feels about the king at this point. We certainly have no indication that she finds him to be as awe-inspiring as in B.

Verse 15. A and B are completely different at this point. Both, however, portray the physical emotion of Esther to either her vision of the king specifically, or more generally to the effect which all of the recent events have had upon her.

In A, Esther just perspires ('upon her face was a measure of perspiration', ἐπὶ τὸ πρόσωπον αὐτῆς μέτρον ἱδρῶτος). Her countenance now displays the fact that she has been affected by what has transpired, as it had also earlier in this episode (cf. vv. 5, 7). We see now that she is physically as well as emotionally upset.

B shows Esther as being much weaker in a physical sense. The proceedings have affected her more severely than in A. She falls for a second time, and is faint and weak. The particular vocabulary used here recalls her reaction in v. 7, in which she also falls (ἔπεσεν) and experiences faintness or exhaustion (ἐκλύσεως/ἐκλύσει). Because the repeated use of this term is key to understanding the progression of this scene, we must translate it in the same manner at both places (contra Moore, who translates 'she sagged with relief' here [*Additions,* p. 219]).

M includes no hint that Esther is emotional, upset, or otherwise influenced at this point. Her encounter with the king does not cause her to lose her composure; she does not fall nor perspire.

Verse 16. In A, everyone tries to encourage Esther, all of the servants as well as the king ('and they encouraged her', καὶ παρεκάλουν αὐτήν). She is the center of attention. In B, the singular form of παρακαλέω (παρακάλει αὐτήν, 'he encouraged her') signifies that only the king is attempting to console Esther. (Within this context, it is much more logical to understand the king as the subject performing the encouraging, in contrast to Dorothy's interpretation that the servant comforts Esther ['Books', p. 160], though either is grammatically possible).

It is more evident why the king is troubled in B, as Esther has just fainted and fallen down for the second time within a matter of minutes. More difficult to understand is why, in A, the king and his servants are all so worried, especially as the overall encouragement rendered to her is greater in A than in B. And, as M does not include this event, we get from it no idea that Esther is either upset or in need of encouragement.

In A and B, the king cares about the welfare of Esther and his emotions towards her. M's absence of these details renders its portrayal of the king to be less affectionate towards her.

In M, to this point in the episode, there has been no sound. In A and B, we have heard the words of Esther and the king to each other, but in M neither of them has yet spoken. All of the events have transpired in silence.

Analysis
A Text. Noticeable links tie this episode to the one which immediately precedes it (Esther's prayer). In the last episode, Esther took away all the signs of her rank and glory in preparation for prayer. At the beginning of this scene, Esther makes efforts to return her appearance to that same glorious state. After so doing, she calls upon God. This progression serves to let the reader know that, though her visible appearance is now again that of her non-praying condition, her inner self continues its prayer. Esther continues to view God as completely omniscient and one who saves, which are two of the characteristics of God she especially stressed throughout her prayer. Furthermore, this narrative continues to portray Esther as less totally alone in the court than the other texts. Here her servants provide some emotional, as well

as physical, support for her. They join with her in her mission to Ahasuerus, and at the end of the scene, servants, perhaps the same ones, join with him in trying to ease Esther's anxiety.

Esther displays greater attention to what people wear. She herself has two complete sets of garments, one appropriate for worshipping and another for activities which require more glorious raiment. In preparing to meet with Ahasuerus, she is careful to put on her best and most beautiful clothing. And it is upon her clothing, the change to the second set of garments, which she relies to make her overall appearance magnificent. Esther is not only aware of her own clothing, but that of other people as well. When first seeing Ahasuerus sitting on the throne, the reader perceives, through her eyes, the king's robe, as it is described in somewhat greater detail.

Esther is a victim of Ahasuerus's wrath. In this narrative, the king's anger is more pronounced. When Esther first sees him, he appears as an angry beast, as a bull at the angriest that it can be, and he directs his rage particularly at her. Later in the episode, Esther views him particularly in terms of his anger, and this aspect is what upsets her from that vision. And when God comes on the scene to affect Ahasuerus's emotional state, it is specifically his state of anger that God must change. However, as in the B text, the king is also concerned about and compassionate towards Esther. She is a recipient of his encouragement and kindness as well. His concern and that of his servants is greater, at a point when she herself is even less visibly upset, than in the B text. The king's emotions towards Esther thus vary to the greatest degree in this narrative, from one extreme to the other.

Esther feels certain emotions at times throughout the events of this episode. At one point the narrative tells us that she is particularly afraid immediately after coming into the king's presence and encountering his angry gaze upon her. Her response of fear at this point is quite understandable, even expected. The king has just been described as inspiring terror, and fear is a logical response to being at the mercy of one who is as angry as a bull. At other places, Esther sometimes appears upset, but the narrative does not reveal a more specific feeling than that. When getting ready for the meeting, her inner being is in distress, though we know less specifically in what manner than in the B text. Then, later, she speaks of her inner self being affected by her vision of Ahasuerus. Although her vision obviously impacts her in some way, exactly what she is feeling or why remains more ambiguous.

Esther's fear and other emotions do not affect her physical strength as much as they might. Upon seeing the king's anger and experiencing fear of him, she does not faint nor even fall down. Her face, though, expresses her exhaustion, and she bends over a bit more, requiring support from the servant upon whom she is already leaning. And after her vision of the king, we can see the perspiration of her face, a physical indication that she is upset or has been somehow affected emotionally over these events, but such remains a relatively minor response.

B Text. Esther makes a greater effort in order to see the king in this narrative. First, we see that she has to work especially hard to disguise her true feelings. On the outside she appears even more happy and cheerful than in the A text. But we also know that on the inside Esther's heart is knotted up with a greater fear. Then she has to travel the furthest distance, walking through a series of doors, just to get where Artaxerxes is.

Esther possesses a certain beauty of her own here. She is a magnificent figure after preparing herself for her meeting, but it is more her and not the clothing she wears which provides this appearance. She removes her garments of prayer and puts on not glorious garments but a glory that is somehow essentially connected with her. At this point, when Esther's beautiful aspect or features are at their extreme, she blushes. But as Esther exhibits passivity in being made into her glorious presence, we are left to assume that it is God who is assisting her. This narrative likewise portrays God as having a greater role elsewhere in the episode. It is important to Esther that God is both visibly aware of all things and is able to save. Later, after her vision of Artaxerxes, she stresses more his gracious and glorious character as one sent by God.

Fear is Esther's predominant emotion. Her feelings of fear are named more explicitly and frequently than in the A text and occur throughout a longer extent of the episode. When this narrative tells of Esther's troubled state of mind, it tends to attribute this state particularly to fear. Even before she sees the king, Esther is afraid. Apparently praying did not help alleviate her anxiety. Then when seeing Artaxerxes in his anger, who himself is terrifying, she cannot bear the added burden in her already fearful state. Even after the king has calmed down, encouraged her, and reassured her that she will not die, she still remains more afraid. Esther's vision in this narrative is obviously a troubling one, and she again speaks of fear as the cause of her distress.

Esther displays greater physical weakness as well as emotional weakness. Her response, upon seeing the king in his anger, is to pass out and fall down. And she drops further upon the servant, requiring greater support. Artaxerxes must run down to her and hold her up until she recovers. Even though the king is actually less angry in this narrative, Esther's physical reaction to him is more severe. Then, later, after telling him about her vision of him and her opinion of him, she faints and falls down for a second time. In sum, all the proceedings seem to affect Esther to a greater extent in this narrative.

The king acts in a more affectionate manner towards Esther in this narrative. In his encouragement of her, Artaxerxes desires to help her. When holding and supporting her until she stands, he is attempting to take away the weakness and fear which caused her to fall. He speaks of a closeness or togetherness between them, and he addresses his words directly to her. This closeness is threefold: emotional, in their brother–sister relationship; political, in their joint rule; and physical, in his request that she walk nearer to him. Artaxerxes also wants to ensure that there are peaceful feelings between the two of them, that they be in agreement rather than conflict. And when she falls for the second time, he is distressed along with the others, but he alone attempts to encourage her. All of these details about Artaxerxes's character show Esther as one who is loved and cared about by her husband.

As in the other narratives, Esther possesses an aspect of royalty here. Yet Esther is subservient to the king. She holds him in high regard, or at least makes him believe that she does, for she stresses how wonderful and glorious he is. Esther even notes how his visage changes over from anger to benevolence and kindness, and she praises him for his second attitude. We can also note, though, that earlier it was this same person of the king whom she found so terrifying.

Effects of the Greek Versions of This Episode on the Esther Story. The greater amount of material in the Greek narratives, the A and B texts, provide numerous details about the story which are not represented in the Hebrew M text. This additional information falls within the general categories of actions comprising the movement of the plot, the religious dimensions, the outward appearance of the characters, the feelings of the characters, and the relationship between Esther and the king.

The two Greek narratives include a story line which is based upon more individual actions within the general framework of Esther's approach to the king in preparation for her petition. First, she does not go alone but takes along with her two servants, and she utilizes their help in carrying her clothing and her person. She goes to the king with a support network of sorts. Later, she bends down (in the A text) or falls (in the B text) when in the king's presence. His actions towards her are also more numerous from this point on in the plot. He gets up out of his throne and comes to embrace her. He speaks to her, and then she replies.

When going in to the king, Esther works to present herself in a certain manner. She again demonstrates herself to be an accomplished actress. After making her appearance splendid, she takes care to allow her maids to support her when going into the king's chamber. Her efforts are in order to make her appear delicate and dainty. Then she forces a pleasant expression on her face, despite her inner anxiety, in order to appear happy and friendly before the king. Esther feigns an appearance of the type of queen the king might want her to be—gentle and cheerful. Unfortunately, she is unable to maintain her façade. Her fear takes control and causes her to display the fear and faintness she feels.

As is not surprising, these narratives also include religious elements. We see Esther as one who prays to God; she is prayerful and reliant upon God for help and success in her venture. She even chooses to describe her impression of the glorious appearance of the king with reference to the divine. And in causing the king's emotions to change God influences him as well as Esther.[1]

More detailed descriptions of the visible demeanor of Esther and the king are provided. The beauty and excellence of Esther and her clothing is highlighted in these narratives, but it is the king's clothing which is described in detail. We are told of the golden threads and precious stones which adorn his royal robe. The expressions upon the characters' faces are also sometimes noted: Esther's blushing complexion and then its loss of color, the king's manifestations of anger and glory, and her expression of happiness. Each narrative, furthermore, indicates a unique detail by means of faces: the king's expression of graciousness (in the B text) and Esther's perspiration (in the A text).

Likewise, the inner characters of Esther and the king are also presented

---

1. Though Esther certainly is a beneficiary of God's assistance at this point, her own actions are not dispensable. It is not so much that 'God, not Esther, is the greater hero of Addition D', as Moore has stated (*Additions*, p. 219), or even that God is responsible for the outcome (as he proposes elsewhere [*Esther*, p. 57]). Rather, both Esther and God play important parts in this scene.

more fully. We are told the feelings that they each have at certain points throughout the story. For instance, the reader knows that though Esther appears cheerful before meeting with the king, she is actually anxious. We know that she feels faint and exhausted in his presence, that she is troubled by her vision, and that she is worried and afraid at particular times. And the king feels anger when Esther first enters the throne room, gentleness and anguish when seeing the effect his anger has upon her, and affection and concern throughout their conversation. However, the king's range of emotions in this scene also gives an idea of the unpredictability with which Esther must deal in the Persian court.

But these narratives also show the degree of affection which the king feels for Esther within their relationship. He physically embraces her when she is upset and several times vocally urges her to feel encouragement. He desires that she be confident before him and considers them to be like siblings in closeness. When touching her with his sceptre or rod, he does so with affection and welcome. And he is interested to hear her viewpoint and ideas, and listens as she speaks. The reader is left with the impression that Esther is loved and cared for by the king and that their marriage is one of affection, at least on his part.

M Text. This narrative provides fewer actions of, and significantly less information about, the characters in this episode. In general, it tends to de-emphasize the religious character of Esther and Ahasuerus. And, in this episode, it tends not to portray their emotions directly, provide many details about their outer impressions or appearances, or give as much insight into the relationship between them.

Esther herself is more active in this narrative. Upon first seeing the king, she wins his favor, attaining his approval in the same manner as when Ahasuerus first chose her to be the new queen. She comes close to him without being asked, and reaches out to touch the sceptre herself rather than waiting to be touched by it. We are left with the impression that Esther is a strong person. No hint of weakness about her is evident. She goes alone, without need of others, to meet with the king. She appears assured, confident, and courageous, and being in the king's presence causes her no anxiety. Esther is in control of the situation, as well as her own response to it.

Esther's royal status is also evident in this narrative. Her aspect of royalty is the only description given of the impression she makes, and is therefore her primary characteristic at this point in the story.[1] As Esther does not change her appearance or her clothing in preparation for meeting with the king, we have no reason to doubt that she always appears as a royal figure. And the nomenclature this narrative uses to refer to her emphasizes her position as queen in the kingdom as well as her importance in this brief encounter. Ahasuerus likewise is not portrayed with any special clothing. His implement for bestowal of audience is most glamorous in this narrative, a sceptre made of gold, and it is only this article which suggests any magnificence or royal power.

Little information is provided about the personal relationship between Esther and Ahasuerus. We see that, when she comes to see him, he is immediately accepting of her. He is pleased with her before she even says a word and apparently has a positive impression of her. Ahasuerus appears as a rational, calm person. But we are left with the general impression that these events are part of a formal procedure. This narrative tells us that Esther stands in a certain place and that the king is sitting in a certain place, all within a certain part of the palace of the kingdom. Their interaction is conducted in total silence; neither speaks to the other. Such details provide a sense of emotional distance between Esther and Ahasuerus.

Episode 5 (5.3-8)

Again, this episode follows immediately upon its predecessor. Esther has approached the king and has been accepted by him. She now stands before him ready to announce why she has come to him without being called. The episode opens with the king asking her to name her desire and vowing to fulfill it. Esther does not answer him directly but instead invites him and Haman to a party. They arrive at the party, during which the king again questions Esther with regard to what she wants. She responds only by inviting the two men to another party the following day.

The three narratives proceed along roughly parallel lines throughout the extent of these six verses. The B text is somewhat shorter. In it, the amount and content of dialogue at certain points is affected, but not the actions of the characters or the events in the plot. And the A text

---

1.   Fox likewise brings to our attention the significance of Esther's donning regal apparal at this point. He, quite correctly, argues that her garments visibly reflect the new stature she is gaining (*Character*, pp. 67-68).

includes a final sentence recording a statement by the king which does not exist in either of the other two narratives.

Text

καὶ εἶπεν ὁ βασιλεύς Τί *ἔστιν*, Εσθηρ; *ἀνάγγειλόν μοι*, καὶ *ποιήσω* σοι· ἕως ἡμίσους τῆς βασιλείας μου.

καὶ εἶπεν ὁ βασιλεύς Τί *θέλεις*, Εσθηρ, καὶ τί σού ἐστιν τὸ ἀξίωμα; ἕως τοῦ ἡμίσους τῆς βασιλείας μου, καὶ *ἔσται* σοι.

ויאמר *לה* המלך מה־לך אסתר 3
המלכה ומה־בקשתך עד־חצי המלכות
ותן לך

And the king said, 'What is (it), Esther? Tell me, and I will do (it) for you, as much as half of my kingdom.'

And the king said, 'What do you wish, Esther? And what is your petition? As much as half of my kingdom, and it will be to you.'

And the king said to her, 'What is (it) for you, Esther the queen? And what is your request? Up to half of the kingdom, and it will be given to you.'

καὶ εἶπεν Εσθηρ Ἡμέρα ἐπίσημός μοι *αὔριον*· εἰ δοκεῖ οὖν τῷ βασιλεῖ, *εἴσελθε σὺ* καὶ Αμαν *ὁ φίλος σου* εἰς τὸν πότον, ὃν ποιήσω *αὔριον*.

εἶπεν *δὲ* Εσθηρ Ἡμέρα μου ἐπίσημος *σήμερόν ἐστιν*· εἰ οὖν δοκεῖ τῷ βασιλεῖ, ἐλθάτω *καὶ αὐτὸς* καὶ Αμαν εἰς *τὴν δοχήν*, ἣν ποιήσω σήμερον.

ותאמר אסתר אם־על־המלך טוב יבוא 4
המלך והמן היום אל־המשתה אשר־
עשיתי לו

And Esther said, 'Tomorrow (is) a special day for me. Therefore, if it seems good to the king, you must enter in, and Haman your friend, to the drinking-party which I will prepare tomorrow.'

But Esther said, 'Today is a special day for me. Therefore, if it seems good to the king, he himself must come, and Haman, to the banquet which I will prepare today.'

And Esther said, 'If it is good to the king, may the king come, and Haman, today to the drinking-party which I have prepared for him.'

καὶ εἶπεν ὁ βασιλεύς Κατασπεύσατε τὸν Αμαν, ὅπως ποιήσωμεν τὸν λόγον Εσθηρ. καὶ παραγίνονται ἀμφότεροι εἰς τὴν δοχήν, ἣν ἐποίησεν Εσθηρ, *δεῖπνον πολυτελές*.

καὶ εἶπεν ὁ βασιλεύς Κατασπεύσατε Αμαν, ὅπως ποιήσωμεν τὸν λόγον Εσθηρ. καὶ παραγίνονται ἀμφότεροι εἰς τὴν δοχήν, ἣν *εἶπεν* Εσθηρ.

ויאמר המלך מהרו את־המן לעשות 5
את־דבר אסתר *ויבא המלך והמן* אל־
המשתה אשר־עשתה אסתר

And the king said, 'Hasten Haman along, so that we may do the word of Esther.' And both arrived to the banquet which Esther prepared, an expensive supper.

And the king said, 'Hasten Haman along, so that we may do the word of Esther.' And both arrived to the banquet about which Esther had spoken.

And the king said, 'Hasten Haman along, to do the word of Esther.' And the king came, and Haman, to the drinking-party which Esther had prepared.

καὶ εἶπεν ὁ βασιλεὺς
πρὸς Εσθηρ ἡ βασίλισσα,
τί *τὸ θέλημά* σου;
αἴτησαι ἕως ἡμίσους τῆς
βασιλείας *μου*, καὶ
ἔσται *σοι* ὅσα ἀξιοῖς.

ἐν *δὲ* τῷ πότῳ εἶπεν ὁ
βασιλεὺς πρὸς Εσθηρ Τί
ἐστιν, Βασίλισσά Εσθηρ;
καὶ ἔσται ὅσα ἀξιοῖς.

הַיַּיִן מַה־ וַיֹּאמֶר הַמֶּלֶךְ לְאֶסְתֵּר בְּמִשְׁתֵּה 6
שְׁאֵלָתֵךְ יִנָּתֵן לָךְ וּמַה־בַּקָּשָׁתֵךְ עַד־
חֲצִי הַמַּלְכוּת וְתֵעָשׂ

And the king said to
Esther 'O queen, what is
your desire? To request as
much as half of my
kingdom, and it will be to
you as much as you deem
worthy.'

So during the drinking, the
king said to Esther, 'What
is it, queen Esther? And it
will be as much as you
deem worthy.'

And the king said to Esther
during the drinking of wine,
'What is your petition? And it
will be given to you. And what is
your request? Up to half of the
kingdom, and it will be done.'

καὶ εἶπεν Εσθηρ Τὸ
αἴτημά μου καὶ τὸ
ἀξίωμά μου·

καὶ εἶπεν Τὸ αἴτημά μου
καὶ τὸ ἀξίωμα·

וַתַּעַן אֶסְתֵּר וַתֹּאמַר שְׁאֵלָתִי וּבַקָּשָׁתִי 7

And Esther said, 'My
request and my petition:

And she said, 'My request
and petition:

And Esther answered and said,
'My petition and my request:

εἰ εὗρον χάριν *ἐναντίον*
σου, βασιλεῦ, καὶ εἰ ἐπὶ
τὸν Βασιλεά ἀγαθὸν
δοῦναι τὸ αἴτημά μου
καὶ ποιῆσαι τὸ αἴτημά
μου, ἐλθέτω ὁ βασιλεὺς
καὶ Αμαν εἰς τὴν δοξήν,
ἣν ποιήσω αὐτοῖς *καὶ* τῇ
αὔριον· καὶ αὔριον *γὰρ*
ποιήσω *κατὰ* τὰ αὐτά.
καὶ εἶπεν ὁ βασιλεύς
Ποίησον κατὰ τὸ θέλημά
σου.

εἰ εὗρον χάριν *ἐνώπιον*
τοῦ βασιλέως, ἐλθάτω ὁ
βασιλεὺς καὶ Αμαν *ἔτι*
τὴν αὔριον εἰς τὴν δοχήν,
ἣν ποιήσω αὐτοῖς· καὶ
αὔριον ποιήσω τὰ αὐτά.

אִם־מָצָאתִי חֵן בְּעֵינֵי הַמֶּלֶךְ וְאִם־עַל־ 8
הַמֶּלֶךְ טוֹב לָתֵת אֶת־שְׁאֵלָתִי וְלַעֲשׂוֹת
אֶת־בַּקָּשָׁתִי יָבוֹא הַמֶּלֶךְ וְהָמָן אֶל־
הַמִּשְׁתֶּה אֲשֶׁר אֶעֱשֶׂה לָהֶם וּמָחָר
אֶעֱשֶׂה כִּדְבַר הַמֶּלֶךְ

If I have found favor before
you, king, and if it is good
to the king to grant my
request and to do my
petition, the king must
come, and Haman, to the
banquet which I will
prepare for them and (will
be) tomorrow, for also
tomorrow I will do
accordingly the same.' And
the king said, 'Do
according to your desire.'

If I have found favor before
the king, the king must
come, and Haman, again
tomorrow to the banquet
which I will prepare for
them, and tomorrow I will
do the same.'

If I have found favor in the eyes
of the king, and if to the king it
is good to grant my petition and
to do my request, may the king
come, and Haman, to the
drinking-party which I will
prepare for them, and tomorrow I
will do according to the word of
the king.'

Notes

Verse 3. In B, the king just asks what Esther wants or what she intends
('what do you wish' Τί θέλεις) right away, and then secondly speaks in

terms of her more formal decree or request ('and what is your petition?', καὶ τί σου ἐστιν τὸ ἀξίωμα). This progression gives the impression that he anticipates that Esther will express to him her desire, but as told in an articulated petition or stated decision of some sort. In M, also, the king is concerned about her request.

In A, the king asks Esther only one question, but then gives her a command ('tell me', ἀνάγγειλόν μοι). Here the king does not speak in the language of a request, petition, or even the desire, of Esther, which would give the sense of a less formal procedure.

Esther appears more regal in M. The king addresses her not only by her personal name, as in A and B, but also by her title ('Esther the queen', אסתר המלכה).

A shows the king as more willing to make a personal effort in securing Esther's request; he pledges that he himself will provide Esther with what she wants ('I will do for you', ποιήσω σοι). And he seems to imagine Esther's desire as a task to be done rather than an object to be given. In B and M, no agent at all is stated for making Esther's petition come to be. In M, the king just assures her that it will be provided, but not necessarily that he will be the one who takes care of it ('it will be given to you', ינתן לך). We can assume that the king will give it to her, but it is not clear exactly how. In any event, his promise is less specific than in A and he is taking less personal responsibility for fulfilling Esther's desire. And in B, the king merely states that her petition will be hers, in vague language ('it will be to you', ἔσται σοι).

A and B show the kingdom as belonging particularly to the king. He refers to it as 'my kingdom' (τῆς βασιλείας μου). In M, the king does not speak of the kingdom as exclusively his, using no possessive pronoun ('the kingdom', המלכות), but yet he still speaks of being willing or able to have it given away.

In A, in contrast with B and M, the king mentions the item 'half of my kingdom' (ἡμίσους τῆς βασιλείας μου) only after he makes his promise that he will do for Esther whatever she wants. With this ordering, along with the king's promise to do something rather than to give her something, this phrase stands to suggest more the degree to which he is willing to respond to her rather than being the item itself that she might request.

Verse 4. Esther is in less of a hurry in A, for she does not plan on hosting her festivities until the following day ('tomorrow', αὔριον). In B and M, she plans on having the event the same day as when she invites the king and Haman ('today', σήμερον, היום). This detail prolongs the literary suspense (which Paton [*Esther*, p. 234] and Moore [*Esther*, p. 56] note regarding the M text) even longer than in the M and B texts.

In A and B, Esther states that the feast day is somehow distinctive or notable ('a special day for me', ἡμέρα ἐπίσημός μοι), but in M she does not provide any rationale for throwing a banquet for the king.

In A, Esther views the king and Haman as having a relationship of affection or love, as she refers to Haman as 'your friend' (ὁ φίλος σου). Perhaps Esther sees them working together as a more united front against which she must fight. Or perhaps, as Moore suggests, she is intentionally describing Haman as the king's social equal (*Esther*, p. 56). In any case, she makes an explicit connection between the two men.

A portrays Esther as being more personal with the king in her invitation. She speaks directly to him in the second person ('you must enter in', εἴσελθε σὺ) rather than the third person of B and M ('he will come', ἐλθάτω, יבוא). M shows Esther as being the most formal, or expressing distance from the king, for she speaks of him twice as 'the king' (המלך), repeating his title rather than using a personal pronoun the second time.

Both B and M emphasize the king in this verse, though in different ways. B stresses that the king himself must come in person, adding the phrase καὶ αὐτός (which means the same as αὐτός alone, 'himself'), and M twice refers to the 'the king'. Also in M, if we understand the לו to refer to the king and not to Haman, Esther makes her banquet particularly for the king. It appears that it is more specifically the king she hopes to affect or win over to her cause than Haman. Uniquely in A, Esther does not stress the person of the king in a similar way, but she does describe Haman. These two details give the impression that A is placing as much, or more, emphasis upon Haman as upon the king.

In A, Esther is requesting more specifically that he and Haman come or enter *in* to the banquet, with the verb εἰσέρχομαι. Perhaps she is already planning the place where she will host the event.

In M, Esther has already readied her banquet ('I have prepared', עשׂיתי, using the perfect tense). This detail suggests two things, that Esther is certain that the king and Haman would come and that she is in the greatest haste of all here. She anticipates the king's own sense of hurry and urgency of v. 5.

There is a question with regard to what type of festivities Esther provides for the two men in this episode of the three narratives. B refers to Esther's party thrice (in vv. 4, 5, 8), and each time uses the term δοχή, a 'reception' or 'banquet'. A also uses this same term later (vv. 5 and 8), but in this verse uses πότος, a 'drinking-bout' or 'drinking carousal'. πότος is a more specific term, related to the verb πίνω, 'to drink'. In these same three places (vv. 4, 5, 8, and v. 6 in the construct form), M uses the term מִשְׁתֶּה, which can be used for both types of occasions, either festivities which feature drinking or general banqueting. Etymologically, מִשְׁתֶּה is very much similar to πότος, being derived also from a verb meaning 'to drink' (שׁתה). However, we cannot immediately assume that מִשְׁתֶּה is being used here in its more specific sense, as a drinking bout, as there is not a Hebrew word which is used only for general feasting or banqueting. The term חַג (from the root חגג, 'to make pilgrimage, keep a pilgrim feast') is also used for feasting in the biblical literature, but likewise with a specific sense, in terms of feasting that is related to religious celebrations or appointed legal festival times. (Though later in the book of Esther, even when referring to the appointed religious festivities of Purim, M still retains the term מִשְׁתֶּה [cf. 9.17, 18, 19, 22]). A key to understanding exactly what the מִשְׁתֶּה represents in this episode may be in v. 6, where the narrative (and only M) notes the banquet as being 'of wine'. This distinction is significant. In A and M, in this verse, Esther is most likely inviting the king and Haman to a smaller affair, a 'cocktail party' if you will, where the focus would be on drinking and conversation rather than on the foods served, as would be for an actual feast or banquet.

Verse 5. A provides less of an explanation for the king's haste, as Esther invites them to a party not that same day but on the following day (cf. v. 4), a curiosity also noted by Dorothy ('Books', p. 165).

M refers to the king and Haman individually a second time ('and the king came, and Haman', ויבא המלך והמן), in contrast to A's and B's notes just that they both came ('and both arrived', καὶ παραγίνονται ἀμφότεροι).

In B, here, there is less of an emphasis upon Esther's actually having put together or prepared the banquet herself; it is noted only as the banquet about which she had said something ('the banquet about which Esther had spoken', τὴν δοχήν, ἣν εἶπεν Εσθηρ).

In A, Esther's banquet is described more explicitly. Only here do we know it to be costly or extravagant (πολυτελές) and the principal

evening meal, or supper (δεῖπνον). Just a few verses back, in the last
episode (15.6), the king's robe was also described by a form of the
adjective πολυτελής (πολυτελεῖς). The king first exhibited his
extravagance through an article (his robe), but now Esther expresses the
same type of extravagance through another article (her meal). The
language used suggests that her actions here are on the same level as
those of the king. It serves to give the impression that she is imitating
him in reflecting the same type of lavishness that is representative of the
Persian court.

The progression of terminology A uses to speak of Esther's banquet
makes her appear rather deceptive. When inviting the king in the
previous verse, Esther asks him to attend a drinking festivity (τὸν
πότον). However, when he and Haman arrive there they discover that it
is an actual feast or banquet (τὴν δοχήν). (As discussed earlier, the term
πότος specifically signifies a drinking-party or drinking festivity of some
sort, whereas δοχή suggests a more formal banquet or reception.) Then
the narrative adds that it is even more lavish and expensive than an
average banquet ('an expensive supper', δεῖπνον πολυτελές). This
change in terminology is significant for the portrayal of Esther. Either
Esther changes her mind about the type of festivity to offer or she
designedly misrepresents her intentions to the king.

Verse 6. M notes that these events are occurring while the three are
drinking wine ('during the drinking of wine', במשתה היין), and B notes
just that they are in the act of drinking but not specifically what ('during
the drinking', ἐν δὲ τῷ πότῳ). Fox understands this phrase to signify a
special course at the end of a meal (*Character*, p. 67), which is possible.
With the inclusion of this information, both M and B tend to portray the
present time as having a more social or leisurely quality.

In M, the king speaks in terms of petition, using both of the synonyms
שאלתך ('your petition') and בקשתך ('your request') in this statement. He
envisions an interaction which is more procedural and formal, stressing
the formulated petition that Esther is to make. However, here the king is
even more generous, promising twice that he will give her whatever her
petition is ('and it will be given to you', וינתן לך, 'up to half of the
kingdom, and it will be done', עד־חצי המלכות ותעש).

A speaks in terms of Esther's will rather than a more formulated
petition. The king asks to know her design or inclination ('what is your
desire?', τί τὸ θέλημά σου). And he envisions the expression of her

will as the action of asking on her part, not as presenting a request, by using an infinitive verb ('to request as much as ...', αἴτησαι ἕως ...). A gives the impression that the king will satisfy her desire or whim whatever it might be, and it does not even necessarily have to be something that is supported by a logical argument or a formal petition.

B is the most general in terms of the king's statement. He does not ask Esther either for her petition nor even her desire, but only questions, 'what is it' (Τί ἐστιν). With regard to his response, he does not promise either to give her or to do for her any certain thing, stating only that whatever is Esther's reply 'will be' (ἔσται). Also, the king is not nearly as generous here. He does not offer up to half of the kingdom or suggest anything at all to her.

In A, the king sees the kingdom as particularly belonging to him ('my kingdom', τῆς βασιλείας μου), whereas in M he speaks of it more neutrally ('the kingdom', המלכות). But after mentioning 'my kingdom' in A, the king goes on to say that it would be hers ('it will be to you', ἔσται σοι) if she so desires, a detail not as explicit in M.

A and B speak in terms not only of the extent to which Esther desires and makes request but also of what she thinks is proper ('and it will be [to you] as much as you deem worthy', καὶ ἔσται [σοι] ὅσα ἀξιοῖς). The king's hinting at a moral or ethical aspect to Esther's request here anticipates the justice that Esther argues has not been done when she finally does state her request during the second banquet (7.4-6).

Verse 7. M presents two verbs to represent Esther's action of verbal response ('And Esther replied and said', ותען אסתר ותאמר), whereas A and B exhibit only one ('and [Esther] said', καὶ εἶπεν [Εσθηρ]). However, this difference reflects the particularities of Hebrew narrative style more than any significant differences in the characterizations of Esther.

Verse 8. In A and B, the ἐναντίον (A) and the ἐνώπιον (B) are so similar in meaning that this textual difference does not affect the sense of this verse.

A portrays Esther as first speaking directly to the king in the second person ('if I have found favor before you', εἰ εὗρον χάριν ἐναντίον σου), before addressing him by title numerous times (as do B and M as well). Esther is calling the king to acknowledge his part in their relationship and, at least partially, basing her argument on a more personal or relational note.

In A and M, Esther puts forward two types of arguments regarding why the king should come to her second banquet. She bases her reasoning upon his good opinion of her ('if I have attained favor before/in the eyes of the king', εἰ εὗρον χάριν ἐναντίον... βασιλευ, אם־מצאתי חן בעיני המלך) and upon his sense of morality or right behavior ('if it is good to the king', εἰ ἐπὶ τὸν βασιλέα ἀγαθὸν, אם־על־המלך טוב). In B, she appeals to only whether the king is pleased with her ('if I have found favor before the king', εἰ εὗρον χάριν ἐνώπιον τοῦ βασιλέως). At this point Esther appears less persuasive and eloquent in general, including fewer planks in her argument than in A and M.

In B, Esther does not speak in the language of 'petition' and 'request', as do A and M, which each use the two terms again (τὸ αἴτημά μου, τὸ ἀξίωμά μου, שאלתי, בקשתי).

A stresses more than B that Esther will carry out the second banquet just like the first ('I will do accordingly the same', ποιήσω κατὰ τὰ αὐτά in A; 'I will do the same', ποιήσω τὰ αὐτά in B). She seems to have somewhat more of a strategy into which she anticipates the actions of the following day will fall.

In M, Esther states that she will perform according to the 'word of the king' (כדבר המלך). By this detail, M suggests Esther's obedience to the king more than A and B. And this statement stands in contrast to that of v. 5, where the king and Haman 'do the word of Esther' (לעשות את־דבר אסתר), evidencing their obedience to her. Esther is also here acknowledging to the king that the invitation to the second banquet is not her actual petition, but that she will reveal it, as per his request (his 'word'), during the following day's festivities.

The entire last sentence, which repeats the king's response to Esther, is unique to A. It suggests a certain trust that the king has for Esther, for he is here giving her free rein to do whatever she wants, and it concretely demonstrates the approval which she has just questioned whether the king has towards her (in finding favor before him). The θέλημά σου ('your desire') reflects the use of this same term from v. 6. The king first asks her what she desires. Then he grants her the authority to carry it out, before even knowing what her intention might entail.

Analysis

A Text. Esther gives the impression of having more of a strategy in this narrative. With regard to the first banquet, she is not in a hurry to host it, possibly giving her time to make everything right. She eloquently presents thorough and successful arguments for getting Ahasuerus to agree to attend her banquets. Esther also is not above using a bit of deception to make her plans come about. She invites the king to a casual gathering, but when he arrives he finds a formal, lavish dinner. The reader is led to question whether Esther has a logical reason for choosing to underrepresent what she intends. And she seems to have a clearer sense of how she envisions the second banquet.

Esther's simple desire or whim is important, at least to Ahasuerus. He stresses that whatever her will is must be done. This first banquet is a turning point with regard to Esther's control. When beginning the festivities, Ahasuerus states that *he* will do whatever she wants, but by the end he allows *her* to do whatever she wants. Esther's own authority is highlighted in this episode. She is trusted to carry out affairs as she thinks best. And she is given power of her own to fulfill her request and need not wait for Ahasuerus to do it for her. With regard to Esther's request itself, this narrative portrays it more as something Esther desires to happen than an actual object to be given.

Esther accommodates more to Persian customs. She has recognized the lavishness and costly extravagance of the Persian court, and now she takes pains to prepare her banquet on the same scale of grandeur. Perhaps this action is also part of her strategy, to impress her guests or to make them feel at home. And Esther is also more concerned with the person of Haman and his relationship to the king.

Longer and more responsive interaction of Esther with Ahasuerus is exhibited by this narrative. We see more communication between the two. Ahasuerus especially desires her response to his query, in first requesting that she reply to him. Then, at the end of their conversation, he gives her back a final response of approval. Esther herself addresses Ahasuerus more personally, which gives the impression of a greater closeness and less formality between them. She is also a recipient of the promises of a more generous and active king. Though Ahasuerus does speak of the kingdom as specifically his, he is willing to give it over specifically to Esther. And he is himself willing to carry out her desire and not merely arrange that it be done. Finally, Ahasuerus displays a great deal of trust towards Esther in allowing her to do whatever she might want.

B Text. Esther here plans her festivities to be a banquet, or feast, right from the start. She is particularly concerned that Artaxerxes himself attend her party and presents him a reason why he should. However, she herself appears to be less involved in actually putting it together, and hence less in control of the situation. And at the end, when inviting Artaxerxes to her second banquet, she again acts less in charge. Her argument is less rhetorical and she gives the king fewer reasons to grant her request. She bases her proposition solely upon Artaxerxes's feelings of affection and favor towards her, an action which appears risky. But perhaps Esther does indeed know what she is doing, for the king has just evidenced some degree of respect for her in personally addressing her in terms of her position as queen and promising to do what she considers proper.

This narrative describes some of the events with less clarity. In particular, Artaxerxes promises in only vague terms that what Esther wants will come to be. The reader is not quite sure how she will be granted her desires. And the details with regard to the petition itself are similarly vague. Neither Esther nor Artaxerxes speak in terms of request and petition as such overall, and the procedure itself appears less formal or official.

Esther is not treated with the same degree of generosity in this narrative as in the other two. The king does not state as often during the episode that she might request, and be given, as much as half the kingdom, nor does he emphasize as much that she can have whatever her request might be. Furthermore, Artaxerxes does not envision himself as being as personally involved in carrying out Esther's desires.

M Text. This narrative portrays Esther as both more and less authoritative. In Ahasuerus's first statement to her, he addresses her from the start as queen. And every time he speaks of the kingdom, he does not describe it in terms of his exclusive ownership. Thus Esther first appears as already in charge of the kingdom, having some degree of respect and authority. However, she is also portrayed as feeling a certain obedience to the king. At the conclusion of their conversation, she herself promises to do the word of the king. Yet it is less clear that both Ahasuerus and Haman were conscious of doing her word earlier. And Esther is less demanding in this episode; she does not command the men, especially the king, to the same degree. But she also knows how to test the limits of her expected obedience. She does not follow Ahasuerus's request to the letter, for she does not state the petition for which he asks right then but toys with him in requiring him to wait an additional day for it.

Esther plans her first party as more of a drinking festivity, and this narrative emphasizes the drinking of wine. Such details give the impression that it is more a social affair. Esther is in a hurry to give the party, and has already arranged it when she invites Ahasuerus. She is confident that he would accept her offer. Haman is also less important to Esther, for she emphasizes that the king is her primary guest. Her primary concern is that her petition to save the Jews be granted, which would require only Ahasuerus's attendance. She is less concerned about publicly exposing and embarassing Haman in person.[1]

The procedure for the announcing and granting of Esther's desire appears more formal. This narrative uses the language of request and petition most often, which makes the process seem to resemble official government business. However, Ahasuerus also shows a greater concern to know what Esther wants. He asks about the nature of her request most frequently in this narrative, and he asserts most often that whatever it is will be granted. He is prepared to give or perform whatever object or action she might want.

Episode 6 (7.1-8)

Immediately after the last episode, that of Esther's first banquet, Haman returns to his home. He boasts about his successes, but also relates how he is vexed by Mordecai's behavior. His family advises that he have a gallows constructed and then convince the king to hang Mordecai upon it. That evening the king experiences insomnia, so he has the government chronicles read to him. Among the writings is the account of Mordecai's earlier actions to save the king's life. Deciding to reward him and hearing someone in the entryway, the king calls in Haman and asks his counsel regarding an appropriate reward. Haman comes up with an elaborate suggestion, thinking it is for himself. However, the king commands him to carry it out for Mordecai. When back at his home, Haman's family warns him about working against the Jewish people, and he and the king return to the palace for Esther's second banquet.

This episode relates the conversation and events of that second banquet. First, the king repeats his questions about Esther's request and his vow to fulfill it. Esther responds, asking that he give the lives of her

---

1. Fox has also concluded that Esther is not completely obedient to the king in this scene. He suggests that Esther intends her postponement to be a diversionary tactic with the objective of heightening Ahasuerus's curiosity (*Character*, p. 73).

people and herself. She explains to him how they had been sold into distressing circumstances, at which the king demands to know the identity of the perpetrator of this action. Esther identifies Haman. The king becomes upset, stands up, and exits the room, at which point Haman takes the opportunity to beg leniency from Esther. The king, upon returning, finds Haman in a compromising position with his wife and speaks condemningly towards him.

The A text is significantly longer at places throughout these eight verses, including details not found in the B or M texts at vv. 3 and 6. In the A text, before first responding, Esther feels antagonism towards Haman and she prays. Later, Esther notes that the king is angry. She attempts to calm him, but the king insists that she should answer him and again promises to grant her desires. The B text for this episode is shorter than the other two at certain points, providing more concise quotations and fewer narrative details. And the final sentence, in v. 8, differs among all three narratives.

Text

1

καὶ πορευθεὶς ἀνέπεσε μετ' αὐτῶν ἐν ὥρᾳ.	Εἰσῆλθεν δὲ ὁ βασιλεὺς καὶ Αμαν συμπιεῖν τῇ βασιλίσσῃ.	ויבא המלך והמן לשתות עם־*אסתר* המלכה
And proceeding, he reclined at table with them in due time.	So the king and Haman entered in to drink together with the queen.	And the king and Haman entered, to drink with Esther the queen.

2

ὡς δὲ *προῆγεν ἡ πρόποσις,* εἶπεν ὁ βασιλεὺς τῇ Εσθηρ Τί ἐστιν *ὁ κίνδυνος* καὶ τί τὸ αἴτημά σου; ἕως τοῦ ἡμίσους τῆς βασιλείας μου.	εἶπεν δὲ ὁ βασιλεὺς Εσθηρ τῇ δευτέρᾳ ἡμέρᾳ ἐν τῷ πότῳ Τί ἐστιν, Εσθηρ βασίλισσα, καὶ τί τὸ αἴτημά σου καὶ τί τὸ ἀξίωμά σου; καὶ *ἔστω* σοι ἕως τοῦ ἡμίσους τῆς βασιλείας μου.	ויאמר המלך לאסתר *גם* ביום השני במשתה *היין* מה־שאלתך אסתר המלכה *תנתן* לך ומה־בקשתך עד־ חצי המלכות *ותעש*
And as the preliminary drinking progressed, the king said to Esther, 'What is the danger? And what is your request? As much as half of my kingdom.'	And the king said (to) Esther on the second day during the drinking, 'What is it, queen Esther? And what is your request and what is your petition? And be it to you, as much as half of my kingdom.'	And the king said to Esther again on the second day, during the drinking of wine, 'What is your petition, Esther the queen? And it will be given to you. And what is your request? Up to half of the kingdom, and it will be done.'

καὶ ἠγωνίασεν Εσθηρ
τῷ ἀπαγγέλλειν, ὅτι ὁ
ἀντίδικος ἐν ὀφθαλμοῖς
αὐτῆς. καὶ ὁ θεὸς
ἔδωκεν αὐτῇ θάρσος ἐν
τῷ αὐτὴν ἐπικαλεῖσθαι
αὐτόν. καὶ εἶπεν Εσθηρ
Εἰ δοκεῖ τῷ βασιλεῖ, *καὶ*
ἀγαθὴ ἡ κρίσις ἐν
καρδίᾳ αὐτοῦ, δοθήτω ὁ
λαός μου τῷ αἰτήματί
μου *καὶ τὸ ἔθνος* τῆς
ψυχῆς μου.

καὶ ἀποκριθεῖσα εἶπεν
Εἰ εὗρον χάριν *ἐνώπιον*
τοῦ βασιλέως, δοθήτω ἡ
ψυχὴ τῷ αἰτήματί μου
καὶ ὁ λαός μου τῷ
ἀξιώματί μου.

3 ותען אסתר <u>המלכה</u> ותאמר אם־מצאתי
חן <u>בעיניך</u> המלך ואם־על־המלך טוב
תנתן־<u>לי</u> נפשי בשאלתי ועמי בבקשתי

And Esther fought to
respond back, because the
opponent was before her
eyes. And God gave to her
confidence in her calling
upon him. And Esther said,
'If it seems right to the
king, and the judgment is
good in his heart, have my
people be given for my
request, even the nation of
my being.

And she, answering, said,
'If I have found favor
before the king, have life
be given for my request,
and my people for my
petition.

And Esther the queen answered
and said, 'If I have attained favor
in your eyes, O king, and if to the
king it is good, may my life be
given to me as my petition and
my people as my request.

ἐπράθημεν γὰρ ἐγὼ καὶ
ὁ λαός μου εἰς δούλωσιν,
καὶ *τὰ νήπια αὐτῶν* εἰς
διαρπαγήν, καὶ *οὐκ*
ἤθελον ἀπαγγεῖλαι, ἵνα
μὴ λυπήσω τὸν κύριόν
μου· ἐγένετο γὰρ
μεταπεσεῖν τὸν
ἄνθρωπον τὸν
κακοποιήσαντα ἡμᾶς.

ἐπράθημεν γὰρ ἐγώ *τε*
καὶ ὁ λαός μου εἰς
ἀπώλειαν καὶ
διαρπαγὴν καὶ
δουλείαν, *ἡμεῖς* καὶ *τὰ*
τέκνα ἡμῶν εἰς παῖδας
καὶ παιδίσκας, *καὶ*
παρήκουσα· οὐ γὰρ ἄξιος
ὁ διάβολος *τῆς αὐλῆς* τοῦ
βασιλέως.

4 כי נמכרנו אני ועמי להשמיד <u>להרג</u>
<u>ולאבד ואלו</u> לעבדים ולשפחות נמכרנו
<u>החרשתי כי אין הצר שוה בנזק</u> המלך

For we have been sold, I
and my people, for
bondage, and their infants
for plundering. But I did
not wish to report (it), so
that I will not cause grief
to my lord. For it has
occurred that the person
who caused us injury has
undergone reversal.'

For we have been sold,
both I and my people, for
destruction and plundering
and bondage; we and our
children, for male servants
and female servants. And I
have overheard (this). For
the slanderer is not worthy
of the court of the king.'

For we have been sold, I and my
people, for annihilation, for
slaughtering, and for killing. And
if as male servants and female
servants we had been sold, I
would have kept silent, for there
is no distress comparable with
damage of the king.'

118 **Three Faces of a Queen**

καὶ *ἐθυμώθη* ὁ βασιλεὺς
καὶ εἶπεν Τίς *ἐστιν*
οὗτος, ὃς ἐτόλμησε
ταπεινῶσαι τὸ σημεῖον
τῆς βασιλείας μου ὥστε
παρελθεῖν τὸν φόβον
σου;

εἶπεν δὲ ὁ βασιλεύς Τίς
ὅστος, ὅστις ἐτόλημσεν
ποιῆσαι *τὸ πρᾶγμα*
τοῦτο;

ויאמר המלך <u>אחשורוש</u> ויאמר <u>לאסתר</u> 5
<u>המלכה</u> מי הוא זה ו<u>אי־זה הוא</u> אשר־
<u>מלאו לבו</u> לעשות <u>כן</u>

And the king was angered
and said, 'Who is this,
who has presumed to abuse
the sign of my kingdom,
so as to disregard the fear
of you?'

But the king said, 'Who is
this, who has presumed to
do this matter?'

But the king Ahasuerus spoke,
and said to Esther the queen,
'Who is this one? And where is
this one, who has filled his heart
to do such?'

ὡς δὲ εἶδεν ἡ βασίλισσα
ὅτι δεινὸν ἐφάωη τῷ
βασιλεῖ, καὶ μισοπονηρεῖ,
εἶπεν Μὴ ὀργίζου, κύριε·
ἱκανὸν γὰρ ὅτι ἔτυχον
τοῦ ἱλασμοῦ σου· εὐωχοῦ,
βασιλεῦ· αὔριον δὲ
ποιήσω κατὰ τὸ ῥῆμά
σου. καὶ ὤμοσεν ὁ
βασιλεὺς τοῦ
ἀπαγγεῖλαι αὐτὴν
αὐτῷ τὸν
ὑπερηφανευσάμεν τοῦ
ποιῆσαι τοῦτο καὶ μετὰ
ὅρκου ὑπέσχετο ποιῆσαι
αὐτῇ ὁ ἂν βούληται. καὶ
θαρσήσασα ἡ Εσθηρ
εἶπεν Αμαν *ὁ φίλος σου* ὁ
ψευδὴς οὑτοσί, ὁ πονηρὸς
ἄνθρωπος οὗτος.

εἶπεν δὲ Εσθηρ
"Ανθρωπος ἐχθρός· Αμαν
ὁ πονηρὸς οὗτος. Αμαν δὲ
ἐταράχθη ἀπὸ τοῦ
βασιλέως καὶ τῆς
βασιλίσσης.

ותאמר־אסתר איש צר <u>ואויב</u> המן 6
הרע הזה והמן <u>נבעת מלפני</u> המלך
והמלכה

And when the queen saw
that (it) appeared terrible
to the king and he hated
the wickedness, she said,
'Do not be angry, lord. For
it is sufficient that it
happens (that) you are
merciful. Feast
sumptuously, king, and
tomorrow I will do
according to your
direction.' But the king
swore that she should
report back to him the one
who behaved (so)

And Esther said, 'A hostile
person—Haman is this evil
one.' And Haman was
troubled by the king and
the queen.

And Esther said, 'A man—an
adversary and an enemy—Haman
is this wicked one.' And Haman
was terrified before the king and
the queen.

arrogantly as to do this,
and with an oath he
promised to do for her
whatever she might desire.
And Esther, being
confident, said, 'Haman—
your friend—is this
deceiver, this wicked
person.'

7

ἔκθυμος δὲ *γενόμενος* ὁ
βασιλεὺς *καὶ πλησθεὶς*
ὑργῆς *ἀνεπήδησε καὶ ἦν*
περιπατῶν. καὶ ὁ Αμαν
ἐταράχθη καὶ
προσέπεσεν ἐπὶ τοὺς
πόδας Εσθηρ τῆς
βασιλίσσης ἐπὶ *τὴν*
κοίτην ἔτι ἀνακειμένης.

ὁ δὲ βασιλεὺς *ἐξανέστη*
ἐκ τοῦ συμποσίου εἰς τὸν
κῆπον. ὁ δὲ Αμαν
παρῃτεῖτο τὴν
βασίλισσαν· ἑώρα γὰρ
ἑαυτὸν ἐν κακοῖς ὄντα.

והמלך קם בחמתו ממשתה היין אל־
גנת הביתן והמן עמד לבקש על־נפשו
מאסתר המלכה כי ראה כי־כלתה
אליו הרעה מאת המלך

And the king, becoming
vehement and being filled
with anger, jumped up and
was walking about. And
Haman was troubled and
he fell upon the feet of
Esther the queen, who was
still reclining upon the
bed.

And the king rose up from
the drinking together, to
the garden. And Haman
entreated the queen, for he
saw himself as being in
harmful circumstances.

And the king rose up in his rage
from the drinking-party of wine
to the garden of the house. But
Haman remained (there) to
request his life from Esther the
queen, for he saw that injury was
plotted against him from the king.

8

καὶ ὁ βασιλεὺς
ἐπέστρεψεν ἐπὶ τὸ
*συμπό*σιον καὶ *ἰδὼν*
εἶπεν Οὐχ *ἱκανόν σοι ἡ*
ἁμαρτία τῆς βασιλείας,
ἀλλὰ καὶ τὴν γυναῖκά
*μου ἐ*βιάζῃ ἐνώπιόν
μου; *ἀπαχθήτω Αμαν*
καὶ μὴ ζήτω.

ἐπέστρεψεν δὲ ὁ
βασιλεὺς ἐκ τοῦ κήπου.
Αμαν δὲ ἐπιπεπτώκει
ἐπὶ τὴν κλίνην, *ἀξιῶν*
τὴν βασίλισσαν. εἶπεν
δὲ ὁ βασιλεύς *"Ωστε*
καὶ τὴν γυναῖκα βιάζῃ
ἐν τῇ οἰκίᾳ *μου*; *Αμαν δὲ*
ἀκούσας διετράπη τῷ
προσώπῳ.

והמלך שב מגנת הביתן אל־בית משתה
היין והמן נפל על־המטה אשר אסתר
עליה ויאמר המלך הגם לכבוש את־
המלכה עמי בבית הדבר יצא מפי
המלך ופני המן חפו

And the king returned to
the drinking together, and
when he saw he said, 'Is an
offense of the kingdom not
sufficient for you? But
must he also force my wife
before me? Let Haman be
led away, and not inquire.'

And the king returned from
the garden. And Haman
had fallen upon the couch,
asking of the queen. And
the king said, 'And
therefore must he force the
woman in my house?' And
Haman, hearing, turned
away (his) face.

And the king returned from the
garden of the house to the house
of the drinking-party of wine, and
Haman was falling upon the
couch which Esther was upon.
And the king said, 'Will he also
force the queen before me in the
house?' The word went out from
the mouth of the king, and they
covered the face of Haman.

Notes

Verse 2. M and B locate this scene within time, making it clear that these events are occurring at Esther's second banquet ('on the second day', τῇ δευτέρᾳ ἡμέρᾳ, ביום השני), and M highlights the repetition even further by noting that actions are being done again ('again, also', גם). They stress that this has all happened before, at least as the scene begins.

A gives the sense that the first part of the festivities are only a prelude to Esther's intent with the term πρόποσις ('drinking before, to someone, before food'), though the text does not state exactly to what the drinking is a prelude. The meal itself would be the most plausible possibility, which is suggested further by Esther's reference to eating later on in the evening (v. 6). This terminology provides an impression that the main import of Esther's initiative is not on the food or drink but on what she has to say. The use of the verb προάγω ('to lead forward, bring before') adds to this sense of anticipation.

M notes that the banqueting is particularly of wine ('drinking of wine', משתה היין), a detail which is noted elsewhere throughout this episode and exclusively by M (cf. vv. 7, 8). It appears that the social aspect of this second banquet, like that of the first, is important.

M again gives an impression of a more formal procedure. The king speaks of both items which were mentioned frequently before and during the first banquet, Esther's request and petition ('your petition', 'your request', שאלתך, בקשתך). That this verse is almost a verbatim repetition of 5.6 calls the reader to understand the present conversation in light of the former banquet scene. Though B also mentions both of the items (τὸ αἴτημά σου, τὸ ἀξίωμά σου), it does so in a more condensed fashion, together in the same question. And A mentions only one ('your request', τὸ αἴτημά σου).

In A, the king now recognizes that Esther is at risk. His use of κίνδυνος, 'danger, risk, hazard', makes clear the element of peril in Esther's venture. The term here also recalls Esther's earlier expression to God of her feeling of danger at hand, when she herself used this same description (14.4). Right from the start, the stakes are higher; the fact that the situation is focused not around a whim or fancy of Esther but a literal danger puts her request in a new perspective.

The king acts more generously to Esther in M. He tells her twice that she will be given what she wants ('and it will be given to you', ותנתן לך; 'and it will be done', ותעש). In B, he promises that what she wants will come to be ('and be it to you', καὶ ἔστω), but only once. However, its use of the third person imperative (ἔστω) lends forcefulness and assurance to the king's statement of meeting her desires. And in A, the king does not actually say that he will do anything or give Esther anything. He speaks with a shorthanded approach, in referring again to a portion of the kingdom ('as much as half of my kingdom', ἕως τοῦ ἡμίσους τῆς βασιλείας μου). Only by recalling his similar promises during the first banquet can we understand the reference here.

B places the most emphasis upon what Esther wants, for the king asks her thrice what her request is ('what is it?', τί ἐστιν; 'what is your request?', τί τὸ αἴτημά σου; 'what is your petition?', τί τὸ ἀξίωμά σου).

M presents the kingdom as not exclusively the king's. He mentions it as only 'the kingdom' (הַמַּלְכוּת).

Verse 3. In A, Esther is portrayed as pious. She is dependent upon the help of God at this point, for she invokes God's help ('her calling upon him [God]', τῷ αὐτὴν ἐπικαλεῖσθαι αὐτόν). Her present action recalls her long prayer to God (14.3-19) as well as her calling upon God before approaching the king with her request (15.2). Here we see Esther's praying to be effective, for she receives the courage she needs for the situation ('God gave to her confidence', ὁ θεὸς ἔδωκεν αὐτῇ θάρσος). This verse does not serve to show women as tender and in need of support, a suggestion proposed by Dorothy ('Books', p. 206), but serves to emphasize Esther's personal strength in successfully overcoming the anxiety she feels.

A introduces this scene with language of the courtroom or legal system. First, Haman is referred to as ὁ ἀντίδικος, a term used most particularly for one's adversary in a lawsuit or legal battle. This term is used in contrast with the more general terms for adversaries found elsewhere in the Esther narratives, which do not carry similar legal implications. For instance, ἐχθρός ('enemy, adversary, hated one') is used frequently by Esther in her prayer (cf. 14.6, 10, 11, especially in A), and διάβολος ('slanderer, enemy, backbiter') is used in B's text of the next verse (v. 4). Second, κρίσις, which refers to the king's decision, can reflect a judgment in general, but also carries the specific meaning of a judgment made in court or in a legal trial. And the verb ἀγωνίζομαι can also refer specifically to contending with someone in court. The accumulation of these three terms in these few sentences renders the impression that Esther feels herself to be in a sort of courtroom trial and is calling for justice in her appeal to the king.

In M, Esther is more royal in her position as queen ('Esther the queen', אסתר המלכה), but in B she is not even named again.

Esther speaks more personally to the king in M, addressing him in the second person ('in your eyes', בעיניך).

Esther appeals to different things when making her argument. In M, she appeals to two distinct judgments of the king, that of his favor or pleasure ('if I have attained favor in your eyes', אם־מצאתי חן בעיניך) and that of his ethical standards and sense of propriety ('if to the king it is good', אם־על־המלך טוב). In A, Esther uses two phrases as well, but she appeals to the king's sense of goodness and justice in both ('if it seems right to the king', εἰ δοκεῖ τῷ βασιλεῖ, and if 'the judgment is good in his heart', ἀγαθὴ ἡ κρίσις ἐν καρδίᾳ αὐτοῦ). B's argument is the least elaborate of the three, being comprised of only one plank rather than two. In it, Esther appeals solely to her favored status by the king ('if I have found favor before the king', εἰ εὗρον χάριν ἐνώπιον τοῦ βασιλέως).

M shows Esther as more self-centered. She asks first for her own life ('my life', נפשי), then that of her people ('and my people', ועמי). In B, she requests only life in general (ἡ ψυχὴ), not necessarily her own, which lends the idea that she is pleading for the lives of all the people whom she mentions next. As Fox suggests, she is here equating herself with her people (*Character*, p. 83). And in A, Esther seems to ask for only one thing, though using two terms: her people and nation (ὁ λαός τὸν ἔθνος).

In A, Esther does refer to her life, but connects it with the nation. She uses the phrase τὸ ἔθνος τῆς ψυχῆς μου ('the nation of my being' or 'the nation of my life'), which gives the impression that Esther finds her identity, her very life, in her people.

In B and M, Esther again speaks with both terms for her petition (τῷ αἰτήματί μου, τῷ ἀξιώματί μου, בבקשתי, בשאלתי). And A again uses only the one (τῷ αἰτήματί μου), which suggests that the petitioning is now less important. Convincing the king to take the just and right action is more important.

Verse 4. Esther interprets the results of Haman's edict somewhat differently in the three narratives. In A, the possibilities are the least severe. Esther envisions servitude or slavery (δούλωσιν) and the plundering of small children ('their infants for plunder', τὰ νήπια αὐτῶν εἰς διαρπαγήν). In B, she mentions three actions: destruction or ruin (ἀπώλειαν), plundering (διαρπαγὴν), and servitude (δουλείαν). M's portrayal is by far the most violent and the most lethal. Though also speaking of three actions, they all involve the actual killing of people: extermination or annihilation (הֹשׁמִיד), violent slaying or slaughter (הרוֹג), and destruction or killing (אבד [אבד in the piel]). In M, Esther does not see bondage as a result of the edict, as she does in the other two narratives, but instead as less than the edict requires.

B portrays a greater solidarity of Esther with her people. She specifies for a second time who the edict would affect ('we', ἡμεῖς) and claims the children as part of her community ('our children', τὰ τέκνα ἡμῶν). A expresses more separation, at least with the people's children, for Esther does not view them as hers also ('their infants', τὰ νήπια αὐτῶν). M does not note any particular treatment of the children of the community.

In M, Esther expresses a greater tolerance for abuse. She informs the king that if her people had been sold into slavery, such action would be acceptable to her and she would not complain ('if as male servants and female servants we had been sold, I would have kept silent', אלוּ לעבדים ולשפחות נמכרנו החרשתי). Apparently the killing of them is the cause of her objection. Interestingly, M's Esther would not have complained about the type of abuse A's Esther laments, in which the people are only placed in servitude and plundered but not destroyed.

A shows Esther to be concerned not to trouble the king, hoping not to cause him the distress that the information would inflict ('so that I will not cause grief to my lord', ἵνα μὴ λυπήσω τὸν κύριόν μου). Esther obviously anticipates the king's possible response correctly, for after telling him, he does become upset and angry (vv. 5-7).

B provides the detail that Esther learned her information through accidentally overhearing or even intentionally eavesdropping ('I have overheard [this]', παρήκουσα).

Both A and B present Esther's view of Haman. In A, she identifies him, though not by name, as one who has personally affected herself and her people by causing them harm ('the person who caused us injury', τὸν ἄνθρωπον τὸν κακοποιήσαντα ἡμᾶς). She here exhibits concern for the fate of the people. However, in B, Esther does not speak of what he has done directly to her people, but instead in terms of the Persian court. She identifies him as one who is deceitful in general character ('the slanderer', ὁ διάβολος), and then passes a value judgment upon him as one whom she does not deem worthy of the standards of the court ('for [he] ... is not worthy of the court of the king', οὐ γὰρ ἄξιος ... τῆς αὐλῆς τοῦ βασιλέως). Esther focuses not upon Haman's threat against her people nor even against the person of the king, but against the court as a whole. Perhaps she feels that one as deceitful as Haman would harm the reputation of the Persian government. In M, Esther does not refer to the action of any one particular person at all.

The final phrase in M, כי אין הצר שוה בנזק המלך, is difficult to understand with precision. It includes one term which has a variety of meanings (צר, from the root צרר), and another which is a *hapax legomenon* and most likely derives its meaning from the Aramaic נזק, 'injury, damage' (as suggested by Francis Brown, S.R. Driver and Charles H. Briggs, *A Hebrew and English Lexicon of the Old Testament* [Oxford: Clarendon, 1907], p. 634). Paton concludes that the text is corrupt (*Esther*, pp. 261-62) and Moore reads this sentence as agreeing in substance with A (*Esther,* p. 70). BHS proposes (without textual evidence) הצלה שוה ('the deliverance is equal, comparable') for הצר שוה, but there is no reason to do so, as the text is comprehensible as it stands. The הצר can be understood in its meaning of 'distress, travail, straits'. Esther is here weighing the distress caused to her people with the injury and damage that would be caused to the king if he were advised of the situation, perhaps either in causing him grief (as in A) or in bringing shame upon him (but not necessarily the monetary loss which Fox asserts [*Character,* pp. 84-85, 282]). She displays a divided loyalty. She is concerned both for the pain of her people and for the welfare of the king and his government. It is the fact that the people will be destroyed, and not just sold as servants, which tilts the balance and makes her decide to inform the king.

Verse 5. In M, the king is named personally for the first time in this scene, as well as by his title ('the king Ahasuerus', המלך אחשורוש). It likewise refers to Esther by both her position and name ('Esther the queen', אסתר המלכה). This nomenclature causes the king to appear more personal than he usually does and designates Esther by her royal position.

A portrays the king as being more emotional at this point in Esther's proceedings. He responds to her information (of v. 4) with rage ('and the king was angered', καὶ ἐθυμώθη ὁ βασιλεὺς). As Dorothy correctly notes, the king's emotions in this verse render him as a more sympathetic character at this point ('Books', p. 197).

In A, it is of great importance, at least to the king, that Esther is feared and respected. He is enraged that someone has not revered her properly, asking her who 'disregarded the fear of you' (παρελθεῖν τὸν φόβον σου). Yet he is also concerned that his kingdom is treated respectfully, wanting to know the identity of the one who had attempted to abuse or deface it ('who has presumed to abuse the sign of my kingdom', ὃς ἐτόλμησε ταπεινῶσαι τὸ σημεῖον τῆς βασιλείας μου). Hence, the king is equally concerned for Esther and for his kingdom, and it appears that he is even viewing Esther herself as the sign of this kingdom.

B's language is quite vague. The phrase τὸ πρᾶγμα τοῦτο ('this matter') leaves it uncertain with what exactly the king is taking issue. And M is not clear, either, about the actual character of the offense. The king asks only the identity of the one who had 'done so' (לעשׂות כן).

In A, what seems wrong to the king is not that an entire people is to be destroyed but how the situation has affected Esther. He exhibits a special concern for her honor and authority. In M, the king instead speaks about the effect Haman's action has had upon himself, in feelings of personal fulfillment ('who has filled his heart', אשׁר־מלאו לבו), but not upon Esther or the kingdom.

Verse 6. In general, the material unique to A at this point reveals more interaction between Esther and the king, particularly in a greater amount of their dialogue. She responds to his feelings, speaks to him, then he responds to her and tells her to answer him again.

In A, Esther pays attention to, and cares about, the feelings of the king. She responds to his emotions. She notes his opinions about the situation she just revealed to him, that he views it negatively ('the queen saw that [it] appeared terrible to the king', εἶδεν ἡ βασίλισσα ὅτι δεινὸν ἐφάνη τῷ βασιλεῖ) and with antipathy ('he hated the wickedness', μισοπονηρεῖ). In the previous verse, the king appeared angry, but now Esther urges him not to be ('do not be angry', Μὴ ὀργίζου).

A portrays the king as much more emotional at this point in the plot, and we know that he perceives the events as terrible and wrong. Esther first observes his strong feelings about the treatment of her people. Then, later, he himself evidences his heightened emotional state. He swears in asking for the identity of the one accountable for such a situation ('the king swore', ὤμοσεν ὁ βασιλεὺς) and promises with a vow to do whatever she thinks will remedy this situation ('with an oath he promised', μετὰ ὅρκου ὑπέσχετο), actions which enforce what he is saying.

In A, Esther views the king as being appeasing or merciful ('you are merciful', ἱλασμοῦ σου).

In A, Esther appears concerned that her guests eat well, and she encourages the king to continue with the banqueting after their early drinks of v. 2. And it suggests that this second banquet is lavish like the first (cf. 5.5). She commands the king not just to eat but to eat with relish ('feast sumptuously', εὐωχοῦ).

The king and Esther express reciprocal actions in A. She tells him that she will do what he wants ('I will do according to your direction', ποιήσω κατὰ τὸ ῥῆμά σου). And then he vows the same thing to her, that he will do what she wants ('he promised to do for her whatever she might desire', ὑπέσχετο ποιῆσαι αὐτῇ ὃ ἂν βούληται).

A shows Esther to be anxious to calm down the king. She appears as concerned that he not be upset right now as she wants to present her petition to him. Esther commands him not to be provoked ('do not be angry, lord', Μὴ ὀργίζου, κύριε), and is willing to postpone her request until the following day, perhaps at yet a third banquet. These details suggest either that Esther wishes to stretch out the revelation of the problem over time, or that she may want the king to be in a calm and rational state of mind when she finally does make her petition.

In A, the king is quite receptive to Esther's request. He first shows that he wants to hear what she has to say, especially desiring that she respond back to him ('the king swore that she should report back to him', ὤμοσεν ὁ βασιλεὺς τοῦ ἀπαγγεῖλαι αὐτὴν αὐτῷ), and then yet again promises to do whatever she wants ('he promised to do for her whatever she might desire', ὑπέσχετο ποιῆσαι αὐτῇ ὃ ἂν βούληται). He appears not just to be granting a supplicant's petition but genuinely concerned about her desires.

A alone notes that Esther feels confident or hopeful when revealing Haman's identity ('Esther, being confident, said ...', θαρήσασα ἡ Εσθηρ εἶπεν...). Her reference to courage recalls v. 3, in which she called upon God for courage. Apparently God is still influencing her similarly now.

Each of the three narratives portrays Haman, or at least Esther's view of him, differently. M emphasizes his hostility and wickedness, using three descriptive terms which lend this impression: צר ('adversary, foe'), אויב ('enemy, one who is hostile'), and רע ('evil, bad'). B describes Haman to a lesser extent than M and A, with only two terms which suggest, as does M, his hostility and evil character: ἐχθρός ('adversary, hated one') and ὁ πονηρός ('evil, malevolent one'). And as in M, A uses three descriptions, but it portrays Haman as the king's friend and one who deceives as well as being wicked: ὁ φίλος σου ('your friend, loved one'), ὁ ψευδής ('lying, deceiving one'), and ὁ πονηρός ('evil, bad, malevolent one'). Moreover, the king himself has just identified him as one who behaves arrogantly (τὸν ὑπερηφανευσάμενον). The substantive ὁ φίλος can represent a title of a court official as well as a friend. B regularly employs the term as a title for government officials elsewhere throughout the story (cf. 1.3, 13; 3.1; 6.9; 16.5) but A does not. It instead chooses other terms to describe the king's officials in the rest of the story (the sole possible exception is 3.1). That the term ὁ φίλος is now used here by A suggests that the king's relationship with Haman includes some degree of affection (in the sense of a friend or loved one) and is not only an official title.

Both M and B report how Haman is affected by Esther's revelation. M specifically notes that he is afraid ('and Haman was terrified', והמן נבעת) and B notes more generally that he is anxious and upset ('and Haman was troubled', Αμαν δὲ ἐταράχθη). These two verbs are not synonomous, as this is the sole instance in the LXX where ταράσσω translates נבעת. B's use of ταράσσω here (in the aorist passive) recalls Esther's approach before the king, when her heart was similarly troubled (15.13). Esther has shifted positions by this point in the proceedings. Haman now feels the same type of anxiety before her that she felt earlier before the king.

Verse 7. The emotional reaction of the king is provided by M and A. In M, we are told that the king is angry ('and the king rose up in his rage', והמלך קם בחמתו). In A, though he is also angry, he acts significantly more upset, full of anger and vexation ('and the king, becoming vehement and being filled with anger', ἔκθυμος δὲ γενόμενος ὁ βασιλεὺς καὶ πλησθεὶς ὀργῆς). He also shows his agitation physically through his greater motion. He leaps up (ἀνεπήδησε), instead of merely rising up (ἐξανέστη, קם in B and M), and he paces about (ἦν περιπατῶν). B focuses less upon the king's emotions. We are not given information about how he feels or how the news about Haman affects him.

M is most specific with regard to place. The king goes out to the palace garden ('the garden of the house', גנת הביתן). In B, he just goes to a garden or orchard (τὸν κῆπον), and in A we do not know where the king goes. We can only assume that in his pacing about he leaves the room because v. 8 mentions his return.

In M, Haman asks Esther particularly for his life ('but Haman remained [there] to request his life from Esther the queen', והמן עמד לבקש על־נפשו מאסתר המלכה). This detail suggests that Esther's revelation of his actions would result in his extermination. He interprets the king as being out for his life ('he saw that injury was plotted against him from the king', ראה כי־כלתה אליו הרעה מאת המלך), so the fact that he asks for his life from Esther, and not from the king, highlights Esther's power in the court and her influence over the king.

B is not as detailed regarding the actions and fate of Haman. He only sees that he is in trouble, but not exactly what will come to him nor from whom it will come ('he saw himself as being in harmful circumstances', ἑώρα ... ἑαυτὸν ἐν κακοῖς ὄντα).

The placement of the description of Haman's falling upon Esther varies. In A, it is found in this verse, but in the next verse (v. 8) in B and M. The ordering of this detail makes A appear more centered upon Esther. The reader sees the scene from Esther's perspective, when only she is in the room. In contrast, in B and M this action is described through the king's eyes, when he himself sees the scene upon re-entering the room. A also does not include certain details about Haman which are found in B and M.

In A, Esther's announcement has the power to make Haman anxious ('and Haman was troubled', καὶ ὁ Αμαν ἐταράχθη). And that he falls upon her feet suggests his attitude of subservience towards her ('and he fell upon the feet of Esther the queen', καὶ προσέπεσεν ἐπὶ τοὺς πόδος Εσθηρ τῆς βασιλίσσης).

All three of the narratives include a sexual allusion in Haman's actions towards Esther. He throws himself upon her as she is reclining (v. 7 in A, v. 8 in B and M), and his use of force, as described by the king in v. 8, implies sexual advances. (Dorothy's reasoning that B's version of this scene is the most sexually suggestive because Haman falls at Esther's feet is questionable ['Books', pp. 198-99]). Dorothy has neglected to note that it is A's unique terminology for the bed which makes clear Haman's sexual interactions in that narrative. κοίτη, which is used by A alone, reflects not only a bed for sleeping, but a conjugal bed or the act of sexual intercourse itself.) Overall, the sexual element is clear in each of the narratives, and to an equal degree.

Verse 8. M is the most complete version of this verse, including various details from both A and B. It states that 'the king returned from the garden of the house to the house of the drinking of wine' (המלך שב מגנת הביתן אל־בית משתה היין). Like B, M notes that he came from the garden ('the king returned from the garden', ἐπέστρεψεν δὲ ὁ βασιλεὺς ἐκ τοῦ κήπου). And like A it notes that he came back to drinking festivities ('the king returned to the drinking together', ὁ βασιλεὺς ἐπέστρεψεν ἐπὶ τὸ συμπόσιον). Then M relates the king's questioning, 'will he also force the queen before me in the house?' (הגם לכבוש את־המלכה עמי בבית). Like A, it notes that the event occurs in his presence ('must he also force my wife before me?', τὴν γυναῖκά μου ἐκβιάζῃ ἐνώπιόν μου), and like B it notes the house as its location ('must he force the woman in my house?', τὴν γυναῖκα βιάζῃ ἐν τῇ οἰκίᾳ μου). M is also the most complete in detail of place, providing the locations in the house of the garden and of the banquet.

B alone provides the particular reason why Haman falls upon Esther: to make a request ('asking of the queen', ἀξιῶν τὴν βασίλισσαν).

B refers to Esther in the king's question as just the woman but not necessarily the wife (τὴν γυναῖκα). A, including the possessive pronoun, makes it clear that the king is referring to his marital partner ('my wife', τὴν γυναῖκά μου). And in M, Esther instead appears regal, for the king refers to her as 'the queen' (המלכה). Her political position is important, not just her relationship as his spouse.

In B, the king claims exclusive ownership of the palace ('my house', τῇ οἰκίᾳ μου), in contrast with M ('the house', בית).

A portrays the king as being concerned about two things, the kingdom and Esther. He first views Haman as working against the entire kingdom, not just one people, in making his edict ('an offense of the kingdom', ἡ ἁμαρτία τῆς βασιλείας). Then he chides him for pressing upon Esther ('force my wife', τὴν γυναῖκά μου ἐκβιάζῃ). In both B and M, the king expresses concern for only Esther, without any reference to the kingdom or its court.

The final sentence of this verse is completely different among the three narratives. A continues the king's speech, in which he commands consequences for Haman; he is to be silenced and taken from their presence. B records Haman's own response to the events. When hearing the king's accusing question, he averts his face. And M reports, as A, consequences towards Haman. After the king is done speaking, Haman's face is covered. It is not entirely clear, though, who performs this concealment. As the verb (חפו) requires a plural subject, it is grammatically possible that Esther and the king perform the action. However, in the larger context of the narrative, it is more likely performed by the eunuchs who go to bring Haman for the banquet (6.14), hang Haman (7.10), one of whom speaks in the very next verse (7.9), and who thus appear to have been present also throughout this entire interchange between Esther, the king, and Haman. (It is not necessary to emend the חפו to חפרו, 'was shamed', as Fox suggests [*Character*, p. 283], to give the general impression that Haman is in disfavor at this point.)

Analysis
A Text. Esther displays a great sense of confidence and courage in this narrative. Twice it explicitly states that she is confident and bold, near the beginning of the conversation between her and Ahasuerus, before she even speaks to him, and then again right before she announces to him that Haman is the one who harmed her people. And Esther strives to actively fight her feelings of fear. However, Esther's courage is also emphasized implicitly. As Ahasuerus's anger is greater here, Esther shows a certain amount of boldness merely in standing up to him. And as she views Haman even more as her enemy and he has the power to upset her, Esther exhibits courage in facing up to him as well. But Esther's courage is inseparably linked with her piety, for it is only because she first prays to God that she is emboldened in this situation. And she feels dependent upon God for the success of her mission.

Esther is also logical and rational throughout the events of this episode. In making her request to Ahasuerus, she appeals to his heart and mind. She herself remains calm, even to the point of being uncomfortable with his display of emotion. This narrative portrays Esther as quite concerned to keep Ahasuerus in a similar calm state. She does not want to report the results of Haman's actions to him because she knows the information will upset him. And later, when he does indeed become extremely upset, Esther tries her best to appease his anger and to calm him down. Furthermore, she is patient, willing to postpone her request until the king is likewise in a rational state of mind. In this narrative, we also see Esther as a good hostess, generous and giving attention to detail, as she plans her banquet with pre-dinner drinks and desires that her guests partake abundantly of the dinner.

Justice is a primary concern for Esther. She here attempts to get Ahasuerus to make what is the ethical or moral decision in this situation. When presenting her request, she bases her entire argument upon an appeal to what he sees as the right thing to do. Even the language used is evocative of a legal trial, wherein the goal is to work in the most just manner. The heart of the matter is not so much Esther revealing her petition and request but convincing Ahasuerus to act properly.

This narrative portrays Esther as being important to the kingdom overall. Her honor is linked with that of the kingdom, and when she is abused, the whole kingdom is as well. Indeed, Ahasuerus perceives her as an extension of the kingdom, its mark or sign. Twice he interprets an offense against the individual, Esther, as one against the entire kingdom. The proper attitude towards Esther is honor and respect, and Haman's sin, at least in the mind of the king, is that he did not so reverence her.

Though the stated ramifications of Haman's edict are not as severe in this narrative, they are portrayed as having a stronger effect. From the start, Esther and her people are suggested to be in actual danger, and she makes her request within the framework of a perilous situation. Thus the Jews' need for Esther to perform well at this juncture is heightened. Not only are the Jewish people understandably horrified but even the Persian king finds this situation terrible, evil, and wrong. Esther, then, as spokesperson for the Jews, acts in a highly important role. Esther finds her identity and very life in her nation, and she selflessly requests only that their lives be spared and does not think of her own. Yet she does not speak in terms that suggest her loss will be as great as theirs, especially with regard to the fate of the children.

More extensive detail about the relationship Esther has with the king is provided by this narrative. The two interact with each other to a much greater extent. We get the sense that Esther is quite close to Ahasuerus, as she is able to anticipate and read his emotional states well. She views him as kind and merciful, and obviously respects him. And we also see his special care for her. He stresses that he wants to know what concerns her and wants her to express it to him. And he swears strongly that he will do for her whatever she might desire. She is a recipient of Ahasuerus's allegiance, for in matters of dispute he quickly and vehemently sides with her. Though Esther has told him of the demise of an entire sector of his population, what concerns Ahasuerus most is only how this destruction has especially affected her.

However, the reader is not left with the impression that theirs is an ideal or completely equal relationship. Ahasuerus is quite emotional, and Esther apparently feels responsible for soothing these emotions and keeping him serene—a challenging task. She exhibits an amount of deference to him and pledges to do what he says if that will aid the situation. Nor does Ahasuerus here share the royal power equally with her. He mentions the kingdom as particularly his and does not address her at all by her title as queen in their conversations. Instead, he refers to her as his wife.

In this narrative Esther is also portrayed as having a certain relationship with Haman. From the start, he appears particularly as her opponent and she obviously feels antagonism towards him. Haman's mere presence upsets her, throwing off her ability to respond to Ahasuerus. But such is to be expected, for she sees him as personally responsible for causing injury to her people. Though recognizing that Haman is her husband's friend, Esther perceives his true character as fraudulent, deceptive, and evil. At the end of the encounter, Haman is even more subservient to Esther, falling at her feet in the very same gesture that he faults her relative Mordecai for not performing towards him. But though he exhibits an upset, emotional state before her, just as Ahasuerus does earlier, Esther holds no sympathy for Haman.

B Text. In this narrative Esther exhibits a concern for the Jewish people. She feels for them and considers herself more as a part of them. When appealing to Artaxerxes, Esther does not ask particularly for her own life but for the life of all. And she stresses that the destructive events will occur to her as well as to the rest of the Jews.

With regard to the king, he is most inquisitive towards Esther at the beginning of their interaction. But his line of questioning tends as much to want to know what is occurring and why Esther called a second banquet as to express concern for her personal desires. Less of a sense of close relationship of Esther with Artaxerxes is evident. He refers to the palace as particularly his dwelling, and he does not refer to Esther specifically as his wife. However, instead of interest in him, Esther has interest in the Persian court. She is concerned for the honor and reputation of the court and desires that it not be shamed, and she condemns Haman because he has not shown himself to be worthy of its standard. Moreover, Esther knows how to get around in the court, for she eavesdrops and manages to obtain the information she needs without being told outright.

Esther is oriented more towards emotion than rhetoric and intellectual argumentation. When presenting her request, she does it simply and appeals only to her being held in a pleasing and favored manner by Artaxerxes. However, Esther exhibits a certain amount of power in this narrative, as she, along with Artaxerxes, has a troubling effect upon Haman. She herself is not now afraid but instead actively causes anxiety in others. And Esther passes judgment upon Haman. Though her characterization of Haman overall is less descriptive, she emphasizes that he slanders, deceives, is wicked, and holds animosity.

M Text. This episode begins very much like Esther's first banquet. Esther must have planned it to be, or at least is experiencing it, as an exact repetition. It is the same type of festivity and Ahasuerus speaks again to her and says exactly the same thing. Once again the mood begins as quite formal. But it is Esther herself who breaks this mood. She is careful to respond punctiliously to Ahasuerus's questions, but she breaks the solemn atmosphere by introducing the nasty topics of partisanship and extreme violence against innocents.

Esther is an extremely balanced person in this narrative. She bases her argument to Ahasuerus on both reason and emotion, and she exhibits concern with both individual and community, in asking for her own life and for the lives of her people. When informing the king about what has happened to the Jews, she expresses her concern for the pain of both the Jews and the Persians (through harm to their king). And Esther holds to a median level of acceptable behavior, as she will tolerate a certain amount of abuse but not to the extreme.

The personal destruction which Esther envisions is great. When explaining to Ahasuerus what will happen to her people, she emphasizes the death that will be a part of the violence. The sense of lethal violence includes that from Esther herself. Her very presence is formidable enough to terrify Haman, a person who has proven himself not to be of a peaceful inclination. And it is certain, at least to Haman, that she will have him killed for his actions.

Haman's response of appealing to Esther rather than to Ahasuerus demonstrates that she must hold a certain amount of power in the decision-making of the kingdom. This narrative suggests that she and the king share rulership and authority more equally. Ahasuerus does not name the kingdom nor the palace as exclusively his, and Esther is identified by her position as queen more often. He also speaks more directly to her and emphasizes his willingness to grant her petition and her request.

Esther has less interaction with and concern for Haman. When outlining the distressing circumstances into which her people are to come, she does not even note him as their cause. Later, when Ahasuerus asks the identity of the one responsible, he likewise does not speak in terms of Haman's interaction with Esther but only how he affected himself. When she does think of him individually, though, Esther stresses his particular trait as that of an enemy. She does not describe him as having a generally hostile character but merely as antagonistic towards the Jews.

Episode 7 (8.1-8)

After the king banishes Haman in the previous episode, he wonders what to do with him. Upon being told of the gallows which Haman had prepared for Mordecai, the king commands that Haman himself be hung upon it. And the order is carried out.

The three narratives vary in the events which follow next in the plot of the story. The B and M texts parallel each other closely in this episode. In them, the king gives Haman's possessions to Esther. She reveals her relationship with Mordecai, and he also comes before the king. The king presents to Mordecai his ring and Esther places him in management of Haman's possessions. She then speaks before the king, with the purpose of asking him to overturn Haman's actions against the Jews. He extends his sceptre to her, at which she stands and presents her argument. The king responds by recalling what he has already done and commanding her and Mordecai to write an edict as they see appropriate.

The A text differs in the events by which the king hears Esther's and Mordecai's further requests and gives them authority to change the situation. The king begins by conversing with Esther about the wrong of Haman's actions. He calls forth Mordecai, gives him Haman's possessions, and asks what else Mordecai might want. Mordecai requests that the king overturn Haman's edict, and he does so. Then Esther asks to be allowed to punish the adversaries. The king gives her permission, they confer together, and he allows that she might punish Haman's family and men throughout the kingdom. And she does so. These events in the plot of the A text are represented by the versification of 7.14-21 in the Göttingen edition. In the Text section, the A text will be placed alongside the B and M texts as best it corresponds to certain details of the plot they present.

Text

καὶ *εἶπεν* ὁ βασιλεὺς τῇ Εσθηρ *Καὶ Μαρδοχαῖον ἐβουλεύσατο κρεμάσαι τὸν σώσαντά με ἐκ χειρὸς τῶν εὐνούχων*; *οὐκ ᾔδει* ὅτι *πατρῷον απτοῦ γένος ἐστὶν* ἡ Εσθηρ; καὶ *ἐκάλεσεν* ὁ βασιλεὺς τὸν Μαρδοχαῖον	Καὶ ἐν αὐτῇ τῇ ἡμέρᾳ ὁ βασιλεὺς Ἀρταξέρξης ἐδωρήσατο Εσθηρ *ὅσα ὑπῆρχεν* Αμαν τῷ *διαβόλῳ*, καὶ Μαρδοχαῖος *προσεκλήθη ὑπὸ* τοῦ βασιλέως· ὑπέδειξεν γὰρ Εσθηρ ὅτι *ἐνοικείωται* αὐτῇ.	ביום ההוא נתן המלך נתן אחשורוס לאסתר 1 *המלכה אדביח* המן *צרר היהודיים* ומרדכי *בא לפני* המלך כי־הגידה אסתר *מה הוא*־לה
And the king said to Esther, 'Did he determine to hang even Mordecai, who saved me from the hand of the eunuchs? Had he not known that Esther is of his ancestral lineage?' And the king called Mordecai,	And on the same day, the king Artaxerxes granted to Esther as much as belonged to Haman the slanderer. And Mordecai was summoned by the king, for Esther had indicated that he was related to her.	On the same day, the king Ahasuerus granted to Esther the queen the house of Haman, the one who was hostile to the Jews. And Mordecai came before the king, for Esther had reported what he was to her.
καὶ *ἐχαρίσατο αὐτῷ* πάντα *τὰ* τοῦ Αμαν.	*ἔλαβεν* δὲ ὁ βασιλεὺς τὸν δακτύλιον, ὃν ἀφείλατο Αμαν, καὶ ἔδωκεν αὐτὸν Μαρδοχαίῳ, καὶ κατέστησεν Εσθηρ Μαρδοχαῖον ἐπὶ πάντων τῶν Αμαν.	*רסר* המלך את־טבעתg אשר העביר 2 מהמן ויתנה למרדכי ותשם אסתר את־ מרדכי על־*בית* המן
and bestowed to him everything which was of Haman.	And the king took the ring, which he had removed from Haman, and gave it to Mordecai. And Esther appointed Mordecai over everything of Haman.	And the king removed his ring, which he had taken away from Haman, and he gave it to Mordecai. And Esther set Mordecai over the house of Haman.
	καὶ προσθεῖσα ἐλάλησεν πρὸς τὸν βασιλέα καὶ προσέπεσεν πρὸς τοὺς πόδας αὐτοῦ καὶ *ἠξίου* ἀφελεῖν τὴν Αμαν κακίαν καὶ *ὅσα ἐποίησεν τοῖς* Ἰουδαιοις.	ותוסף *אסתר* ותדבר לפני המלך ותפל 3 לפני רגליו *תבך ותתחנן־לו* להעביר את־רעת המן *האגגי* ואת *מחשבתו אשר חשב על־*היהודים

And she spoke again to the king and she fell to his feet, and asked to remove the evil of Haman and as much as he did to the Jews.

And Esther added (to this) and she spoke before the king. And she fell before his feet, and she wept and sought favor of him, to take away the evil of Haman the Agagite and his plan which he had planned against the Jews.

4

καὶ εἶπεν αὐτῷ Τί θέλεις, καὶ ποιήσω σοι.

ἐξέτεινεν δὲ ὁ βασιλεὺς Εσθηρ τὴν *ῥάβδον* τὴν χρυσῆν. *ἐξηγέρθη* δὲ Εσθηρ παρεστηκέναι τῷ Βασιλεῖ.

ויושט המלך לאסתר את שרבט הזהב
תקם אסתר ותעמד לפני המלך

And he said to him, 'What do you wish? And I will do (it) for you.'

And the king extended to Esther the golden rod. And Esther was raised up to stand before the king.

And the king extended to Esther the golden sceptre. And Esther rose and she stood before the king.

5

καὶ εἶπε *Μαρδοχαῖος* *Ὅπως ἀνέλης τὴν ἐπιστολὴν τοῦ* Αμαν. *καὶ ἐνεχείρισεν αὐτῷ ὁ Βασιλεὺς τὰ κατὰ τὴν βασιλείαν.*

καὶ εἶπεν *Εσθηρ* Εἰ δοκεῖ *σοι,* καὶ εὗρον χάριν, *πεμφθήτω ἀποστραφῆναι* τὰ γράμματα *τὰ ἀπεσταλμένα ὑπὸ* Αμαν *τὰ γραφέντα ἀπολέσθαι* τοὺς Ἰουδαίος, οἵ εἰσιν ἐν *τῇ βασιλείᾳ σου.*

ותאמר אם־על־המלך טוב ואם־מצאתי
חן לפניו וכשר הדבר לפני המלך וטובה
אני בעיניו יכתב להשיב את־הספרים
מחשבת המן בן־המדתא האגגי אשר
כתב לאבד את־היהודים אשר בכל־
מדינות המלך

And Mordecai said, 'That you might take away the message of Haman.' And the king handed over to him that regarding the kingdom.

And Esther said, 'If it seems right to you, and I have found favor, have it dispatched to rescind the documents, which have been sent out by Haman, which were written, (that) the Jews, who are in your kingdom, were to be destroyed.

And she said, 'If to the king it is good, and if I have found favor before him, and the matter is advantageous before the king, and I myself am good in his eyes, may it be written to turn aside the documents, the plan of Haman the son of Hammadatha the Agagite, which he wrote to kill the Jews who are in all the provinces of the king.

6

καὶ εἶπεν Εσθηρ τῷ βασιλεῖ τῇ ἐξῆς Δός μοι κολάσαι τοὺς ἐχθρούς μου φόνῳ.

πῶς γὰρ δυνήσομαι ἰδεῖν τὴν κάκωσιν τοῦ λαοῦ μου, καὶ πῶς δυνήσομαι *σωθῆναι* ἐν τῇ ἀπωλείᾳ τῆς *πατρίδος* μου;

כי איככה אוכל וראיתי ברעה אשר־
ימצא את־עמי ואיככה אוכל וראיתי
באבדן מולדתי

And next Esther said to the king, 'Allow me to punish my adversaries by killing.'

For how will I be able to see the affliction of my people? And how will I be able to be saved in the destruction of my native country?'

For how will I be able to look upon the evil which will come upon my people? And how will I be able to look upon the destruction of my kindred?'

<table>
<tr><td>

ἐνέτυχε δὲ ἡ βασίλισσα
Εσθηρ *καὶ κατὰ τῶν*
τέκνων Αμαν τῷ
βασιλεῖ, ὅπως
ἀποθάνωσι καὶ αὐτοὶ
μετὰ τοῦ πατρὸς αὐτῶν.
καὶ εἶπεν ὁ βασιλεύς
Γινέσθω. καὶ ἐπάταξε
τοὺς ἐχθροὺς εἰς πλῆθος.

</td><td>

καὶ εἶπεν ὁ βασιλεὺς
πρὸς Εσθηρ *Εἰ πάντα τὰ*
ὑπάρχοντα Αμαν ἔδωκα
καὶ ἐχαρισάμην σοι καὶ
αὐτὸν *ἐκρέμασα* ἐπὶ
ξύλου, ὅτι τὰς *χεῖρας*
ἐπήνεγκεν τοῖς
Ἰουδαίοις, *τί ἔτι*
ἐπιζητεῖς;

</td><td dir="rtl">

7 ויאמר המלך *אחשורש* לאסתר המלכה
ולמרדכי היהודי הנה בית־המן נתתי
לאסתר *ואתו תלו* על־העץ על אשר־
שלח ידו ביהודיים

</td></tr>
<tr><td>

And the queen Esther
conversed with the king,
also regarding the children
of Haman, that they also
might die with their father.
And the king said, 'Have it
be (so).' And she struck
the adversaries in great
number.

</td><td>

And the king said to
Esther, 'If I gave
everything which belongs
to Haman and bestowed
(it) to you, and hung him
upon a tree because he
placed hands upon the
Jews, what still do you
require?

</td><td>

And the king Ahasuerus said to
Esther the queen and to Mordecai
the Jew, 'Indeed, the house of
Haman I have given to Esther, and
they hung him upon the tree
because he had stretched out his
hand upon the Jews.

</td></tr>
<tr><td>

ἐν δὲ Σούσοις
ἀνθωμολογήσατο ὁ
βασιλεὺς τῇ βασιλίσσῃ
ἀποκτανθῆναι ἄνδρας
καὶ εἶπεν Ἰδοὺ δίδωμί
σοι τοῦ κρεμάσαι. καὶ
ἐγένετο οὕτως.

</td><td>

γράψατε *καὶ* ὑμεῖς ἐκ
τοῦ ὀνόματός *μου* ὡς
δοκεῖ *ὑμῖν* καὶ
σφραγίσατε τῷ
δακτυλίῳ *μου · ὅσα* γὰρ
γράφεται τοῦ βασιλέως
ἐπιτάξαντος καὶ
σφραγισθῇ τῷ δακτυλίῳ
μου, οὐκ ἔστιν *αὐτοῖς*
ἀντειπεῖν,

</td><td dir="rtl">

8 ואתם כתבו *על־היהודים* כטוב *בעיניכם*
בשם *המלך* וחתמו בטבעת *המלך* כי־
כתב אשר־נכתב *בשם*־המלך ונחתום
בטבעת *המלך* אין *להשיב*

</td></tr>
<tr><td>

And in Susa the king came
to agreement with the
queen that men were to be
killed, and said, 'See, I
grant to you to hang.' And
it came to be so.

</td><td>

Write, both of you, in my
name as seems right to
you, and seal (it) with my
ring. For as much as is
written, which was
commanded by the king
and was sealed by my ring,
is not to be opposed by
them.'

</td><td>

And you yourselves, write
concerning the Jews as it is good in
your eyes in the name of the king,
and seal (it) with the ring of the
king. For a document which is
written in the name of the king and
is sealed with the ring of the king
cannot be taken away.'

</td></tr>
</table>

Notes

Verse 1. A relates the direct speech of the king, within the context of addressing Esther ('and the king said to Esther', καὶ εἶπεν ὁ βασιλεὺς τῇ Εσθηρ). The king appears to feel closer to her and his remarks are more personal and conversational than official and formal, even though he is considering matters of the kingdom. He gives an impression of confiding in Esther and wanting her to agree with his assessment of, and indignation at, the situation.

In B and M, the king does not speak to Esther but gives her things ('the king Artaxerxes/Ahasuerus granted to Esther', ὁ βασιλεὺς Ἀρταξέρξης ἐδωπήσατο Εσθηρ, נתן המלך אחשורוש לאסתר). But in A he speaks to her but actually gives things to Mordecai, to whom he does not speak ('the king … bestowed to him', ὁ βασιλεὺς … ἐχαρισατο αὐτῷ, in v. 2).

In M, Esther appears as more royal, for her title is indicated ('Esther the queen', אסתר המלכה).

In A, the king expresses concern about the proper honor given to royalty through his marvelling at Haman's actions. He thinks that Haman has acted wrongly for two reasons. The first reason concerns Mordecai: he tried to harm the one who had saved the king's life ('did he determine to hang even Mordecai, who saved me from the hand of the eunuchs?', Καὶ Μαρδοχαῖον ἐβουλεύσατο κρεμάσαι τὸν σῶσαντά με ἐκ χειρὸς τῶν εὐνούχων;). The second reason concerns the queen ('had he not known that Esther is of his ancestral lineage?', οὐκ ᾔδει ὅτι πατρῷον αὐτοῦ γένος ἐστὶν ἡ Εσθηρ;). Here the king does not speak in terms of immoral action or concern for the Jews of the kingdom as a whole. B and M, in contrast, present Haman differently. In B he is deceitful or traitorous in general character ('the slanderer', τῷ διαβόλῳ). In M, Haman is more directly antagonistic to the Jewish people ('the one who was hostile to the Jews', צרר היהודיים).

In B and M, there is more emphasis upon Mordecai in his coming to the king. M presents him as most active, coming of his own initiative ('and Mordecai came before the king', ומרדכי בא לפני המלך). In B he is more passive, in being first called by the king ('and Mordecai was summoned by the king', καὶ Μαρδοχαῖος προσεκλήθη ὑπὸ τοῦ βασιλέως). In contrast, A reveals Mordecai as the object rather than the subject of this action, and obedient to the king's command ('and the king called Mordecai', καὶ ἐκάλεσεν ὁ βασιλεὺς τὸν Μαρδοχαῖον).

B and M mention Esther's informing people of the relationship between her and Mordecai. Apparently, they have not known of it all this time. In A, as the king chastises Haman for not according their relationship respect, it must have been common knowledge that Mordecai is related to Esther, and hence that Esther is Jewish. In speaking of the character of their connection, M is the most vague. It merely notes that Mordecai is somehow important to Esther ('what he [was] to her', מה הוא־לה). B gives the impression that there is some type of relation or connection but not precisely what ('that he was related to her', ὅτι ἐνοικείωται αὐτῇ). A delineates a greater familial and ethnic closeness of Esther with Mordecai ('that Esther is of his ancestral lineage', ὅτι πατρῷον αὐτοῦ γένος ἐστὶν ἡ Εσθηρ).

Verse 2. B and M portray the process of Mordecai's getting Haman's possessions as being composed of two steps: the king gives them to Esther, then she places Mordecai in control of them. Esther is important in the process and the rightful recipient of the articles. In A, Esther is sidelined at this point. After the king's speaking to her, he gives Haman's things directly to Mordecai and she herself is not granted any of these items.

In B and M, the king's ring acts as a symbol of political power. When Mordecai is given the ring, he is given power in the Persian government. The transfer of power from Haman to Mordecai, as Mordecai takes over Haman's position, is symbolized by the ring. And in M, it is particularly the king's ring ('his ring', טבעתו). Being more intimately related to the king provides an impression of yet greater power. A does not suggest a similar transfer of authority or political power, as it does not mention the king's ring here at all.

The language of B and M, and especially the verbs καθίστημι and שׂים ('to place, appoint, cause to be'), suggests that Esther places Mordecai in a certain position in giving over Haman's possessions to him ('and Esther appointed Mordecai over everything of/the house of Haman', καὶ κατέστησεν Εσθηρ Μαρδοχαῖον ἐπι πάντων τῶν Αμαν, ותשם אסתר את־מרדכי על־בית המן). In A, Mordecai does not appear so much to be set in a position or given control, but only given a gift of physical items, Haman's wealth ('and he bestowed to him everything which was of Haman', καὶ ἐχαρίσατο αὐτῷ πάντα τὰ τοῦ Αμαν).

At this point in the episode, B and M show Esther as having a great deal of authority in the kingdom, as she has the power to appoint people. Moreover, Esther works as one with the king with regard to Mordecai: he gives Mordecai the ring, she gives him Haman's job or management of his possessions. It is only because of Esther and her generosity that Mordecai is such a beneficiary, a fact which Paton (*Esther*, p. 268) and Fox (*Character*, p. 90) have noted as well. A hints here that Mordecai is a person of worth and may himself be deserving of the honor bestowed upon him, in the king's mention of Mordecai's saving his life (v. 1). But as B and M note nothing about Mordecai's character at this point, we are left with the understanding that Mordecai receives what he does not because of his own worth or exemplary actions but only because he is related to Esther.

Verse 3. B's participle προσθεῖσα ('to continue, repeat') refers to Esther's speaking as a repeated action. However, in this scene Esther is much less emotional and more matter-of-fact than she was when approaching the king the first time (15.1-16).

In M, Esther performs two more actions than she does in B. At the king's feet, she weeps or bewails (חבך) and she implores favor of him (תתחנן־לו). In this context it is not clear how upset Esther really is. Unlike A and B, which earlier reported Esther's inner emotions when she appeared agitated before the king (Episodes 3 and 4), M does not tell the reader Esther's emotional state at this time. We cannot assume that Esther is displaying weakness by her crying. Within the context of her request in general, she may be using her tears as a way to further influence the king's decision, along with bowing in deference before him and her choice of especially pleasing speech (v. 5).

Esther speaks more descriptively of Haman in M. She notes his nationality ('Haman the Agagite', המן האגגי) and his intentions ('his plan which he had planned against the Jews', מחשבתו אשר חשב על־היהודים). The על־היהודים ('against the Jews') suggests a greater antagonism to the Jews than B's simple dative τοῖς Ἰουδαίοις ('to the Jews'). B's language is more vague. As Esther only refers to 'as much as he did to the Jews' (ὅσα ἐποίησεν τοῖς Ἰουδαίοις), we cannot be certain to what Esther objects. However, the ὅσα ('as much as') provides a somewhat larger sense of the results of Haman's evil.

Verse 4. In A, these two verses, vv. 4-5, represent a significant difference in the events and progression of this scene than that of B and M. Only in A does Mordecai make a request and have it granted prior to Esther's request, which begins in v. 6 However, it is the king who first approaches Mordecai, inquiring about his desires, and Mordecai only then replies back (v. 5). The king does not require another sceptre-scene. Indeed, he himself initiates the petition and not Mordecai, in contrast with Esther's making the first move in B and M, and later in A as well (v. 6). Such details give an impression of a less formal process, if the characters are following an established Persian process at all. In this verse the king asks what Mordecai wants and then promises to grant it, the same thing he has done often with Esther earlier (cf. 5.3, 6, 8; 7.2).

In B and M, Esther is in a situation where she stands before the king, but she does not speak until he raises his sceptre and gives her permission. They repeat actions that occurred only a few days before

(15.11-12). This scene is so similar to the previous one just two chapters earlier that it is difficult not to understand it in terms of the earlier scene (a comparison Moore would avoid [*Esther,* pp. 78, 82]). In contrast, Esther simply asks the king in A (v. 6).

The wording of the first half of this verse in M, ויושט המלך לאסתר את שרבט הזהב ('and the king extended to Esther the golden sceptre') is exactly the same as in her first entrance scene (15.12 [5.2 in BHS versification]), which encourages us to understand her request here in light of her earlier approach and petition even more than we might in B.

M provides the king with a more regal appearance. He stretches forth his sceptre ('the golden sceptre', את שרבט הזהב) rather than the 'golden rod' (τὴν ῥάβδον τὴν χρυσῆν) of B, both narratives exhibiting here the particular terminology they each used earlier (cf. 15.12, and notes).

In B, Esther is more passive, for she needs the king's assistance to stand up again after falling at his feet ('and Esther was raised up to stand before the king', ἐξηγέρθη δὲ Εσθηρ παρεστηκέναι τῷ βασιλεῖ). M's use of the active voice and two finite verbs present Esther as more active ('and Esther rose and she stood before the king', ותקם אסתר ותעמד לפני המלך).

Verse 5. In A, it is Mordecai who requests particularly that Haman's work be undone, not Esther as in B and M. He requests that the king would 'take away the message of Haman' (ἀνέλῃς τὴν ἐπιστολὴν τοῦ Αμαν). In speaking of the commission, Mordecai is also less specific regarding the details of Haman's command in terms of its intent, the manner in which he wrote and sent it, and the effects it would have upon the Jewish people. B and M present more the idea that Esther has knowledge of exactly what Haman had attempted to do.

In B, Esther speaks more directly to the king. She addresses him in the second person ('to you', σοι) and speaks similarly of the kingdom ('your kingdom', τῇ βασιλείᾳ σου). In M, Esther's words suggest a sense of distance and respect, as she refers to him thrice as only 'the king' (המלך), and uses third person pronouns ('before him', לפניו; 'his eyes', עיניו).

In M, Esther presents a longer, fuller, and more detailed argument before the king, comprised of four planks in contrast with two in B. The first two considerations are the same: 'if it seems good to you/the king' (εἰ δοκεῖ σοι, אם־על־המלך טוב) and '(if) I have found favor (before him)' (εὗρον χάριν, אם־מצאתי חן לפניו). However, in M Esther also bases her

argument upon whether her request will profit the king as well as seem
ethically right to him ('and the matter is advantageous before the king',
וכשר הדבר לפני המלך) and upon whether she herself has his approval as
well as her speech ('and I myself am good in his eyes', וטובה אני בעיניו).
Similarly, she shows concern in her second plank that she finds favor
particularly before him (לפניו) and not just in general. In her rhetoric,
Esther covers all the bases in M, appealing to whether the king likes
either herself or her idea, or if it seems either the right or the profitable
thing to do.

In M, Esther identifies Haman more fully. As in v. 3, she notes his
family's nationality ('the Agagite', האגגי), but now also his parentage
('Haman the son of Hammadatha', המן בן־המדתא). She also envisions him
as having a certain planned intention ('the plan of Haman', מחשבת המן).
Moore suggests that by including mention of Haman's scheme, Esther is
placing all the blame upon Haman for the enactment of the edict and
absolving the king of any responsibility (*Esther*, p. 78). Thus, she
continues to take care to present the situation in a way that will sound
best to the king.

In A, it is uncertain what exactly the king gives to Mordecai, noting it
only as 'things regarding the kingdom' (τὰ κατὰ τὴν βασιλείαν). We
might suppose it to be the message of Haman (τὴν ἐπιστολὴν τοῦ
Αμαν) which Mordecai had just requested, but as ἐπιστολὴν is a
feminine singular noun and τά the neuter plural relative pronoun, such
an understanding is grammatically problematic. This neuter plural more
likely suggests the abstract 'powers of the kingdom' (as Moore
understands it [*Esther*, p. 77]) by which Mordecai can rescind Haman's
edict.

Verse 6. In A, this is the first time that Esther speaks in this scene. She
directly addresses the king ('and Esther said to the king', καὶ εἶπεν
Εσθηρ τῷ βασιλεῖ), in contrast to Esther's first quoted speaking in B
and M ('and Esther/she said', καὶ εἶπεν Εσθηρ, ותאמר, in v. 5).
Apparently Esther, as Mordecai immediately before this, does not need
the king's official permission to speak to him either. The absence of
another sceptre-scene in A renders Esther more authoritative than in B
and M, since she does not have to wait to speak and beg for another
favor. Esther now initiates her request of the king in A as well as B and
M, whereas the king initiated the exchange with Mordecai in A (v. 4).

In M, the two instances of וראיתי (ו with the perfect) are to be understood in the same way as would be an infinitive following אוכל (cf. Brown, Driver, Briggs, *Hebrew and English Lexicon*, pp. 407-408; note meaning 1.f). Hence, the occurrences of this phrase (אוכל וראיתי, 'I will be able to see') are grammatically equivalent to B's phrases consisting of a finite verb followed by an infinitive (δυνήσομαι ἰδεῖν, 'I will be able to see'; δυνήσομαι σωθῆναι, 'I will be able to be saved').

A does not show Esther as being rhetorical here or presenting a crafted argument, nor does she appeal to the king's sense of rightness or favor. She only boldly states her request, without preamble: 'allow me to punish my adversaries by killing' (Δός μοι κολάσαι τοὺς ἐχθρούς μου φόνῳ).

A presents Esther as both desirous of control and extremely violent. Whereas in B and M she asks the king to do the action which will fulfill her request, to revoke Haman's decree, here Esther herself demands to bring about the result she desires ('allow me', Δός μοι). The action she envisions performing is savage. She asks to be enabled to slaughter or murder (φόνῳ) those she dislikes, and by means of a manner which leaves no room for error or reversal.

In B and M, Esther reveals the reason why she asks the king to turn back Haman's demand as concern for her people. In contrast to A's destruction of others, she here imagines the destruction and misery of the Jews in two phrases: 'the evil of/which will come to my people' (τὴν κάκωσιν τοῦ λαοῦ μου, רעה אשר־ימצא את־עמי) and 'the destruction of my country/kindred' (τῇ ἀπωλείᾳ τῆς πατρίδος μου, אבדן מולדתי). Esther's primary consideration is for her people, and she feels their pain.

In A, Esther only exhibits concern about the Jews' enemies, here and in the following two verses. In contrast, B and M in this episode refer only to the individual Haman as working against the Jews. In A, Esther envisions a class of people who are hostile to the Jews and names them as such ('my adversaries', τοὺς ἐχθρούς μου). She appears vindictive in wanting to chastise them for their action ('to punish', κολάσαι). Esther does not request compassion for her own people, but instead justice and retribution for the ones opposing them.

B portrays Esther as being concerned for her own deliverance. She wonders 'how will I be able to be saved?' (πῶς δυνήσομαι σωθῆναι). She also exhibits passivity in expecting someone else to rescue her rather than thinking in terms of saving herself, or even her people as well.

B's use of the term πατρίς ('fatherland, hometown, one's native place or country') lends the impression that Esther's concern with regard to the Jews is more oriented to the people as a nation or as being from a particular area ('my native country', τῆς πατρίδος μου). In M, Esther is interested more in her family, offspring, or kindred ('my kindred', מולדתי).

Verse 7. In B and M, the king rehearses all that he has done for Esther. In B he concludes by asking her what else she could possibly want ('what still do you require?', τί ἔτι ἐπιζητεῖς;). Within the context of this scene, the final question is not the rebuke that Moore understands it to be (*Additions*, p. 229), but a genuine inquiry.

In A, Esther takes the initiative in her continuing discussion with the king ('and the queen Esther conversed with ... the king', ἐνέτυχε δὲ ἡ βασίλισσα Εσθηρ ... τῷ βασιλεῖ).

B presents Esther as less regal. It identifies her by name only (Εσθηρ), but A and M include her title as well ('Esther the queen', ἡ βασίλισσα Εσθηρ, אסתר המלכה). And in M the king is identified again by personal name as well as title ('the king Ahasuerus', המלך אחשורש).

M states that the king is now addressing Mordecai as well as Esther. As he is in the conversation again, the emphasis upon Esther alone during her appeal has shifted. But while Esther is identified by her position in the Persian government, Mordecai is not. Though by this time Mordecai has been given an official appointment, perhaps even Haman's position of being second in command, he is still only viewed in terms of his ethnic and religious character ('Mordecai the Jew', מרדכי היהודי). Esther still appears as more the authority figure. In B, the king continues here to address only Esther with his question. He is only concerned with what Esther, and not necessarily Mordecai, wants.

In A, instead of being concerned about the actions of Haman himself, Esther mentions his children to the king ('the children of Haman', τῶν τέκνων Αμαν). She apparently no longer views Haman or his letter as threatening, but does find his family still to be so.

A portrays the king as having trust in Esther ('and the king said, "Have it be [so]"', καὶ εἶπεν ὁ βασιλεύς Γινέσθω). He gives free power to her to do whatever she might want to Haman's children.

In B, the king appears more generous towards Esther. First, he reminds her that he has given her 'everything which belongs to Haman' (πάντα τὰ ὑπάρχοντα Αμαν). Secondly, two verbs of giving are used to describe the king's past action: ἔδωκα ('I gave') and ἐχαρισάμην σοι ('I bestowed to you'), in contrast to M's one reference נתתי לאסתר ('I have given to Esther'). And, at the end, he asks explicitly what more Esther might want ('what still do you require?', τί ἔτι ἐπιζητεῖς;).

Esther continues to express violence in A, and more than in the previous verse. Now, she desires to act against two groups of people, Haman's children (τῶν τέκνων Αμαν) in particular and the adversaries (τοὺς ἐχθροὺς) in general. And she kills and harms a great many people in her actions ('and she struck ... in great number', καὶ ἐπάταξε ... εἰς πλῆθος). Furthermore, though the king is complicitous in Esther's violence by agreeing to its being done, Esther is quite active in A. It is unquestionably she who is performing, or at least directing, the striking and slaying.

B presents the king as being personally responsible for Haman's death ('I hung him upon a tree', αὐτὸν ἐκρέμασα ἐπὶ ξύλου). M is vague at this point. It states only that 'they hung him upon the tree' (אתו תלו על־העץ), without saying what group of people performed this action.

Verse 8. B's ὑμεῖς at the beginning of this verse makes it clear that the king is now speaking to Mordecai as well as to Esther. Because the καὶ preceding it is not the first word in the sentence, as is typical for conjunctive or continuative use in Greek narrative style, it might best be understood as emphasizing the plurality of the ὑμεῖς ('you both'). In B and M, Mordecai's re-introduction into the king's direction at the end of the episode (here in B, v. 7 in M) makes Esther alone seem less important. The king is now giving power to them both and no longer just to her.

In A's version of this episode, Esther alone is significant at its conclusion. The scene both begins and ends with the king in conversation with only her.

In A, Esther and the king agree together and mutually share the decision-making ('the king came to agreement with the queen', ἀνθωμολογήσατο ὁ βασιλεὺς τῇ βασιλίσσῃ). In B and M, the king does not consult with Esther but only commands her. He appears more authoritarian and she more under his control.

A names Esther and the king exclusively by their royal titles ('the queen', τῇ βασιλίσσῃ; 'the king', ὁ βασιλεὺς). Esther is now clearly acting according to her position in the Persian court. That these events also occur in the capital city Susa (ἐν ... Σούσαις) shows that their decision is now an official government transaction rather than an agreement between wife and husband. (Note also the naming of Esther as queen, with the king, in v. 7.)

In M, the king allows Esther and Mordecai to give orders about just the Jews ('write concerning the Jews', כתבו על־היהודים). They have control over only the Jewish population of the kingdom. But the two can, apparently, write about anything at all in B.

The process the king describes in M is more formal and business-like, and the process in B is more personal and informal. B notes only once that any order is to be in the king's name ('write ... in my name', γράψατε ... ἐκ τοῦ ὀνόματός μου), but M notes this information twice ('write ... in the name of the king', ...כתבו ... בשם המלך; 'a document which is written in the name of the king', כתב אשר־נכתב בשם־המלך). In B, the king refers to the name and the ring with the first person ('my name', τοῦ ὀνόματός μου; 'my ring', τῷ δακτυλίῳ μου), but in M these articles are identified more in terms of their official use ('the name of the king', שם המלך; 'the ring of the king', טבעת המלך).

Yet again in A, Esther desires actions of violence. She kills harshly ('the king came to agreement with the queen that men were to be killed', ἀνθωμολογήσατο ὁ βασιλεὺς τῇ βασιλίσσῃ ἀποκτανθῆναι), and she does so particularly by means of hanging ('I grant to you to hang', δίδωμί σοι τοῦ κρεμάσαι). The king also shares in her decision to perform violence.

In M, the king speaks specifically about something written, a letter, edict, or document (כתב) which Esther and Mordecai may prepare. B is more vague, ambiguously referring to 'as much as' (ὅσα) is written under the king's direction.

In A, the king again gives Esther control by letting her carry out what she wants to do ('see, I grant to you to hang', Ἰδοὺ δίδωμί σοι τοῦ κρεμάσαι).

In all three narratives, the issue at the conclusion of this episode is the power to make official decisions. Esther is granted different types of power. In B and M, the king gives her the authority to make laws—a constructive power in the realm of public policy. In A, she is granted authority to kill and destroy—a punishing or destructive power in the judicial and military realms.

Analysis
A Text. Esther's most striking characteristic at this point in the story is her violence. Because Esther has not exhibited violent tendencies prior to this episode, her so doing now takes the reader by surprise. And because she says relatively little here, and all that she is quoted as saying

refers to the use of force, we can only assume that killing others is at the forefront of her mind. The manner in which Esther envisions the death of those who oppose her is brutal—killing, striking, hanging, and utterly destroying them—and she acts against a great many people. Esther is vindictive in her desire to punish and chastise the ones who have worked against the Jews. Yet she also is concerned about justice, especially in the sense of retribution. Esther does not desire to kill for the sport of it, but so that justice might be done and punishment meted out to those whom she thinks have done actions that deserve such treatment.

Similarly, Esther is still concerned with the adversaries of the Jewish people. She speaks of certain groups of people who are enemies and no longer of Haman as an individual nor even the edict he originated. She first desires to punish her adversaries in general, but then later she specifically asks to harm Haman's children. As Haman is dead, she no longer worries about him, but finds his children to be as guilty as he was.

Esther possesses a great deal of authority. She is very much in control throughout the events of this episode, both of herself and the situation as a whole. Ahasuerus makes it clear that she is to be respected, and punishment results for those who do not pay her proper regard. With regard to Ahasuerus, she does not need his permission to speak to him, and she herself commands him more than makes a request from him. And he gives to her the power to perform that which she requests. They share together the making of decisions, by discussing issues and agreeing upon the actions to be taken. As their decisions at the conclusion of the episode are official government business, Esther is thus portrayed as intimately involved in the process by which the Persian government adjudicates and delivers justice for its people.

Linked with Esther's authority in her position as queen is her level of activity. In this narrative, she does not so much exhibit power to appoint or to create written legislation but to carry out the decisions which she makes with Ahasuerus. She is a person of few words but much action at this point in the story. As well as speaking directly only late into this episode, her statements to Ahasuerus are extremely brief. She only includes that which she wants to do. Esther is anxious to get to the business at hand.

With regard to activity and authority, Esther's qualities are in contrast with those of Mordecai. Mordecai holds less political power than in the other two narratives at this point. He is not given the king's ring, is not appointed over Haman's things but is only given them, and does not speak commandingly to Ahasuerus. And he is not involved with Esther and the king in the making of official decisions. Esther and Mordecai do not share authority in this narrative. She does not share control of Haman's possessions with Mordecai, nor does Ahasuerus give them joint authority to write legislation. Instead, each is given their own separate realm of influence. Though Esther acts on her own initiative in speaking with the king, Ahasuerus must take the initiative with Mordecai by calling him forth and in speaking to him about his desires. Mordecai asks that the king might do something for him, but Esther asks that she herself might do that which she requests. Mordecai's passivity highlights Esther's activity, and his lack of influence in government highlights her authority.[1]

In some respects, this narrative portrays Esther as more closely related to the Jewish people. She has all along been known in the court to be Jewish. And her relationship with Mordecai is as a blood relative, based upon family and racial lineage. Yet Esther does not show much concern for the Jews themselves. Though quite concerned about enemies, Esther sees them as her own adversaries and does not detail whom they harmed or whom their extermination will benefit.

Esther has a relationship with Ahasuerus which includes mutuality, generosity, and respect. She speaks personally and conversationally with him about governmental matters and works with him in making decisions. She does not need to placate him nor plead with him at this point. Ahasuerus is also more generous to Esther and Mordecai, giving them latitude in their requests and actions and requiring them to be less accountable to him, his ring, or his name. He allows Esther the freedom to take her own action to get the result she wants. And Ahasuerus values and honors Esther, and insists that others in his court do likewise.

B Text. Esther likewise possesses a degree of authority in this narrative, but in different areas. She uses her power to appoint Mordecai to be in control of Haman's possessions. Esther understands more completely the actions involved in Haman's making his edict, as well as what is necessary for Artaxerxes to overturn it. And she is demanding of Artaxerxes's action in asking him to do so. Esther also enjoys a certain

---

1.   Dorothy asserts, without explanation, that it is Mordecai who displays more importance in this scene in the A text. But it is difficult to think of reasons why one might interpret Mordecai to be more important here ('Books', p. 207).

sense of authority and respect from the king. He is interested in what she alone desires, not Mordecai as well. Though she exhibits subservience in having to ask for permission to speak, she does not need to argue as much to convince him to hear her petition. However, Esther's authority is limited. Artaxerxes allows her and Mordecai to write orders about everything and to make as great a number as they might want, but he keeps tighter command over them.

However, Esther displays passivity as well. When speaking of the possible destruction coming to her people, Esther is afraid for her life. But instead of wondering how she might save herself from the situation, she expects someone else to rescue her. Earlier in the episode she does not stand up herself at Artaxerxes's extended rod, but apparently feels weak and needs help. However, Esther also exhibits a certain new strength, in contrast with her first effort. When approaching Artaxerxes this time she is truly calm and confident, not attempting to pretend, with no suggestion that she is bothered at all by the exchange.

Esther extends concern about the Jewish people. As she worries about her own salvation in their destruction, she must see herself as one of the Jews who is likewise in danger. And she is somehow connected or related to Mordecai. Esther speaks of her people more in a political or nationalistic sense, and she cares about the pain that they will experience. She is also concerned about those who work against them. Though having a vague sense of opposition coming from a group of people, she sees in Haman their primary adversary. She finds him to be deceitful and even traitorous, and as doing a great deal against the Jewish people.

Esther speaks directly to Artaxerxes and in a manner which tends to be more personal and less formal, and the same is true of the king's words to her. She spends a longer period of time conversing with him alone, without Mordecai. And the king is especially generous to her, in giving her all that was Haman's and then asking whether she wants even more. He allows her, along with Mordecai, to write as many new regulations as they want.

M Text. Esther has a great desire to win over Ahasuerus, a characteristic she exhibits particularly when speaking before him. She says significantly more to him than in the B text, yet is careful to be deferential. Esther bases her appeal both upon his approval of her request and upon his approval of her. By means of her approach before Ahasuerus, Esther reveals significant aspects of her character and state of mind at this point in the story. She is intelligent and speaks persuasively, traits which are apparent in her presentation of a very complete argument. And Esther knows that Ahasuerus cares for her. To appeal to whether he likes her and finds her favorable, she must already be confident that she has his approval. She makes her case so comprehensively that there is no way he can refuse her request.

But Esther's tears also show her to be more emotional this time than during her first approach. She falls before Ahasuerus and weeps in his presence, in direct contrast to her actions when approaching him previously. Esther apparently feels she must do more to obtain Ahasuerus's permission to speak and must say more to convince him to act on her behalf.

Esther's authority is particularly regal. Even now, after her ethnic heritage has been revealed, she is still primarily identified as the queen and not as a Jew. She is important in her position in the king's court. Esther also knows about the particularities of Persian governmental procedure. She realizes the importance of documentation, and that writing something down makes it so. Esther is also cognizant about what Haman has done and about the plan he has enacted. However, there are areas in which she is less in control. She, along with Mordecai, controls orders written for only the Jews, not the entire population of the kingdom.

Even though Esther's connection to Mordecai is the most vague in this narrative, she is most concerned about the Jews. She cares much about the people's pain and destruction, and this narrative provides a greater sense that she cannot bear to see them harmed. In thinking about the Jews, Esther sees them as family and kindred. And at the end of this episode, she and Mordecai are in control especially of these Jewish people.

Likewise, Esther is concerned with Haman as the Jews' enemy. She describes him in terms of hostility, not in general character but in his antagonism particularly against her people. Esther knows about him in an official sense, in her knowledge of his calculated plan against the Jewish people. But she also knows of him in a personal sense, in terms of his nationality and family history.

Esther's interaction with Ahasuerus is more formal and less personal in this narrative. She must first ask permission even to speak to him of her request. And when appealing to him, she speaks in a stately and business-like manner, and she also stands at a greater physical distance from him. Ahasuerus himself also acts at this time more in his office as king. And later, when allowing Esther and Mordecai permission to make legislation, he proposes more official obligations which their orders must meet.

Episode 8 (9.11-15)

After Esther's three-way conversation with the king and Mordecai, the events vary among the three narratives but proceed along the same general plot line. The king's secretaries are called, and an edict is written (by the king in the A and B texts, by Mordecai in the M text) which allows the Jews to defend themselves in response to the upcoming attack. The text of the edict itself is provided by the A and B texts. It denounces Haman, elevates the Jews, permits their defense, and commands celebration of the deliverance. Copies of the edict are dispatched throughout the kingdom. In the A text, the king gives Mordecai permission to write a letter, and the text of the document itself is provided, in which Mordecai informs them of events and commands a religious festival. In all three texts, Mordecai then appears to the Jewish people in magnificent clothing, at which they rejoice. And when the appointed day arrives, the Jews fight and have great success.

Now as this episode opens, in the B and M texts the king is informed of the destruction. He speaks with Esther about the situation and again promises to grant her a petition. In all three texts, Esther presents her desires with regard to the Jews' activities on the following day and the king helps to implement them. The Jews again kill many, and in the B and M texts they also hang the bodies of Haman's family.

This episode in the A text is represented by the versification 9.12-16 in the Göttingen edition of the text.

Text

ἐν αὐτῇ τῇ ἡμέρᾳ· *ἐπεδόθη* *τε* ὁ ἀριθμὸς τῷ βασιλεῖ τῶν ἀπολωλότων ἐν Σούσοις.	ביום ההוא <u>בא</u> מספר ההרוגים בשושן <u>הבירה לפני</u> המלך
On the same day, then, the number of those who had been destroyed in Susa was delivered over to the king.	On the same day, the number who were killed in Susa, the fortress, came before the king.

καὶ εἶπεν ὁ βασιλεὺς τῇ Εσθηρ Πῶς *σοι οἱ ἐνταῦθα* καὶ οἱ ἐν τῇ περιχώρῳ κέχρηνται;

εἶπεν δὲ ὁ βασιλεὺς πρὸς Εσθηρ Ἀπώλεσαν οἱ Ἰουδαῖοι ἐν Σούσοις *τῇ πόλει* ἄνδρας πεντακοσίους· ἐν δὲ τῇ περιχώρῳ πῶς *οἴει* ἐχρήσαντο; τί οὖν ἀξιοῖς ἔτι; καὶ *ἔσται* σοι.

12 ויאמר המלך לאסתר המלכה בשושן הבירה הרגו היהודים ואבד חמש מאות איש ואת עשרת בני־המן בשאר מדינות המלך מה עשו ומה־שאלתך וינתן לך ומה־בקשתך עוד ותעש

And the king said to Esther, 'How, for you, have those here and those in the surrounding area, availed themselves?'

And the king said to Esther, 'The Jews have destroyed, in Susa, the city, five hundred men. And in the surrounding area, how do you suppose they availed themselves? Therefore, what still do you request? And it will be to you.'

And the king said to Esther the queen, 'In Susa, the fortress, the Jews have destroyed, and by killing, five hundred men, and the ten children of Haman. In the rest of the provinces of the king what have they done? So what is your petition? And it will be given to you. And what more is your request? And it will be done.'

καὶ εἶπεν Εσθηρ Δοθήτω τοῖς Ἰουδαίοις *οὓς ἐὰν θέλωσιν ἀνελεῖν καὶ διαρπάζειν.*

καὶ εἶπεν Εσθηρ *τῷ βασιλεῖ* Δοθήτω τοῖς Ἰουδαίοις *χρῆσθαι ὡσαύτως* τὴν αὔριον, *ὥστε* τοὺς δέκα υἱοὺς *κρεμάσαι* Αμαν.

13 ותאמר אסתר אם־על־המלך טוב ינתן גם־מחר ליהודים אשר בשושן לעשות כדת היום ואת עשרת בני־המן יתלו על־העץ

And Esther said, 'Have it granted to the Jews to kill and to plunder whomever they might desire.'

And Esther said to the king, 'Have it granted to the Jews to avail themselves in the same manner tomorrow, so as to hang the ten sons of Haman.'

And Esther said, 'If to the king it is good, may it be granted also tomorrow to the Jews who are in Susa to do according to the decree of today. And the ten children of Haman, may they hang upon the tree.'

καὶ *συνεχώρμσεν.*

καὶ *ἐπέτρεψεν* οὕτως *γενέσθαι* καὶ *ἐξέθηκεν τοῖς Ἰουδαίοις τῆς πόλεως τὰ σώματα* τῶν υἱῶν Αμαν *κρεμάσαι.*

14 ויאמר המלך להעשות כן ותנתן דת בשושן ואת עשרת בני־המן תלו

And he conceded.

And he permitted it to be thus. And he put forth to the Jews of the city the bodies of the sons of Haman, to hang.

And the king said to have it done thus. And a decree was given in Susa, and they hung the ten children of Haman.

καὶ *ἀπώλεσαν μυριάδας ἑπτὰ καὶ ἑκατὸν* ἄνδρας.

καὶ συνήχθησαν οἱ Ἰουδαῖοι ἐν Σούσοις τῇ τεσσαρεσκαιδεκάτῃ τοῦ Αδαρ καὶ ἀπέκτειναν ἄνδρας τριακοσίους καὶ οὐδὲν διήρπασαν.

15 ויקהלו היהודיים אשר־בשושן גם ביום ארבעה עשר לחדש אדר ויהרגו בשושן שלש מאות איש ובבזה לא שלחו את־ידם

And they destroyed 70,100 men.	And the Jews in Susa came together on the fourteenth of Adar. And they killed three hundred men, but they plundered no one.	And the Jews who were in Susa gathered again on the fourteenth day of the month of Adar. And they killed in Susa three hundred men, but they did not lay their hand on plunder.

Notes

Verse 11. Both B and M emphasize that the events and decisions about which Esther and the king speak affect the capital city. In these few verses, Susa is referred to three times in B (vv. 11, 12, 15) and six times in M (vv. 11, 12, 13, 14, 15 [twice]). A does not exhibit a similar emphasis.

Verse 12. M first names Esther according to her regal status ('Esther the queen', אסתר המלכה), whereas she is only named in A and B (Εσθηρ).

In A, the king asks Esther herself for the results of the day's destruction in Susa ('How ... have those here ... availed themselves?', Πῶς ... οἱ ἐνταῦθα ... κέχρηται;), rather than getting the information from another source as he does in B and M (v. 11). Esther is one who is knowledgeable and a source of necessary information. But she is also in control. As the destruction is her project, the king is merely asking her how successful it was. In B and M, the king apparently assumes that Esther would not know of the day's events, for he instead tells her what has happened.

M portrays the Jews of Susa as being more active and more lethally violent in the events of that day. Like B, it notes that the Jews have utterly destroyed or annihilated ('the Jews have destroyed', ἀπώλεσαν οἱ Ἰουδαῖοι, הרגו היהודים), but then also adds that they did so particularly by killing ('and by killing', ואבד). And M furthermore provides the information that they killed Haman's family in addition to the five hundred ('and the ten children of Haman', ואת עשרת בני־המן), a detail not in B. In A, of course, Haman's children were killed and also presumably hung by Esther's hand in the preceding episode (8.7-8).

In A, the king directly addresses Esther. It is not entirely clear how the σοι is to be understood, as it is used here in the dative. (One manuscript in the A tradition reads πόσοι, 'how have they', in place of the πῶς σοι, as Clines also chooses to do [*Story*, p. 245].) But we can recognize A's reference to these events as somehow especially affecting Esther herself. The actions of the Jews are happening for her, or possibly by her, and we are reminded that this destruction is all occurring according to her own direction (cf. 8.6-8).

In B, Esther is more involved in the discussion of the actions of the Jews than in M. The king asks Esther for her thoughts or opinion on the matter ('how do you suppose they availed themselves?', πῶς οἴει ἐκρήσατο;), rather than M's impersonal question ('what have they done?', מה עשׂו).

Both B and M present the king as wanting to know what Esther still desires. Apparently he feels that there remains unfinished business in the Jews' salvation and revenge. In B, he questions her only once ('therefore, what still do you request?', τί οἶν ἀξιοῖς ἔτι;), but in M he does so twice ('and what is your petition?', וּמה־שׁאלתך; 'and what more is your request?', וּמה־בקשׁתך עוד). This second question makes the king appear more concerned about Esther's wishes and makes their conversation here feel more formal, official, and balanced.

In M, the king also is shown as more generous to Esther, for he promises twice that whatever she wants she will have ('and it will be given to you', וינתן לך; 'and it will be done', ותעשׂ). He is more specific in his promises by speaking of things to be given to Esther and actions to be done for her. The king in B speaks more vaguely and is somewhat less involved, vowing only that what she requests 'will be' (ἔσται). He also promises her only once.

Verse 13. M portrays Esther as still concerned with the approval of the king and as presenting her arguments in language crafted to be pleasing. She prefaces her response by appealing to his sense of morality or propriety ('if to the king it is good ...', אם־על־המלך טוב). In A and B, Esther straightforwardly asks, without condition.

The three narratives portray Esther as asking for three different things. In A, she would like the Jews to be able 'to kill and to plunder whomever they might desire' (οὓς ἐὰν θέλωσιν ἀνελεῖν καὶ διαρπάζειν). In B, Esther requests that they might 'avail themselves in the same manner tomorrow' (χρῆσθαι ὡσαύτως τὴν αὔριον). It is the least specific. And in M she wants 'to do according to the decree of today' (לעשׂות כדת היום). M further stresses that this is to be a repeat action ('also tomorrow', גם־מחר), and that it applies only to the Jews who are in Susa (ליהודים אשׁר בשׁושׁן). Moreover, Esther suggests, in B and M, that things go in just the same way as they previously have.

The request of Esther is more violent in A than in B and M, an impression rendered by three factors. First, Esther anticipates the action not just for the Jews in Susa, as do M and B (cf. vv. 14, 15), but in general. Hence, the results of her command will be kingdom-wide. Second, she asks for two things, both actions of force: to put to death (ἀνελεῖν) and to plunder (διαρπιάζειν). The communities of the victims will be completely annihilated, losing both persons and possessions. And furthermore, the Jews will be able to attack anyone in the population, 'whomever they may wish' (οὗ ἐὰν θέλωσιν)

M stresses the importance of law and regulation to Esther. She asks that things be done 'according to decree' (כדת).

The reference in B and M to repeated actions reflects Esther's submission of authority to others. Esther here has the chance to make her own policy, but she does not. In B, she wants the regulations which were enacted for this day repeated. In this narrative, it was the king who made the command for how the Jews were to respond (cf. 8.10; 16.1; 9.1, 4). Therefore it is the king to whom Esther is now deferring. In M, though, it was actually Mordecai who commanded the first killing, albeit in the king's name (cf. 8.9), and thus here she is exhibiting subservience to him.

In B, the killing of many is not the main purpose of the Jews' actions ('avail themselves ... so as to hang the ten sons of Haman', χρῆσθαι ... ὥστε τοὺς δέκα υἱοὺς κρεμάσαι Αμαν). As ὥστε with the infinitive (κρεμάσαι) tends to express result, the wording gives the impression that the hanging of Haman's sons is their primary goal. M, instead, treats the hanging more as a separate action from that of the general destruction. It specifies how the children are to be hung ('upon the tree', על-העץ), and highlights the children themselves (through the inverted ordering of subject-verb in this phrase). Both details demonstrate Esther's increased attention to the family of Haman.

Verse 14. M portrays the king as controlling. He commands ('and the king said to have it done', ויאמר המלך להעשות), and a law is actually formulated, presumably also by him ('and a decree was given', ותנתן דת). The king takes over, turning Esther's request into his own command and decree. In B, the king is more passive. He simply allows the idea which Esther suggests (though it was originally his own) to be done ('and he permitted it to be', καὶ ἐπέτρεψεν ... γενέσθαι). A instead gives the impression that the king is won over to Esther's suggestion and that they possibly even had some disagreement regarding it, with its use of the verb συγχωρέω ('to come together, assent, or acquiesce').

In B, the king facilitates the actions of the Jews. He is more involved in the hanging, by giving out the bodies ('he put forth to the Jews of the city the bodies of the sons of Haman', ἐξέθηκεν τοῖς Ἰουδαίοις τῆς πόλεως τὰ σώματα τῶν υἱῶν Αμαν).

Verse 15. B and M present an increased sense of community among the Jews, as they assemble together as a unit for their purpose ('and the Jews who were in Susa gathered', καὶ συνήχθησαν οἱ Ἰουδαῖοι ἐν Σούσοις, ויקהלו היהודיים אשר־בשושן). M further emphasizes that this organization is a repetition of such action ('again, also', גם), which causes it to be understood in light of the first time the Jews destroyed.

A does not state at this point where the described destruction takes place, nor when, nor by whom.

The actions summarized by A are more violent and have greater ramifications than those of B and M. First, the means itself of destruction is somewhat more forceful and brutal. The verb ἀπόλλυμι, 'to destroy, utterly lay waste, demolish', suggests that the attackers utterly destroy in their killing. B's ἀποκτείνω (ἀπέκτειναν, 'they killed, slayed') and M's הרג (יהרגו, 'they killed, slayed') suggest a killing not quite as compelling. Secondly, the results of the action are more severe; 70,100 men (μυριάδας ἑπτὰ καὶ ἑκατὸν ἄνδρας) in contrast to 300 men (ἄνδρας τριακοσίους, שלש מאות איש). And B and M take care to except the Jews from plundering anyone ('but they plundered no one', καὶ οὐδὲν διήρπασαν; 'but they did not lay their hand on plunder', ובבזה לא שלחו את־ידם). In A, however, plundering is one of their intentions (v. 13).

Analysis

A Text. Esther acts very much in control during this episode. The Jews' defense is her undertaking, not the project of Ahasuerus. Esther has her own ideas about how she wants the Jews to act on their second day of fighting, and she has no reservations about commanding them. By her greater description of what she desires them to do, she shows herself to be personally involved in how the Jews will defend themselves, even though she herself does not fight or kill in this episode. Esther's influence also extends over a wider geographical area. The destruction is not performed by only those Jews of Susa nor in only the capital city; it involves the entire kingdom. And in terms of death toll, her command has a great impact upon its population. She possesses authority throughout the whole of Persia.

Furthermore, Ahasuerus treats her with esteem. He relies upon her for information and displays respect for her knowledge about contemporary affairs affecting the kingdom. He trusts her as one who is in charge and not as though he were granting her a favor. Ahasuerus concedes to Esther's power, is convinced by her, and yields to her command over the Jews.

Esther continues to express violent tendencies during the events of this episode. She gives greater latitude to the Jews to attack, both in the types of destruction and the choice of whom they might harm. More persons lose their lives because of her, and the destruction to the victims is complete. However, this narrative characterizes the Jews as also violent themselves, not just as pacifist people being obedient to a bloodthirsty queen. Esther does not command the killing itself but only that the Jews might do so if they desire it—which they apparently do.

B Text. Esther exhibits a certain degree of authority, but her control is more limited in this narrative. Artaxerxes is interested in what she thinks about the Jews' past actions. Then, Esther commands Artaxerxes regarding what the Jews should do, and he allows what she requests to be done. In contrast, though, Esther affects only that which occurs in the city of Susa and not in the kingdom as a whole. And Esther herself limits her influence and authority. When given the chance to make a new regulation, she opts to go along with the status quo and not to formulate her own ideas. She defers to Artaxerxes when requesting to retain his regulation, thus agreeing with how he did things. Esther lacks originality in formulating her own public policy.

The encounter between Esther and Artaxerxes has a more personal and informal quality. Esther speaks directly to him, and he uses less official language to her. She is also a recipient of Artaxerxes' helpfulness, generosity, and kindness. He is concerned that she still might need something, and he promises that what she requests will be hers. And when recognizing that her primary desire is to hang Haman's sons, he helps her towards that goal by giving over their bodies.

M Text. Esther is more regal in this narrative, in her position as queen. It is in this manner that she speaks with Ahasuerus. Their conversation is formal and business-like. Esther presents her request as an official decree, naming it with governmental terminology, and she emphasizes that this decree be carried out. When requesting the hanging of Haman's children, she provides more detailed instructions. Even within this framework, though, Ahasuerus is the most concerned about her desires and the most willing to grant them.

But Esther is less commanding, and she exhibits subservience to both Ahasuerus and Mordecai. Rather than introduce a regulation of her own, she defers to Mordecai's past decree. And Esther is still trying to win Ahasuerus over. She makes her request appear in a favorable light, using somewhat placating language, rather than commanding him to accede to it. Ahasuerus instead is the one who acts authoritatively in this episode.

Esther's actions affect a more limited group of people, namely, the Jews and non-Jews in Susa. Her physical realm of influence is the least in this narrative. And her actions seem least necessary. The next day's action will be only a repetition of this day's—again following the decree, again gathering together. We wonder what the need is for her or for this conversation with Ahasuerus, and we question what she herself actually contributes to the situation.

Episode 9 (9.29-32)

After the Jews perform Esther's request of the preceding episode, in the B and M texts the Jewish people in the entire kingdom act. During the next two days they kill thousands of their enemies, then they rest and celebrate. Mordecai writes to all the Jews, giving them instructions about keeping a yearly holiday. The recent past events are summarized, an explanation is provided for why this new festival is to be called Purim, and a policy is stated of how the holiday should be commemorated by all Jews at all times.

In this episode Esther writes a document about Purim, along with the help of Mordecai. It is reported that Esther and Mordecai establish this document, and Esther's message is incorporated within it. In the M text, Mordecai sends copies throughout the kingdom. Following this episode, the king enacts a tax upon the kingdom and his greatness is recorded in the official Persian annals. Mordecai is described as also important to the kingdom and honored by many. And finally, in the B text, Mordecai reports the insight he has received about his dream.

The progression of the events at the conclusion of the story in the A text differs from that of the B and M texts. After Esther's command is carried out by the Jews of the kingdom, Mordecai writes to all of them.

He tells them, quite briefly, how to celebrate this incident and he gives generously to the poor. The holiday is named. The king writes about his own magnificence, then Mordecai writes similar things in the government annals. Mordecai's greatness in the kingdom is noted, and that he is respected by all the Jews. He then provides an explanation of his dream.

The events of this episode have no counterpart in the A text. Therefore, only these verses in the B and M texts will be compared with each other, in the usual fashion. Then the primary areas in which this material affects the overall portrayal of Esther will be considered.

Text

καὶ ἔγραψεν Εσθηρ ἡ βασίλισσα θυγάτηρ Αμιναδαβ καὶ Μαρδοχαῖος ὁ Ἰουδαῖος *ὅσα ἐποίησαν τό τε στερέωμα* τῆς ἐπιστολῆς τῶν φρουραι.

29 ותכתב אסתר המלכה בת־אביחיל ומרדכי היהודי את־
כל־תקף לקים את אגרת הפורים הזאת השנית

And Esther the queen, the daughter of Aminadab, wrote, and Mordecai the Jew, as much as they did, the ratification of the letter of Purim.

And Esther the queen, the daughter of Abihail, wrote, and Mordecai the Jew, (with) complete power, to establish this second letter of Purim.

30 וישלח ספרים אל־כל־היהודים אל־שבע ועשרים ומאה
מדינה מלכות אחשורוש דברי שלום ואמת

And he sent documents to all the Jews, to 127 provinces of the kingdom of Ahasuerus; words of well-being and truth,

καὶ Μαρδοχαῖος καὶ Εσθηρ ἡ βασίλισσα ἔστησαν *ἑαυτοῖς καθ' ἑαυτῶν* καὶ *τότε* στήσαντες *κατὰ τῆς ὑγιείας ἑαυτῶν καὶ τὴν βουλὴν αὐτῶν.*

31 לקים את־ימי הפרים האלה בזמניהם כאשר קים עליהם
מרדכי היהודי ואסתר המלכה וכאשר קימו על־נפשם
ועל־זרעם דברי הצמות וזעקתם

And Mordecai and Esther the queen established (this), by themselves alone, and thereupon establishing (it) according to their own intent and their purpose.

to establish these days of Purim at their appointed times, just as Mordecai the Jew imposed upon them, and Esther the queen, and just as they established, upon themselves and upon their offspring, words of fasts and their lamentation.

καὶ Εσθηρ λόγῳ ἔστησεν *εἰς τὸν αἰῶνα,* καὶ ἐγράφη *εἰς μνημόσυνον.*

32 ומאמר אסתר קים דברי הפרים האלה ונכתב בספר

And Esther established (it) for a statement forever, and it was written as a memorial.

And the command of Esther established these words of Purim, and (it) was written in the document.

Notes

Verse 29. In B, the content of the document written by Esther includes a record of all of the past actions, of her own and Mordecai's ('as much as they did', ὅσα ἐποίησαν). The purpose of her writing is thus informational.

For M, because the verb ותכתב is feminine singular, some have suggested that the phrase ומרדכי היהודי ('and Mordecai the Jew') is a later addition to the text (Paton, *Esther*, p. 300; Moore, *Esther,* p. 95; Fox, *Character,* pp. 123-25, 286). Though such may indeed be the case, the text can be understood as it now stands if we think of this verse as speaking of Esther and Mordecai generally in establishing regulation about Purim. For this present document, both Esther and Mordecai are presented as performing certain actions which each do alone. Esther writes (v. 29) and commands (v. 32) by herself, and Mordecai dispatches her letter throughout the kingdom by himself (v. 30). The inclusion of the phrase 'and Mordecai the Jew' emphasizes that this second letter represents a joint effort by the two of them.

M states that Esther writes in 'all strength' or 'complete power' (את־כל־תקף). This notation gives the sense of her writing from the position of her own power and authority within the government.

M identifies this document as a repeat missive about Purim ('this second letter of Purim', אגרת הפורים הזאת השנית). Presumably the first document was that written by Mordecai regarding the keeping of a commemorative festival (9.20-23). And now Esther is writing the Jews another letter, a second document, about other issues pertaining to Purim. (Certain commentators have questioned this reference to a second letter, including Moore [*Esther,* p. 96] and Fox [*Character,* pp. 123-25], the latter who chooses to omit the phrase.) B does not designate this writing as second in order, but only as 'the letter of Purim' (τῆς ἐπιστολῆς τῶν φρουραι).

From the start, M emphasizes the action of confirming or establishing. The purpose of Esther's writing is particularly to set up or establish (לקים) something about Purim. In B, Esther only writes and does not in this verse establish anything.

Verse 30. In M, in this action of sending Esther's message, Mordecai works alone ('and he sent documents', וישלח ספרים); it de-emphasizes Esther at this point. Some have suggested emending the masculine singular וישלח ('he sent') to the feminine singular 'she sent' (Paton,

Esther, p. 300) or to the niphal masculine plural '(documents) were sent' (Fox, *Character,* pp. 125, 286; Moore, *Esther,* p. 93). Yet it is not illogical to understand Mordecai to be actually performing the action of sending out the letter which Esther (or he and Esther) had just written.

M portrays the effect of Esther's document as being more widespread, for it will be dispatched to every Jew and throughout the entire kingdom ('to all the Jews, to 127 provinces of the kingdom of Ahasuerus', אל־כל־היהודים אל־שבע ועשרים ומאה מדינה מלכות אחשורוש).

In M, Esther desires peace and truth for the Jews of the kingdom; her letter is composed of such a message ('words of well-being and truth', דברי שלום ואמת). She apparently finds it to be her role to give good tidings or encouragement to the people.

Verse 31. In B, both Esther and Mordecai perform together all the actions of this verse.

In M, the report of which is spoken has been often understood as Mordecai's earlier letter about Purim (9.20-23). Because the formation of that letter was an action performed by only Mordecai and in which Esther did not assist, and because the verb קום here is in the masculine singular, certain scholars have suggested that the phrase ואסתר המלכה ('and Esther the queen') is a later addition and should be deleted (BHS; Paton, *Esther*, p. 301; Moore, *Esther,* pp. 93, 96; Fox, *Character,* p. 125). As we have it now, the verse appears to be a conjunction of details. The entire verse cannot be easily interpreted as referring to Mordecai's earlier document, for he made no reference to memorial fasts or mourning acts in it. He established, instead, the precise times Purim is to be celebrated and the feasting and acts of benevolence to be performed. This verse gives the impression that there are dual aspects to the establishment of regulations about the celebration of the holiday, those of Mordecai's earlier letter and those of the present letter, the 'second', enacted by both Mordecai and Esther. Each of their letters individually establishes particular religious requirements for the holiday unique unto itself. The form קום in the latter phrase of this verse (קימו, 'they established') is in the plural, signifying that Esther and Mordecai together establish these present actions of fasting and mourning, in addition to the earlier requirements about the proper times for celebration presented in Mordecai's earlier letter.

B stresses that Esther and Mordecai set forth this document alone, presumably without the influence of the king or other government officials ('and Mordecai and Esther the queen established by themselves alone', καὶ Μαρδοχαῖος καὶ Εσθηρ ἡ βασίλισσα ἔστησαν ἑαυτοῖς καθ᾽ ἑαυτῶν). They also write particularly by their own determination ('according to their own intent and their purpose', κατὰ τῆς ὑγιείας ἑαυτῶν καὶ τὴν βουλὴν αὐτῶν). The term ὑγίεια literally signifies that which is healthy or sound. In the present context it is to be understood as emphasizing that Esther and Mordecai perform their own intents and desires.

M is quite concerned about religious observance. First, it notes that the purpose of the writing and sending out is 'to establish these days of Purim at their appointed times' (לקים את־ימי הפרים האלה בזמניהם). It empha-sizes Purim as a festival that is to be celebrated at its proper times during the liturgical year. Then M states that the document includes a command about the proper manner in which the Jews should fast and lament at these times ('words of fasts and their lamentation', דברי הצמות וזעקתם). B does not mention Purim or any such religious concerns at all.

M exhibits interest in the future of the Jewish people. It, and possibly also Esther in her letter, recognize the regulations as affecting not only the present population but also future generations ('upon themselves and upon their offspring', על־נפשם ועל־זרעם).

Verse 32. M portrays Esther as authoritative. It is a commanding word which she is giving to the Jews ('the command of Esther', מאמר אסתר). This final verse makes us think of this letter as more individually Esther's decree, just as the first letter was more individually Mordecai's.

In B, Esther puts forth her document for all time ('and Esther established [it] for a statement forever', καὶ Εσθηρ λόγῳ ἔστησεν εἰς τὸν αἰῶνα). The actions which she describes are to be known well into the future.

M specifically designates Esther's writing as pertaining to Purim ('these words of Purim', דברי הפרים האלה).

The purpose of Esther's letter in B is not religious but historical. As she and Mordecai write about the things which they had done, they do so particularly to serve to remember these actions ('and it was written as a memorial', καὶ ἐγράφη εἰς μνημόσυνον).

The document in which Esther's command is included can logically be seen as the present one. As the same term (ספר) is used here as in v. 30, there is reason to assume that the same document is being referred to. A separate book or historical annal does not need to be postulated to understand the referent of this term (contra Moore, *Esther*, pp. 93, 97; Fox, *Character*, p. 127). This verse emphasizes that Esther's command is now committed to writing.

Analysis

B Text. Esther's primary concern is with history. The reason that she writes her document is to provide a record of the events which have just transpired, of which she has been an instrumental part and eyewitness observer. She wants this record to influence future generations, as a memorial, so that the events of Purim are remembered. There is, furthermore, authority to Esther's document. And she and Mordecai are very much in control of the writing of this history. As in this narrative Esther does not write specifically for the Jewish people in Persia, her document may even be the official Persian record of these events. At any rate, Esther exhibits authority and initiative in preparing it, as she evidently decides to do something and then establishes a statement according to her purpose and desire.

Esther and Mordecai work more as a team in this narrative. Though she primarily writes the document by herself, he performs with her in establishing it. They have the same purpose in their endeavor, and the two act alone, without influence from Persian officials. They, together, possess a degree of autonomy within the governmental system.

M Text. Esther, and Mordecai as well, does a great deal of establishing, confirming, or setting things up in this narrative. What they establish, however, is not Esther's document itself, but regulations regarding the observance of Purim. Esther's interest is primarily religious. The purpose of her writing is to command the Jews to celebrate the holiday properly. In so doing, Esther writes to bring a positive word to the people, a message of encouragement, peace, and steadfastness, and desires good things for them. Her writing and establishing regulations is an act of authority, for she does so in total power and strength. Esther is commanding in this narrative. And the effects of her directive extend the greatest distance, over Jews throughout the entire kingdom.

Esther and Mordecai perform almost parallel actions. He has written to the Jews earlier regarding the celebration of Purim, and now she writes to them.[1] They both write to the same people and establish

1. Esther's purpose in writing is not merely to accentuate Mordecai's earlier directive (as Paton has suggested [*Esther*, p. 301]) or because the Jews had neglected

certain cultic practices of the same holiday. However, Esther shows herself to be a more serious, solemn person than Mordecai. While he chooses to command the Jews to be joyful and no longer dejected, Esther chooses to require them to fast and to lament, actions of abstinence and penitence. In this narrative, Esther and Mordecai tend to work more separately than together, each performing individual tasks which help the other.

Effects of This Episode on the Esther Story

Certain details which influence the overall character of Esther are provided to the B and the M texts but not to the A text. For one thing, Esther appears as an authoritative and commanding person in this episode, both in general character and towards the Jewish people in particular. She is twice identified as the queen in these few verses. More significant, though, is that Esther is now herself giving a written command in the form of a letter to the citizens, just as Haman, the king, and Mordecai have done prior to this point in the story. She no longer gives only oral ordinances but makes her requests known directly to the people and not through the intermediary of the king. Esther is also concerned about the future of these people, that they know of the importance of Purim and the events which occurred in the Jews' salvation. Through the message of her letter, Esther's influence will last beyond herself and this incident in Persian and Jewish history. Esther remains important on a public level, even after she has successfully convinced the king to change his policy and the Jews have had their revenge.

Esther is further involved with the Jewish community in these two narratives. She here now acts boldly as their leader. And the repetition of her parentage in this episode makes her appear more Jewish, within her family, just as she was introduced to the readers at the beginning of the story. This reminder about Esther's familial background also emphasizes her relationship with Mordecai, who is identified as a Jew throughout this episode. And Esther operates closely with Mordecai at this point in the plot of the story. Now is the first and only time that the two really work together and for the same purpose throughout all of these happenings.

his earlier instructions (a possibility raised by Moore [*Esther*, p. 95]). Instead, Esther writes because she has something new to say, to add to Mordecai's earlier ideas about how this new holiday should be remembered by the Jewish people.

Minor References to Esther

Esther 2.22

B   καὶ ἐδηλώθη Μαρδοχαίῳ ὁ λόγος, καὶ ἐσήμανεν Εσθηρ, καὶ αὐτὴ
     ἐνεφάνισεν τῷ βασιλεῖ τὰ τῆς ἐπιβουλῆς

And the matter was known to Mordecai, and he notified Esther, and she
revealed the plot to the king.

M   ויודע הדבר למרדכי ויגד לאסתר המלכה ותאמר אסתר למלך בשם מרדכי

And the matter was known to Mordecai, and he reported (it) to Esther the
queen, and Esther spoke to the king in the name of Mordecai.

This transaction occurs quite soon after the selection process for the new
queen. Mordecai manages to overhear two of the court servants
planning to kill the king. Mordecai, from his position outside the court,
tells Esther (who is now inside the court), and she informs the king. This
plot detail is not present in A, in which Mordecai becomes aware of the
plot against the king much earlier in the story, before we have even
been introduced to Esther, and tells the king himself.

The inclusion of this exchange serves to strengthen the link between
Esther and Mordecai in these two versions. The two meet, converse, and
work together for the benefit of the kingdom. However, we find certain
differences between B and M. In M, Esther is described according to her
newly-gained royal position, as 'queen Esther'. It also specifically notes
that Esther recognizes Mordecai when telling Ahasuerus the news, doing
so 'in the name of Mordecai' (בשם מרדכי). In B, the information which
she tells the king is more accurately described. The message is not only
the neutral 'word' or 'matter' (דבר) of M, but is noted as an actual plot
or conspiracy (ἐπιβουλῆς). Such terminology suggests that, as there is
such danger at stake, Esther and Mordecai are performing a greater, and
possibly more dangerous, service.

In B, Esther acts more autonomously. It seems to be her idea and
initiative to tell Artaxerxes what she has just learned from Mordecai,
because she recognizes Mordecai's news as reflecting danger to the
king. Esther acts somewhat more passively and obediently in M. She is
presented as more reliant upon Mordecai, more as the one who relays a
message and less as the one who is instrumental in saving the king from
harm. In M, Esther acts on Mordecai's behalf, whereas in B she acts on
Artaxerxes's behalf.

Esther 16.13

A τὸν δὲ ἡμέτερον σωτῆρα διὰ παντὸς Μσρδοχαῖον καὶ τὴν
ἄμεμπτον τούτου κοινωνὸν Εσθηρ

and Mordecai, our savior through everything, and Esther, the blameless
partner of that one

B τόν τε ἡμέτερον σωτῆρα καὶ διὰ παντὸς εὐεργέτην Μαρδσχαῖον
καὶ τὴν ἄμεμπτον τῆς βασιλείας κοινωνὸν Εσθηρ

and Mordecai, our savior and benefactor through everything, and Esther,
the blameless partner of the kingdom

This mention of Esther occurs within the letter which the king writes to
the people explaining Haman's actions and allowing the Jews to defend
themselves. Mordecai and Esther are listed by the king as part of that
which Haman attempted to destroy. In both of the narratives, Esther is
described as blameless, without reproach, or perfect (ἄμεμπτον) and as
a companion or co-worker with someone (κοινωνὸν). But there is a
difference between them. B portrays Esther as a partner to the kingdom;
that is, she is identified in terms of her role within Persia. A instead
portrays her as a partner with Mordecai. It is unclear exactly to what the
demonstrative pronoun τούτου refers, but as Μαρδοχαῖον is the only
singular masculine noun in the vicinity, it must refer to Mordecai. Of
course, as Esther conceals her Jewish identity from the Persian court in
B, the king would not be expected to link her with the Jew Mordecai.
Thus, in A, Esther is not termed as one working for the kingdom as a
whole, as in B, but only as working with Mordecai as his partner. In A,
Esther is described in relationship with Mordecai, but in B her alliance is
linked to the nation. (This verse is designated as E.13 in the Göttingen
texts.)

Esther 9.24-25

M כי המן בן־המדתא האגגי צרר כל־היהודים חשב על־היהודים לאבדם והפיל פור הוא הגורל
להמם ולאבדם ובבאה לפני המלך אמר עם־הספר ישוב מחשבתו הרעה אשר־חשב על־
היהודים על־ראשו ותלו אתו ואת־בניו על־העץ

For Haman, the son of Hammedatha the Agagite, the enemy of all Jews,
planned against the Jews, to kill them, and he cast Pur, which is the lot, to vex
and to kill them. And when she came before the king, he said, in the
document, (that) the evil plan which he had planned against the Jews would
return upon his head, and he and his sons would hang on the tree.

Though Esther is not directly named here, it is unquestionable that the ובבאה ('and when she came') refers to her actions in approaching the king. These two verses are part of the narrative's summary of the recent events in the kingdom. In its interpretation of events, M presents Esther as instrumental in the Jews' salvation. At this point, only her efforts towards that end, and not any of Mordecai's, are noted. It is Esther's boldness before the king which is responsible for the ultimate defeat of Haman, and thus the credit for the Jews' victory rests solely upon her shoulders.

Esther 11.10 and 10.6

A ἐγένετο ἐκ πηγῆς μικρᾶς ὕδωρ πολύ, ποταμὸς μέγας

'Η μικρὰ πηγὴ Εσθηρ ἐστίν... ποταμὸς τὰ ἔθνη τὰ συναχθέντα ἀπολέσαι τοὺς Ἰουδαίους

much water, a great river, came out of a small spring

the small spring is Esther ... the river (is) the nations which came together to destroy the Jews

B ἐγένετο ὡσανεὶ ἀπὸ μικρᾶς πηγῆς ποταμὸς μέγας, ὕδωρ πολύ

ἡ μικρὰ πηγή, ἣ ἐγένετο ποταμός ... Εσθηρ ἐστιν ὁ ποταμός, ἣ ἐγάμησεν ὁ βασιλεὺς καὶ ἐποίησεν βασίλισσαν

a great river, (with) much water, came as if from a small spring

the small spring, which became a river ... Esther is the river, whom the king married and made queen

These two phrases occur in the recitation of Mordecai's dream at the beginning of the story (11.10) and his interpretation of that dream at the conclusion of the story (10.6). The first reference to Esther, with which she is not yet identified, is fundamentally the same between the two narratives. The difference between their portrayals of Esther is the manner in which Mordecai understands the symbolism of his dream. In A, Esther remains only the small fountain or spring (ἡ μικρὰ πηγὴ), and the enemies who attack the Jews are interpreted as the river. It is, however, unclear how the plot of the story allows for the nations as coming out from or existing because of (ἐγένετο ἐκ) Esther. In B, in contrast, Esther is identified as the little spring (μικρᾶς πηγῆς), but it is she herself who becomes the great river with abundant water (ποταμὸς μέγας, ὕδωρ πολύ). B further notes that she marries the king and becomes queen, information not in A's interpretation. Hence, B renders

Esther as more important to the events of the story, in being given a greater role by Mordecai's interpretation. She is likened to a large river, an object of great power.[1] Her rise to importance is also highlighted, as Esther is understood to have begun as only a small fountain, an orphaned girl of a foreign race in Persian society. And B emphasizes her position as queen, along with her good relationship with the king. In A, though, Esther remains only that little stream. Nothing more comes from her, nor does she grow in stature. She does not appear to be very significant at all in its interpretation of events. (These verses are represented by A.9 and F.3, 5 in the Göttingen edition.)

1. This fact is also noted by Moore about this text. Speaking of the B text, he states that 'the great hero in Addition A ... is Esther, symbolized by the mighty river, not Mordecai, one of the great dragons' (*Additions*, p. 181).

Chapter 3

COMPREHENSIVE ANALYSIS

This chapter will consider the characterization of Esther throughout the extent of each narrative. The analysis will be made according to those conclusions about her character as a whole which can be drawn from the individual differences of details and events which have been presented in the previous chapter. Throughout the previous analyses of the individual episodes, certain themes about the portrayal of Esther in these three texts have begun to emerge. Particular traits of Esther's character have become important across the extent of the individual scenes as categories into which the differences of detail about her fall. These categories can be determined as: the level and type of authority she exhibits; the activity or passivity with which she acts; the emotions she expresses; how religious belief affects her; her relationships with the Jews, the king, and Mordecai; how she views the Jews' adversaries and interacts with them; the way in which she exists in the Persian court; and her sexuality. All three of the texts' characterizations of Esther include these general character traits, but in differing degrees and with differing emphases. It is according to these ten categories that conclusions about her character in the whole of the story will be assessed. Within these categories each of the texts will be discussed individually as well as how it compares to the other two texts.

Certain aspects about Esther are emphasized more strongly by only one of the three texts. These will also be included for each text. For instance, throughout the story of the A text, Esther's general intelligence, her concern for justice, her use of violence and physical force, how she is affected by outward appearances, and her altruistic quality are traits particularly significant to her characterization. The B text, in addition to the general traits, stresses Esther's interest in knowledge, her physical weakness, her beauty, the optimistic tendency of her outlook, and how she grows throughout the story. And consideration of the M text reveals Esther's great strength, the manner in which she speaks, the degree of balance she exhibits, and the continuity and discontinuity of her actions to be of unique significance in its portrayal of Esther's character.

Furthermore, the major differences among the narratives will also affect the degree to which we are able to assess Esther's character on the whole. For instance, the unique ending of the A text presents a significantly different view of Esther with regard to the traits she is portrayed as possessing. And the B text incorporates the most actions involving Esther of all the three, for it includes her prayer and her writing of a letter. It often lies between the A and M texts with regard to differences in detail, and it frequently uses more vague terminology in the places at which it differs. These qualities all render it more difficult to obtain a precise, comprehensive portrait of Esther's character at times.

The final section of this chapter will include a consideration of the portion of the story which deals with Vashti, the first queen. In this story, Vashti, a secondary female character, functions as a comparative figure to Esther, the primary female character. The three texts exhibit differences in detail which affect their presentations of Vashti and what attributes are expected of the new queen. For assessment of the characterization of Esther, these differences are of secondary importance to those details about Esther herself. Yet they set up the reader's expectations for the introduction of the main protagonist later in the story.

Authority

The amount of power and authority which Esther displays varies among the three versions. The degree of authority she possesses in general, the type of power she wields, what is beneath her control, and with whom she shares her authority are areas in which we can find distinctions. In the A text, Esther exhibits the greatest growth in the level and type of influence she holds. And her power is particularly manifested within her relationship with Ahasuerus. As in the other two narratives, at the beginning of the story she lies under the control of the court servants and Ahasuerus (2.8, 9, 14). But upon receiving her crown, she immediately begins to act in an authoritative capacity. By the conclusion of her approach to the king, Ahasuerus speaks and acts in recognition of her power (5.8). However, Esther's full power does not come about until the end of her second banquet. Ahasuerus's action at this point initiaties a series of instances in which he allows her the authority to carry out her own desires within the kingdom (5.8; 8.6, 7, 8; 9.12-14). When we last see her, Esther is speaking only to command, a strong image that remains in the reader's mind.

In the A text, Esther's influence is particularly an active, controlling power. By the conclusion of the story, she not only commands but takes action herself. When Ahasuerus grants requests, he does not give Esther physical things but power (8.6-8; 9.12-14). And her greatest influence in the kingdom is primarily in the area of retributive justice and punishment. Esther's actions with regard to the public are not so much constructive in the A text (the making of laws, the writing and sending of documents) but destructive, in carrying out a program of defense and retaliation (8.6, 7, 8; 9.13). The differences in the ending of the A text result in Esther's never sharing power with Mordecai. Instead, she is treated quite individually and her authority belongs only to her. However, it still must be noted that Esther's control is never hers completely, but only what the king permits her to do. Though in every action which she requests from him he grants her full power to do as she wishes, she still must make arrangements with him before doing anything (8.7, 8; 9.14).

In the A text, Esther's influence extends over a wider geographical area. This trend is initiated from the very first, when Ahasuerus gives her a party during which he gives remission to those under his kingdom (2.18). Her actions have national ramifications throughout the story, and she commands the entire kingdom. And Esther helps to legislate official government decisions. By the conclusion of the story, Esther's authority is less localized to the capital city than in the other two texts (9.11-15). Her power affects the entire extent of the kingdom, and she herself is even viewed as the representative of the Persian kingdom (7.5, 8). Esther's position as queen includes the necessity of her being treated with the proper respect by others in the court and throughout the kingdom, at least in the opinion of their king.

In the B text, Esther's authority is more limited than in the other two narratives throughout the bulk of the story. She exhibits control and command at certain times and within certain areas, but her power is not as pronounced. Esther does not use her sovereignty to the extent that she could. As with the M text, Esther shows less control in general during the seventh and eighth episodes here than in the A text. She decides to give over to Mordecai the power that she is given; her power to make official decrees is not hers alone but shared with Mordecai, and they together possess less power to command than in the other two texts. However, Esther is at times her own enemy, in choosing not to act according to the degree of power which her position could provide her, viewing the kingdom as belonging to Artaxerxes alone (as does he) (5.3; 7.2; 8.5), and deferring authority to others in enacting official legislation and decisions (8.2, 5; 9.13, 31). Esther does not take as much power into her own hands on a national or political level. And when she is allowed to make legislation with Mordecai and then to write her own document, her authority lies primarily within Susa and within governmental concerns. Her authority does not affect the whole of the kingdom as much. In the B text overall, Esther's control is the least. It does not extend much beyond the domestic court setting or the capital city and its concerns throughout most of the events.

Esther's authority in the B text occurs most strongly towards the end of the story. That influence is not as evident throughout the events of her rise to queenship and her requests of the king. Rather, her authority emerges after the danger has been averted and in the overall interpretation of the events of her actions. Esther's primary exercise of authority and influence begins in her writing of the letter. That Mordecai does not help her dispatch it shows Esther herself to be more in control of the entire process (9.30, 32). Esther is also characterized as important and authoritative in the two references to her by outside sources (16.13; 10.6). In them, she is presented as the partner of the entire kingdom, important to all of Persia, and acting in a role of high importance to the Jews. It stresses her royal position and her rise to great power. Thus, at the conclusion of the story, the vision with which the reader will be left is that of Esther holding a significant degree of authority. The B text shows Esther's influence to continue far beyond her and her immediate circle. Her own report will be available for all to read for all time (9.32). The entire kingdom knows Esther as the one who is working for their benefit (9.31). And all who read this story will understand her to be the one who rises to great importance in the Jews' battle with evil forces (10.6; 11.10). Though not as much in the portrayal of the events of the story itself, Esther is instead noted in permanent documentation according to her authority.

In the M text, Esther also possesses a good deal of authority, though it differs in type and degree from the other texts. Overall, Esther is portrayed as more authoritative at certain places and less at others.

Especially at the end of the story we are explicitly told of her complete authority (9.29). And the narrative itself indicates that she is responsible for the positive outcome of the events (9.24-25). However, the M text also presents limits to Esther's influence. Her authority extends not to all Persian citizens but only to the Jews of the kingdom (8.8; 9.13, 30). As in the B text, the greatest restriction on Esther's degree of control is a result of the ending of the story. Instead of making her own decisions and carrying them out, she is eclipsed by others. Even in conjunction with Mordecai, though, Esther retains slightly more autonomy than in the B text. The two work together, but they work more as a team in which each has a role and performs separate actions (9.29-31). Hence, Esther exhibits a degree of independence through the end.

The most indicative sign of Esther's authority in the M text is her royal aspect and her royal demeanor. Esther is continually identified by the position of queen and spoken of as living in the palace. From the time of the selection process, Esther is distinguished from the common. She is deemed superior to the previous queen (2.17), approaches Ahasuerus from her queenly position (15.1, 7; 5.3; 7.2-3, 5; 8.7), and claims the royal sceptre herself (15.12). Even Mordecai, who raises her from childhood, recognizes her new royal status (8.2). Esther's queenliness is in contrast to her Jewishness, the trait which continues to identify Mordecai even after he has also been given official royal status. Overall, her royal aspect pervades, albeit subtly, this narrative.

The M text further characterizes Esther's influence by means of her use of decrees and other official statements (8.3, 5, 8; 9.13, 14, 29-32). In this sense, she imitates the Persian manner of doing things, for she recognizes the power that the written word has in Persia, for example, in those documents written by Haman and Ahasuerus. In her actions of referring to decrees and then writing them, Esther reflects the same type of authority which is practiced by the Persian government. This correspondence presents her as quite powerful and makes her place within the court appear to be secure.

The dignity with which Esther speaks and acts further demonstrates her status as the queen of Persia. Her character has an understated quality in the M text. Esther's actions are almost always more solemn and dignified than in the other two texts. Her first approach before Ahasuerus (episode 4) is indicative of her general temperament (though the second is arguably less so). Esther comes to him silently, in a manner quite restrained. In much of her conversation, Esther speaks more formally and less insistently, especially when inviting Ahasuerus to her second banquet (5.7-8) and when presenting her other requests (5.4; 7.3-4; 8.3, 5-6; 9.13). Perhaps the combination of Esther's formal demeanor and her understated speech enables her to get her way so easily. Esther's authority in the M text is of a type which is not pronounced or strident. She realizes that often the best way to get ahead in politics is through well-modulated speech and actions, so that fewer feathers are ruffled.

Activity/Passivity

In the A text Esther exhibits the greatest progression in her level of activity, from the most passive to the most active. As in the other two narratives, she begins the events as a passive child, but then she becomes much more active as the story goes along. It is Mordecai's comments to her during their conversation which act as a catalyst for Esther. His vision of her in an active, necessary role, as saving the Jews (4.8, 14), makes her begin to think in such terms as well. By the first conversation with Ahasuerus about changing the Jews' situation, Esther is fully active in the events and takes control of them. Later, in contrast to Mordecai's passivity, Esther takes the initiative with the king, speaking to him without prior permission (8.1-7), and becomes extremely active with regard to the adversaries—punishing, killing, striking, and hanging by her own hand (8.6, 7, 8). By the conclusion of the story, Esther's actions are as instrumental as Ahasuerus's and Mordecai's in bringing about reversal for the Jews.

The characterization of Esther in the B text tends much more towards passivity. Though at certain individual points she demonstrates personal activity and initiative, Esther is significantly more passive in general. It is particularly Esther's actions throughout the two scenes in which she approaches the king which provide the lasting impression of Esther's greater passivity. In the first of these scenes (episode 4), both the B and A texts portray her as weaker and less in control than the M text, but the B text is the most striking in this trait. And with regard to the second approach (episode 7), the B text shares with the M text more details which suggest Esther's greater passivity than does the A text. In these two scenes, Artaxerxes is the one who really takes the initiative, with Esther dependent upon the position of his sceptre.

In addition, the B text stresses Esther's greater obedience, especially during the early part of the story. As in the M text, we know that she remains obedient to Mordecai even while living in the Persian court (2.10, 20). But in the B text alone, Mordecai thinks of Esther's approach to the king as an act of continuing this early obedience (4.8, 14). And from the beginning, it portrays Esther's relationship with God as being one of fearing and obeying God (2.20). Furthermore, throughout the remainder of the story are several occasions when Esther's actions and the narrative itself enhance the impression of greater passivity. For instance, she expects others to save her (4.11, 12; 14.3, 14, 19; 8.6), to change Artaxerxes's temper (15.8), and to decide how the Jews should act in defense (9.13).

The M text, though, characterizes Esther with a level of activity and passivity that is more mixed. There are some events throughout the course of the story during which she is quite active, particularly her first approach before Ahasuerus. At other times she gives over control to the other characters, especially during the selection of a new queen (2.8, 11, 16). For most of the story, however, her actions do not fall into either extreme.

Esther is most unambiguously active and strong when approaching the king (episodes 4 and 7). She is dependent upon neither servants nor God, but proceeds by means of her own strength and resolve and without fear. Esther is active in winning Ahasuerus's approval and she claims for herself the power bestowed by the sceptre. Her second approach, though somewhat different, still exhibits greater activity and initiative on her part. She again goes before Ahasuerus as her own idea and under her own power. She uses the actions of falling and weeping more to get Ahasuerus to do what she wants than as an indication of her own weakness. The combination of these two approach scenes highlights Esther's self-initiative. And throughout the story, there are other numerous individual suggestions of the degree of Esther's activity.

Likewise, we can see details of the story which portray Esther as more passive in the M text. She speaks in Mordecai's name rather than her own (2.22). At times she is less demanding, and once she even states that she is willing to accept abuse (7.4). It is towards the end of the story when Esther here, along with the B text, is more passive than in the A text. She takes less initiative to get her request for the Jews' retaliation enacted (9.13-14). And, at the conclusion, she does not act alone in establishing her letter but shares the power with Mordecai (9.29-31). Hence, the overall impression of Esther is of one who sometimes acts on her own and at other times allows others to act for her. Neither tendency dominates the M text.

Emotions

The amount and range of emotion expressed by Esther vary significantly among the three narratives. The A and B texts share certain similarities during her prayer and first approach before the king. For instance, we know of Esther's anxiety, her unhappiness in the Persian court, her feelings of need, and her trust in God. It is the A text that exhibits the greatest degree and widest range of emotion throughout the story. Its Esther tends to experience emotion in different situations and in response to different people than in the other narratives. Those who affect her are Ahasuerus, Haman, other non-Jews, and God. What is unique in the A text is Esther's lack of emotional response to the plight of her own people, the Jews. She is not particularly grieved by their situation (4.4, 9-10; 8.3, 6), but instead worries that the king not be grieved (7.4, 6). Esther's emotional investment lies more with Ahasuerus and Haman and not so much with the fate of the Jews or in contact with Mordecai.

Yet Esther's accentuated emotional responses do not hamper her ability to act as she desires. Even though her reasons for being afraid during her first approach to the king (episode 4) are greater in this narrative, Esther is actually less afraid and upset. Though her anxiety does give her pause, she does not allow it to overwhelm her or to impede her progress as much as in the B text. And her new-found courage during the second banquet serves as a sign of her success. Only in the A text is Esther able to turn the fear she feels before Ahasuerus into new confidence (7.3).

The B text characterizes Esther with three particular emotions: fear, loneliness, and concern for the Jewish people. She is more afraid and lonely than in the other texts, and these emotions are interpreted particularly within her relationship to God, as is evident especially in her prayer. And knowing the misery and pain of the Jews causes Esther also to feel emotional pain (4.4; 8.3, 6). It is her worry about the Jews which acts as the catalyst for her even to contemplate taking the risk of going to Artaxerxes. However, the level of emotions which Esther expresses decreases as the story goes along. At one point, she even causes fear in others rather than herself be its victim (7.6). By the end of the story,

Esther overcomes the extreme negative emotions which earlier hold her in their grip.

The B text at times employs physical actions and objects to suggest Esther's emotional state. She uses clothing to express feelings of grief and anxiety (14.2), her face to feign great happiness (15.5). Most indicative, though, is Esther's falling. Her anxiety and fear cause her to feel faint and to fall down twice (15.7, 15). The extremity of her anguish at this time is especially visible in the great impact it has upon her physical strength.

The Esther of the M text is extremely level-headed, and even unemotional. Nor are we told as much about any emotions the other characters feel towards her as in the other texts. Esther's characterization here stands out especially in comparison with the emotional range expressed by the other two texts. She outwardly displays emotion at only three points during the M text's version of the story: when hearing the servants' report about Haman's edict (4.4), when telling Ahasuerus of the difficulty she has in seeing the suffering of her people (8.6), and when approaching the king for the second time (8.3). The last instance is even ambiguous, for though Esther cries, it is not clear how upset she actually feels. Though such is not explicitly stated, there are a few instances in the M text when the reader can infer that Esther feels a certain confidence. She appears, in her sure actions and silence, certain that what she is doing is correct and will yield the results she desires. And her resignation to the possibility of death for herself and of abuse for the people is stoic (4.16). It is significant that in these few instances of emotion, Esther does not feel anything for herself but only for the Jewish people. She is moved by their pain and the threat of their destruction, but not by the danger of her own situation.

Religion

The characterization of Esther in both the A and B texts includes an important religious trait. She is pious and prayerful, has a relationship with God, and refuses to worship foreign deities. However, in the A text Esther's religion affects her to a greater degree in her day-to-day life than in the other two texts. Esther's faith and life are the most integrated. She does not separate her Jewish identity from her life in the Persian court (2.10, 20; 8.1), and she prays on a more continual basis (episode 3; 4.8; 15.2; 7.3). In the A text, personal piety is more important to Esther than outward religious action. Esther recommends prayer, worship, and direct communication with God. And the A text does not depict her with association with religious festivities as such (i.e. Purim). In Esther's mind, prayer is to take on and confess one's error, not to shirk it, and it is to be performed with an attitude of sorrow, alienation, and humility. In addition, she believes more strongly than in the B text that people must take the responsibility for asking for God's saving actions on their behalf (14.5).

Furthermore, Esther experiences particular success in her times of prayer. God's influence upon her and the circumstances in which she works is more strongly evident in the A text. Esther herself is portrayed as working with God, as an instrument of God's intention, in the salvation of the people (4.8, 14; 14.13). She depends upon God most heavily to affect her own action and to influence her own speaking (4.8; 14.13; 15.2; 7.3). The success of Esther's frequent prayer is demonstrated through her receipt of the courage for which she asks and the change of outward circumstances. The Esther of the A text depends upon God more continually throughout her actions and owes her final success particularly to God.

The B text, as well, characterizes Esther as a pious, spiritual person. Yet her religious trait remains distinctive in certain ways. Esther considers individual piety to be important, as in the A text, but religious works important as well. She does not pray as continually nor debase herself as much as in the A text. Instead, Esther stresses the importance of outwardly visible religious actions. For instance, she maintains a lifestyle of religious discipline (2.20; 14.15-18) and is careful to wear the proper clothing for prayer (14.2; 15.1). Not only are such individual religious actions of concern to Esther but community-wide ones as well, especially fasting. And she views the purpose of fasting more as the appropriate response to dire situations than as a response to victorious situations (4.16; 9.31).

As in the A text, Esther shows herself to have a close and personal relationship with God. However, her relationship here differs in the degree that it is founded upon obedience and based firmly within the Jewish community. Practicing piety, not revealing her origins, and obedience to Mordecai are all connected to her attitude and relationship with God. Esther also views her own religiosity in terms of her people and her religious tradition. She links herself more closely with the Jewish community throughout the story, and expects God to work for her and the contemporary Jews as God did for their Israelite ancestors (14.3, 5, 12, 18). In the B text, Esther speaks of herself as part of Israel's heritage and tradition more than in the A text, though in both she emphasizes it less than Mordecai does in his prayer.

Relationship with God, for Esther, is primarily reliance *upon* God. In her prayer, she more readily expresses her and her people's present need for God than in the A text. It is within the relational, rather than the universal, realm that Esther's particular view of God becomes apparent. Within her general need for God's help in her delivering of the Jews, she relies upon God for a variety of things. But most significantly, she relies upon God for help in overcoming her negative emotions of fear and loneliness, as is seen especially in her prayer. In the B text Esther wants more that God would remove her fear and isolation than in the A text. Esther is characterized as expressing her needs before God precisely because she knows that God will understand her similar situation of being alone, will listen, and will remember what God has done for her ancestors.

The Esther of the M text lives primarily in the secular world, not the religious. Her attitude about things religious is not pronounced in comparison with the other two narratives, as would be expected from the M text's overall more secular tone. Because her prayer, her extended approach scene, and the various other references to God or religious actions in the A and B texts are not present in the M text, we know less fully about Esther's religious leanings. As neither her relationship with God nor her piety in personal actions is recorded, we know nothing about that aspect of her character. And the M text does not suggest that Esther is feeling obedient to God in the court or following a certain lifestyle which includes religious regulations.

Still, two places in the M text suggest a religious trait to Esther's character. After she decides to approach Ahasuerus with a petition at the risk of her own life, she commands the Jews of Susa to join her in a fast (4.16). Then at the end of the story, she writes and sends a letter that is particularly about the proper celebration of Purim (9.29-32). From these instances we know that Esther finds it important to perform religious rites both in times of crisis, when hoping for a change in a negative situation, and in times of celebration. These actions are both of a solemn, sober type, of abstinence and of grief and remembrance of the sorrow of the people. In the M text, Esther stresses the serious side of religious action, as over against Mordecai's greater interest in joyous, celebratory action.

Two theological aspects can be discerned from these proposals in the M text. First is the importance that Esther places upon the community, that pious actions to God need to be practiced not in isolation but within the religious community. In the M text, Esther does nothing of a religious nature by herself. Second, Esther finds the celebration of a religious holiday to be important, that performing festival rituals on a regular basis is a good way to keep fresh for future generations the remembrance of a time when the people are saved.

Connection with the Jews

Each narrative characterizes Esther with a unique relationship to the Jewish people. The A text's Esther is the most separated from the people. As with the other two texts, she has a relationship with the Jews, but it is defined in a more limited way. Esther is not as emotionally concerned about the Jewish people, and her place within the community is the most ambiguous. Instead, she is portrayed especially according to the role of the Jews' savior. As in the B text, Mordecai early on in the story describes the goal of her action as particularly to save them from death (4.8). But throughout the remainder of the scene, he continues to view her as being especially responsible for helping and saving them (4.14). And Esther also tends to see herself as primarily linked with the people in terms of their need for salvation during this time (14.3, 5, 13, 14).

In the A text Esther has a great deal of command over the Jews. However, the different ending of this narrative does not render Esther as a leader who will necessarily influence the Jewish community in any ongoing fashion. She is not a future leader, nor a religious leader, of them. Her role is primarily to save them from this particular situation and at this particular time. On the whole, Esther acts as the official representative of the Jews, but she is not as emotionally and ethnically connected with them. She instead is characterized as their spokesperson in the Persian court, an official in a high position who works on their behalf. Esther's concern for the Jews, and their need for her, is distinctively for this situation of threatened destruction.

The B text, in contrast, portrays Esther as very much linked with the Jewish community in Persia. She thinks in terms of the Jews both politically and as part of her own heritage (2.10, 20; 4.14, 16; 14.3, 5; 7.3, 4; 8.6). Her position within her family and within the larger community of Jews is important. From the time she is introduced, and throughout the story, Esther is described in terms of her family relationship (2.7; 4.8; 8.1; 9.29). Her connection to the Jewish people, though, is not only ethnic or cultural but also includes a religious element. She knows the God of the Jews as her own God, and their history as her history(14.5-10, 18). Esther's position among the Jewish people is intimately related to her relationship with God.

Furthermore, the B text emphasizes the temporal, the continual, aspect of Esther's connection to the Jewish people. She has a much more extended view of them and of her role within the community than just this present national crisis. Esther remembers her relationship with them throughout the entire extent of her own life. She sees herself as part of God's inheritance that was begun in ancient history and will continue through eternity. And Esther adds to their tradition through time, for she herself will have influence by writing a document that will last forever (9.32).

Esther, in the B text, feels great concern for these people even while living apart from them in the court. As in the M text, she becomes worried and anxious when hearing what has been happening to them, and she emphasizes how their agony and destruction will affect her (4.4; 14.1-2; 8.3, 6). Esther cares about the Jewish situation within Persia. But in the B text, Esther is less the Jews' leader and more simply another member of the Jewish people. She acts less as their savior than in the A text, and emphasizes herself as more a part of the community. This trait of Esther as less in a leadership position over the Jews is particularly suggested by the details of her letter-writing at the end of the story (episode 9). She does not rule over them, in a religious capacity or otherwise, nor does she distribute material to them. Instead, she writes about her experiences.

The M text's Esther also has a strong identity with the Jewish people. From the very first time that Esther is introduced to the reader, her Hebrew name is given even before we know her Persian one (2.7). She has the closest connection to Mordecai and we are told the most information about both of her parents (2.7, 15; 9.29). When thinking about the Jews, Esther tends to view them in terms of familial ties (2.10, 20; 4.14; 7.3, 4; 8.6). In contrast to the B text, she refers to them not so much as a nation, a political group, but in an ethnic fashion, as people connected by blood relation. Esther's manner of leadership of the Jewish community is two-fold. She commands when and in what manner to perform religious actions and she establishes guidelines for the recognition of a national holiday (4.16; 9.31). But she also tries to encourage the Jews, writing her letter in response to the violence which they have recently experienced. Esther obviously cares about her people. And, as in the B text, her concern is not just for the present community but also for future generations to come.

With regard to her relationship with the Jewish people, Esther progresses through a three-stage transformation in the M text. Though the A and B texts include some of these details, they do not present as systematic a change as does the M text. At first, Esther is very much connected to the Jews and her status within the community is well-defined. She is an orphan who has been taken in by a relative, who has the position of a daughter within his household (2.7, 15). Then her persona shifts from being very Jewish to being very much the Persian queen. At first, this change is emphasized by a change in locale, from the house of Mordecai to the palace, the often repeated house of the king (2.8, 9, 11; 4.13; 15.6). Esther is very much the queen in the king's house, and her status within the Jewish community is no longer as important to her. She appears always and only as Persian royalty. At this point Esther does not appear to be worried about the Jewish people. She is concerned with her own personal life before that of the Jews, and even finds it permissible that they would be enslaved against their will (7.4).

Esther shifts to her third stage at the beginning of the seventh episode. Even though still in the palace, she begins to care about the Jews and to act more as their leader. The turnabout comes when she reveals her Jewish identity to the court (8.1). At this time Esther clearly lets the king and the court know how she is connected to the Jews and how painful it would be for her to see them harmed at all. Here at the conclusion of the story, Esther's Jewish connection is reaffirmed through this repetition of her ancestry and her working with Mordecai in establishing religious practices (episode 9). Though the queen of Persia, she is also the leader of the Jews. Esther's Jewish ancestry and her Persian position finally become integrated.

Relationship with the King

Esther's relationship with the king includes how they speak to each other, the manner in which they rule together, and the support they show one another, as well as other details. Esther is most interactive with the king in the A text. She and Ahasuerus converse with each other more frequently and at greater length, and their speaking is typically more give and take. Her relationship with Ahasuerus is also generally less formal and at times more personal. Esther tends to speak more *with* the king than at him, and he with her.

Though she receives respect and approval from Ahasuerus from the start, Esther is less certain about the solidity of their relationship at the beginning of the story. She suspects her status to be the most unfavored (4.10, 16) and she is awed by his glory (15.6-7, 13). But as the story progresses, Esther gains confidence in Ahasuerus and starts to trust and respect him. She begins to command him directly (5.8; 8.6; 9.13), and she more often appeals to his good judgment than to his favor (5.4, 8; 7.3). By the conclusion of the story, Esther is assured that she has his respect and trust. She no longer considers bowing before him, but speaks directly and forcefully (episode 7). In all, the A text displays the most latitude within their relationship.

Esther's relationship with the king develops into one of mutuality and respect. They act more as equals in the A text than in the other two narratives. Ahasuerus is the most approving of Esther and of her good judgment, and she works with him in the most conjoint manner. They share in the treatment of issues concerning the kingdom. The two often reason together and come to agreement about what should be done, a process into which Esther must also provide important input (8.7, 8; 9.14). At times she even persuades him to make certain decisions. Ahasuerus displays a great deal of confidence in Esther's judgment in political and governmental matters, often entrusting her to do as she thinks best. The unique ending of the A text, which does not incorporate the final scene between Esther and Mordecai, suggests that Esther shares responsibility more with the king than with Mordecai. They work more exclusively as a team.

The relationship between Esther and the king in the A text is also mutual on an emotional level. The two care for and attend to each other. Ahasuerus, overall, displays the most emotion towards Esther. He also exhibits great concern for her welfare and well-being. The two, furthermore, understand each other's feelings. Ahasuerus particularly demonstrates how well he can read her inner thoughts during her first approach (episode 4). He is also more anxious that Esther be happy in the A text, trying hard to please her and being most willing to give her whatever she wants (5.3, 6, 8; 7.6). Esther, likewise, knows Ahasuerus well and cares about his feelings. She anticipates his distress, and when he is upset she recognizes it and speaks of it (7.4, 6). She also cares about his happiness. Esther does not want the king to be grieved, even at great cost to herself, but works hard to keep him calm and happy. In all, the A text portrays Esther as sharing with Ahasuerus the governance of the kingdom more as a loved and valued partner than an obedient wife. She has come to respect Ahasuerus and to expect that he will likewise respect her wishes and ideas for what is to happen in the kingdom.

Esther's relationship with the king is more ambivalently characterized by the B text than by the other two texts. At times we are less certain what Artaxerxes thinks of Esther, what she thinks of him, or what their intentions are towards one another. Sometimes the greater ambiguity of the B text is a result of conflicting actions at different points during the story. It is vagueness in the description of plot events, however, which most adds to the ambiguity of their relationship. For instance, from the selection process, we are uncertain of Esther's status with Artaxerxes. And the manner in which he later describes her does not help to clarify their relationship. The language used by Artaxerxes, and by the B text in general, often obscures information at important points in Esther's interaction with the king. And throughout the story, particularly when Esther is presenting her petitions, their conversations tend to be shorter. Thus, on the whole, it is more difficult to determine the overall degree of affection or respect they hold for each other.

Nonetheless, a great many characteristics can be hypothesized about their relationship in the B text. Artaxerxes's affection for Esther is a primary element. As in the A text, he shows especial concern and care for her when she appears upset during her first approach. But his affection and favor are expressed at other points throughout the events as well, and, with fewer other feelings expressed, they predominate in his treatment of Esther (2.14, 18; 5.8; 7.3, 5, 7-8; 8.5, 12). And Esther herself recognizes that his action towards her is based upon the kindness he feels (15.14). She is assured of at least some level of approval and affection in their relationship.

Artaxerxes's feeling of affection cause him to act in certain ways. In this narrative, he tries more often to do things which are helpful to Esther. Perhaps he is responding to her early kindness to him in informing him of his servants' plot (2.22). We see his helpfulness most clearly during her two approaches before him (episodes 4 and 7). For example, Artaxerxes takes pains to help her to be able to express her petitions, to give her relevant information, to aid the Jews in revenge against Haman, and to be more generous than in the other texts. But, on the whole, he promises Esther less, is the least specific about how her desires will be granted, and does not speak of himself as being personally involved. It appears that she can expect him to be helpful in some situations, but not all. Artaxerxes's affection for Esther is also displayed by the closeness between them. This aspect of their relationship is seen most readily in their conversations. The B text characterizes Esther and Artaxerxes as tending to speak more directly to each other at times than do the other two texts (15.7; 5.6; 7.2; 8.3, 7). The two are also close physically, a characteristic which is seen most clearly in her two approaches before him. In the B text, both their conversational and physical closeness are at times related to emotional closeness. By speaking with peaceful words, Artxerxes tries to remove the conflict between them. And by embracing her and calling her to him, he tries to remove the intimidation Esther feels in his presence.

Esther's own responses to Artaxerxes falls into three types in the B text. She is approving of Artaxerxes, intimidated by him, and deferential to him. From the start, Esther imagines the king in a more positive light, tells him to his face how wonderful she finds him to be, and gives honor to him (15.13-14). Second, when first approaching Artaxerxes, Esther feels extremely intimidated, even terrified, by him and the circumstances in which she finds him. She indeed experiences him as a lion (14.13). Her extreme physical response reflects her extreme intimidation. And third, she responds to Artaxerxes with deference. Esther tends to give over authority to him, and he tends to command her rather than consult with her (episodes 7 and 8). Esther is self-effacing, and more under the control of the king in the B text.

The M text portrays Esther with the most formal and least emotional relationship with the king of the three texts. She and Ahasuerus relate towards each other in a more official manner. Their formality is expressed particularly through their manner of speaking together. Esther and Ahasuerus speak to each other the least often in the M text, and when they do their messages tend to be more formally stated. All throughout the story, most of their transactions have a more legal and procedural than personal mood. Though Esther is often noted to be in closer physical proximity in living quarters and accessibility, the two are more emotionally distanced. That the M text does not exhibit her longer approach before Ahasuerus, during which his affection for her and her awe of him are visible, contributes to such a characterization. Their relationship is more business-like and even professional. Unlike the other two narratives, they do not relate with one another in the sister–brother closeness suggested by the Greek texts (15.9), but according to their offices, the king and the queen of Persia.

It is difficult to know exactly how Ahasuerus feels about Esther in the M text. At the very beginning of the story, he claims actually to feel more love and devotion towards her than towards any other woman in the kingdom (2.17). And Ahasuerus is often the most accepting of Esther's petitions in the M text. Yet any explicit affection for her is not at all obvious throughout the rest of the events. In fact, in contrast to the other two texts, we are not told by the M text what Ahasuerus might be feeling about Esther. It indicates no positive (affection, worry, helpfulness) or negative (anger) emotions. Thus their relationship apparently undergoes change throughout the story. Ahasuerus's early emotional love and affection for Esther changes over to respect for her as queen and formality as they begin to discuss kingdom matters.

The M text's Esther, likewise, does not express a great deal of feeling for Ahasuerus. Her attitude towards him is also distant, professional, and business-like. Unlike in the other texts, Esther is not afraid of the king, nor is she awed by his magnificence or connection to the divine (episode 4). She is only confident before him. From the manner in which Esther formulates her petitions throughout the story, basing them equally upon his approval for her and upon his good judgment, we can surmise her opinion of him as being moderate with regard to these issues. In the M text, Esther is certain that he still esteems her, but not as much as she is in the B text.

With regard to how Esther and Ahasuerus share power in the kingdom, in some ways they do so more equally in the M text than in the other narratives and in some ways less. At least in terms of nomenclature, they act more as counterparts on the same level of administration. The M text refers to Esther more frequently by her title as well as her name (2.22; 4.4; 15.7; 5.3; 7.1, 2, 3, 5, 7, 8; 8.1, 7; 9.12), and to Ahasuerus more frequently by personal name as well as title (2.16; 7.5; 8.7). As in the B text, they share more equally the task of making new appointments, and Esther has a degree of power to influence Ahasuerus's decisions (episodes 7 and 8). Yet her authority within their relationship is also less at times. She directly commands the king less frequently, and he occasionally curtails her level of control. At the conclusion, she here, as well as in the B text, does not have as much control over the kingdom or receive as much respect from the king as in the A text. On the whole, the M text portrays Esther's level of control and influence within her relationship with the king to be mixed, but to tend towards exhibiting greater rather than lesser authority.

Relationship with Mordecai

Factors such as the emotional closeness or distance between Esther and Mordecai, how they influence each other, the degree to which they work together, and Esther's level of obedience constitute Esther's relationship to Mordecai. In the A text, in contrast to her relationship with Ahasuerus, Esther has the least interactive relationship with Mordecai. He does not have as great an influence upon her decisions and actions. She does not tend to rely upon Mordecai for information (4.5, 8) and is less under his command for obedience (2.7, 11, 20). And he does not rely upon her for assistance either (2.22). From the beginning she acts more independently of him, and this early separation sets the tone for their subsequent more distant interaction throughout the events of the story.

The A text does not portray Esther as working with Mordecai to the same extent as do the other two narratives. Although Esther is once identified as Mordecai's partner (16.13), such a description is not borne out at all by the events themselves. They do not act as a team with one member inside and one outside the system, nor do they share joint responsibilities. The Persian authorities, represented by Ahasuerus, treat them quite separately. Mordecai gains in stature less because of his connection to Esther than because of his own independent action on behalf of the king (2.22; 8.1-5). Like Esther, he is important because of what he alone performs. The final scene between the two of them (episode 9) has no counterpart in the A text. Therefore, at the conclusion of the story, Esther and Mordecai do not work together at all, but instead go their separate ways.

The B text represents Esther as the closest to Mordecai during her upbringing. Mordecai has had a greater influence upon her throughout her early years than in the other texts (2.7, 10, 15, 20; 4.8). She has lived her whole life into adulthood with him. And this close and lengthy association renders her particularly obedient to him. Mordecai continues to influence Esther strongly even after she has moved to the Persian court, and her decisions of how to interact with the king are based upon Mordecai's suggestions (2.20; 14.15-18). In the B text, though, Esther further sees her obedience to Mordecai to be linked to religious duty and her relationship with God (2.20).

Esther and Mordecai do, however, interact the most intimately in the B text. They have the ability to communicate well with each other, even through a greater dependence upon messengers, and they speak more comprehensively during their conversations (2.22; 4.4, 7, 8, 9, 12). And as in the M text, Mordecai is the beneficiary of his governmental position and wealth solely because of his relationship to Esther and her generosity towards him (8.1-2). The B text characterizes Esther and Mordecai as working together the most closely. They act as a team, in agreement with each other, and they actually perform tasks together. In the letter writing, the two act in a joint fashion more than in the M text. Hence, the last we see of Esther is her role in a close relationship, working together with Mordecai for the benefit of others, the two of them physically and vocationally separate from the other characters of the story.

The M text portrays the familial relationship between Esther and Mordecai as the strongest. During childhood, Esther's primary family changed to him (2.7, 15, 20). The M text emphasizes Esther's lack of birth parents and the substitution of Mordecai as her father more than the other narratives. She is characterized as more an integral part of his household, and he feels great responsibility for her well-being even when she is in the Persian court (2.11, 19). Yet though their ethnic heritage is the same, there is less a sense of Mordecai's godly or religious influence upon Esther than in the B text.

Esther's level of obedience to Mordecai also undergoes a transformation throughout the story of the M text. First, she is to obey him while living in the court, but during the course of their conversations she displays decreasing obedience to him and increasing influence over him. By the end of the story, Esther exhibits a certain authority within their relationship. She has the power to appoint him to an official position.

Her identity as the Persian queen, in contrast to Mordecai's Jewishness, renders her as more an authority figure, at least from the viewpoint of the Persian government (8.7; 9.29, 31). The two also tend to perform more parallel actions in the M text, which give to their relationship a sense of greater equality. They come before the king independently and are viewed by him more unilaterally. In particular, the M text characterizes the two as performing parallel actions and holding corresponding responsibilities in their establishment of the new holiday.

In the M text Mordecai's action towards Esther vacillates on some points. He is not characterized as being as sure and solid as she is. Mordecai first directs Esther explicitly *not* to speak of her ethnic identity (2.20), but later he faults her for not speaking of her Jewishness (4.14). Ironically, even further into the events it is only because of Esther's action of speaking of her heritage that he himself becomes prosperous (8.1). At first, he apparently does not think Esther is intelligent (4.8), but later he credits her with the ability to think through a difficult decision (4.13). And, as also in the B text, though at the beginning of the story Mordecai refuses to accept Esther's gift of clothing (4.4), at the end he takes her gift of control over Haman's possessions without protest (8.2). Within their relationship, Mordecai is portrayed by the M text as not entirely consistent with regard to his actions towards Esther.

Attitude towards Adversaries

The three narratives characterize Esther with differing views and actions towards those persons antagonistic to the Jewish people. Though in all texts Esther is concerned about both the Jews' enemies as a group and Haman in particular, the level of her concern varies. The A text portrays Esther as the most involved with both categories of adversaries. During the story, Esther pays particular attention to the foremost of the adversaries, Haman (4.8; 14.11, 13; 5.4; 7.3; 8.7). She feels herself to be in individual conflict with him. Esther singles him out as an enemy, distinguished in purpose and action from the general adversaries of the Jews. And she recognizes Haman's true deceptive character (7.6). She is not fooled by his greater gestures of friendship or obeisance (7.7). However, Esther also has control over this chief of the adversaries. She herself commands him, and she influences the king's opinion of him to the greatest degree.

As the story of the A text progresses, Esther's view broadens regarding who she finds responsible for the Jews' predicament. She goes beyond her concern about primarily Haman (leaving Mordecai to deal with his misdemeanor), and she continues on to concern herself with the greater problem of the enemies in general (8.6, 7, 8; 9.13). Her greater early attention to them when praying leads to a greater effect upon them later. She is aware of their evil qualities, considers them to be her personal enemies, and defines them by the most inclusive descriptions. Esther, in the A text, brings the most extreme punishment upon those who oppose the Jews.

The B text characterizes Esther as the least interested in the Jews' adversaries and with the least well-defined relationship with Haman. She concerns herself with the enemies less often, and when she does, tends to consider them less specifically than in the other two texts (14.10, 11, 19). Throughout the events, Esther thinks of the effects which the enemies will have upon the Jewish people in more general terms and does not imagine their destruction to as great a degree. Overall, she is far less vindictive towards them and, as in the M text, causes them far less harm.

In a similar fashion, Esther's relationship with Haman is the most general and least well-defined in the B text. Even though she refuses to eat with him (14.17), Esther is the least interested in him in general, for she does not describe his character or actions against the Jews to such a degree (5.4; 7.3, 4, 5, 6; 8.3, 5; 9.14). In the B text, Esther does not think of Haman as an enemy or as a friend, as do the other two texts, but according to more abstract negative qualities. And Haman likewise feels rather more ambivalent about Esther (7.7, 8). As with the adversaries as a whole, the B text's Esther envisions Haman's actions towards the Jews with the least severity and she is the least interested in punishing him for these actions.

In the M text, in contrast, Esther is portrayed as more concerned with Haman as an individual than the adversaries as a whole. She also sees Haman as especially malicious towards her people and pays the most attention to the hanging of his children (8.3, 5; 9.13, 14). And Haman himself views Esther as having a greater influence over his destiny (7.7). Esther's interest with the adversaries in general centers more upon the destructive impact they will have upon the Jewish people than upon their moral character or their punishment. She anticipates their actions as being more violent and harmful (7.4; 8.6). And it is especially their intention to kill to which she objects. Along with the B text, the overall effects of the Jews upon their adversaries is less in the M text than in the A text. Fewer persons are killed, less destruction is done to them, and only those opponents in the capital city are affected (episode 8).

Court Life

The three texts present Esther's interaction with elements of the Persian court, her daily life within it, and her aptitude for serving there, with certain distinctions. They also portray the atmosphere of the court differently. The A text characterizes Esther as the most integrated into the manners and structure of the Persian court system. She most immediately and most completely meets with the approval of the king's servant (2.8-9) and, immediately afterward, the king himself (2.9). Still, Esther is not as surrounded by court servants nor as dependent upon them as she is in the B text. The relative absence of attendants around her renders Esther as a more independent and autonomous character in the court. But the kindness and concern that those servants who are included by the A text show her when she is upset suggests that Esther must have been able to win their affection by some means (15.16). Though less surrounded by servants, she is still not particularly lonely.

Esther has learned how to accommodate herself to Persian customs in the A text and she has become an accomplished hostess (5.5; 7.2, 6). Her quick rise within the system suggests that the court of the A text is the most open to non-Persians. The court procedures are far less formal and structured than in the other two texts, especially the selection process for a new queen, the manner in which one must get audience with the king, and the way in which requests and petitions are presented and fulfilled.

However, we also know something of Esther's own feelings about her life within the court in the A and B texts through what she expresses in her prayer. This scene is the only time throughout the story that we get any indication of Esther's unhappiness and displeasure with her new home. She speaks of her discomfort with her regal attire, the foreign eating and worshipping practices, and other general duties. But in the B text Esther feels the most unhappy in the court, and extremely lonely in particular. She is most isolated in B, more distant from Mordecai and the outside world (episode 2). And she adheres to Jewish customs most strictly (2.10, 20). Hence, Esther keeps more things secret from the court in the B text, certain actions that she must hide on a daily basis in addition to her Jewish identity. She lives the most fragmented existence, between her duties as the Persian queen and as a Jewish woman, in the B text. This fragmentation of lifestyle enhances her feelings of isolation.

The B text characterizes Esther with a more defined relationship with the court servants, including the supervision of them. She experiences a special rapport with them. Esther relies upon the court servants the most heavily, but she also shows a greater degree of command over them (2.8, 9, 15; 4.4, 5, 10, 12, 15; 15.2-4, 7, 16). The B text's Esther is more officially in charge of the servants within the court system. But it presents her as having certain other official duties, or times of service, as well (2.12; 14.16), and as more concerned for the reputation of the court (7.4). Esther has developed more of an official place within the domestic system at the court than within the government or political systems.

The M text provides less information about Esther's daily life and her feelings towards the court. Instead, three aspects of life and procedure in the Persian court stand out: the placement of women, the formality of process, and the importance of decree. First, the community of women in the court is more segregated and stratified than in the other texts. The M text places emphasis upon different categories of women and their appointed places within the system (2.8, 9, 13, 14, 15, 17). For its women, at least, the court system is structured according to hierarchy.

Second, the M text portrays the various procedures of the court with a great deal of formality. We see this aspect expressed especially in Esther and Ahasuerus's stylized interaction when presenting and accepting petitions (episodes 5, 6, 7 and 8) and the close attention that this narrative gives to physical location all throughout. It is essential that the actions occur exactly how and where they are described to take place. And interactions between the characters of the M text are more official and less spontaneous. It tends to stress the royal aspect of Esther and Ahasuerus and the repetitive nature of certain expressions and procedures (4.15; 7.2; 8.3-4). Such precision and formality depicts the court environment as based upon solemn, restrained communication in which there are certain official procedures that must be followed.

And finally, the M text emphasizes the role played by command and decree in the operation of the Persian court. From the very beginning Esther finds herself under the strong regulations of the court system. She quickly picks up on the importance of decree and adopts it as her own language (8.3, 5, 8; 9.13, 14, 29-32). In the M text actions are carried out within the government system not by consensus or informal manner but by authoritarian power. Overall, daily life is most likely more regulated for Esther as she lives in the palace. The court functions through official procedure, command and obedience, and hierarchy. In the M text, Esther must have had a greater challenge in entering the court to learn the proper way to act within the system to get what she wanted.

Sexuality

All of the narratives attribute a sexual aspect to Esther's character. At two places in the plot Esther's sexuality is specifically suggested: when she undergoes the selection process and is chosen queen (episode 1), and when Haman falls upon her to request mercy (episode 6). In both, Esther is viewed by other characters according to her sexuality—first by the king, then by Haman. She is, furthermore, the victim of unwanted sexual advances in Haman's use of force upon her.

The A and B texts provide the additional information that Esther does not enjoy her marital relations with the king (14.15). We know that the king perceives her to be quite accomplished at lovemaking. In these two texts, Esther's pleasing sexual aspect is part of her dramatic ability, her talent to pretend something before the king that she does not actually feel. The A text does not include a cosmetic component of the selection process itself (2.9, 12), nor indicates a separate dwelling for those women with whom the king has spent the night (2.14). Yet it is particularly Esther's sexual performance that influences the king to deem her most outstanding. The B text, in contrast, emphasizes Esther's sexuality less during the selection process as the reason for the king's choosing her (2.14).

The sexual trait of Esther's character is highlighted the most by the M text. In it we are given no indication that Esther's good lovemaking is an act, so we can assume that it expresses her genuine feelings for Ahasuerus. And Esther is chosen to be the new queen explicitly because she 'pleases' the king (2.14). The structured hierarchy of women within the court system and during the selection process, however, are the most sexual in nature. Women in the Persian court are categorized primarily according to their sexual status (2.14, 17, 19). Thus, the M text leads us to think of Esther as well in a sexual light, knowing that she must also fit into this categorical structure.

Traits Particular to the A Text

Intelligence

The A text characterizes Esther with a good degree of knowledge and a quick mind. In this text, throughout the story she is the most intelligent, in the most comprehensive sense.[1] Esther demonstrates that she is able to think clearly and has an interest in gaining knowledge (14.5, 12). She is literate and educated, at least about religious matters, and, as we see throughout her prayer, has the ability to reason theologically. In the A text Esther similarly requires intelligence and rational thought from other characters—Ahasuerus (5.8; 7.3), Mordecai (4.4, 11), and even God (episode 3). The king, likewise, perceives Esther to be intelligent. She acts as a direct source of information for him and as a discussion partner (8.7, 8; 9.12, 14). His decisions in A to implement her petitions tend to be based less upon his affection for her and more upon whether he finds her suggestions compelling than in the other texts.

Esther's knowledge is not only intellectual but also practical and strategic. She is an independent thinker, not following Mordecai's suggestion to flatter the king to get her way (4.8), but coming up with her own ideas of how best to approach him. The A text portrays Esther as the most knowledgeable regarding current events in the kingdom outside the court (4.4, 5-7; 9.12). And Esther's strategic abilities are seen most fully with regard to her series of banquets. She plans ahead, has a certain scheme in mind for her entertaining, and is cognizant of the atmosphere which will precipitate the best results for her objectives (5.4-5; 7.2). In the A text, on the whole, Esther possesses a range of intellectual abilities, from book-learning to practical planning.

Justice

In the A text especially, Esther tends to think of the Jews' situation in terms of justice. She sees injury as having been done and tries to right the wrong. A clue to her perspective is found in her prayer. As in the B text, Esther understands all of what has happened as God's action of

---

1. Fox (*Character*, p. 201) and Talmon ('Wisdom', pp. 437-43) have noted Esther's wisdom and cunning in their considerations of the M text's Esther. However, the A text presents a characterization of Esther that surpasses the qualities of practical wisdom, strategizing, and overall intelligence that they have quite well observed about her character in general.

justice towards the Jews, as punishment for wrongdoing, but she further thinks of the circumstances in which she is participating as God's working out divine justice. She is judgmental of the Persian government and Haman's part in it, particularly because it has not done right by its citizens and has enacted harm against them (14.11, 19; 7.6, 8). For Esther, God's justice is inseparable from human justice.

Insight into Esther's thought is seen in the A text's version of her second banquet (episode 6). Looking through her eyes, we know that Esther interprets her request to Ahasuerus as being akin to a legal trial. Haman, the adversary, is the one who has violated what is right, and Esther is calling upon the king to act as a judge and adjudicate between them fairly. In the A text, Esther's arguments before Ahasuerus are centered more upon what he deems to be good and right than whether she herself pleases him. She constructs her rhetoric, and hence her presentation of the situation, in terms of morality and ethics. By the end of the story (episodes 7 and 8), Esther's concern that justice be done comes to a head. She is no longer content to wait for God to bring about justice. She also does not trust Ahasuerus to make the right decision, nor does she even consider the Jews' own response to be adequate. Rather, Esther takes matters into her own hands as she deems proper.

Violence
Esther's actions of doing justice are by means of violence. She is a much more forceful, destructive, and violent person in the A text than in the other narratives. This character trait only becomes apparent at the end of the story (episodes 7 and 8), and it is only directed towards those who are the Jews' adversaries. Esther is the most concerned about punishment of the adversaries, and, in general, carries out their punishment more herself, by the most forceful and destructive means, and towards the most persons. Because of Esther's requests, the greatest number of people are killed throughout the greatest extent of the kingdom. In the other two texts, the last we see of Esther is her constructive and peaceful action of informing the people about Purim. In the A text, the last we see of Esther, except for the brief identification in Mordecai's dream interpretation, is her violent and destructive action in Persia.

Physical Appearance
The A text tends to pay more attention to Esther's physical appearance than the B text and significantly more than the M text. Though Esther is

described as exceptionally beautiful (2.7), cosmetics and physical attractiveness are not as important in the king's selection process. After Esther is crowned queen, the type of terminology used to describe her appearance changes from the attractiveness of physical features to more magnificent and royal description (2.17).

More attention is paid to clothing by the A text. It portrays Esther as active in transforming her appearance and with great attention to her garments (14.2; 15.1). Esther's clothing, indeed, is used to reflect her state of mind, as it is also to a certain degree in the B text. In general, Esther is especially aware of the physical appearance of herself and other characters (15.6). And she employs it more in the A text to signify her moods and what she intends to do.

Altruism
Esther's general willingness to put her life at risk and entreat the king for the sake of her people shows her to be unselfish in all three texts. And in the A and B texts we know from her prayer and extended approach to the king how upset Esther is and how great she feels the danger to be. The description of the great difficulty she must undergo enhances the degree of her self-sacrifice in those presentations of her character. However, Esther's trait of altruism is further augmented by the A text. This narrative includes points throughout the story where Esther acts in an especially selfless fashion.

Even from the beginning, Esther does not assume, at least in Mordecai's mind, that she will escape the coming destruction or be treated differently than the rest of the Jews (4.13). She initiates prayer and requests God's deliverance not for her own needs but for the plight of the whole community (4.16). And Esther is the most willing to give of herself for a greater good, to sacrifice her life for the salvation of the Jews and for the good of the Persian court. Esther's lack of concern for her own safety contrasts sharply with Mordecai's more selfish request to her in the A text (4.8). In sum, Esther displays an unsurpassed altruism in her actions on behalf of the Jewish people.

Traits Particular to the B Text

Knowledge
Esther is more interested in the obtaining and the passing along of information in the B text than in the other two texts. In it, her talent is

not with rhetorical or intellectual knowledge, nor is she frequently asked by others for her insight into certain matters. Instead, Esther is characterized as knowledgeable and well-informed in a more general sense. She is one who gathers information from the servants (4.4), Mordecai (4.5, 7-8), and Artaxerxes (9.12). And she requires complete and accurate reports from other sources in order to be well-informed. Yet Esther does not only gather information but also dispenses it. The goal of the document she writes is informational, to report what has just occurred (9.29, 32). The B text portrays Esther as moving from one who is curious to gain as much information as she can to one who serves as a source of information for others.

Interestingly, Esther obtains her information primarily by means of hearing. The B text charcterizes her as one who has her ear to the currents of the times. It is particularly what she hears that upsets her (4.4). Her education (14.5) and obedience to Mordecai (4.14) are similarly described in terms of hearing. Esther has become adept at listening, even possibly to what she is not to hear, and her expertise serves her well. It enables her to obtain information within the court with which she otherwise might not have come into contact (7.4).

Physical Weakness

Esther displays an element of weakness in the B text, but only within a limited sphere. Though in the A text Esther also exhibits a certain degree of weakness, this character trait is much more pronounced here. We see Esther's lack of physical strength in her two approaches before Artaxerxes (episodes 4 and 7). Her fainting, falling, and need of help to stand during the first approach render her as much more weak than in the A text. During the second approach, though her falling is not so much an indication of weakness, she still requires help to stand. Esther's physical reaction to her anxious emotions is, on the whole, far greater in the B text. There is something about the situation of standing before the king to ask a favor which makes Esther lose control of her strength, for elsewhere throughout the story she gives no impression of similar physical weakness.

Beauty

Though Esther's physical attractiveness is not stressed as much by the B text when she is first introduced (2.7), at other points throughout the story this narrative highlights her beauty. Esther's splendor is more innately connected with her person than a result of the clothing she wears (15.1, 2). We know that Esther possesses especially beautiful physical features, and that it is specifically she herself who boasts the glory with which she appears. Before the king, she attempts to appear pleasant to an even greater degree than in the A text (15.5). That Esther does not herself change her appearance to become splendid, as one might do if merely changing clothing, gives the further impression that her beauty is not something she can put on or take off at will. On the whole, Esther herself is characterized as the most physically attractive in the B text.

Optimism

At times during the B text's version of the story, Esther assesses situations with a more positive viewpoint than in the other two texts. She is more optimistic about her chances when first contemplating the idea of going before Artaxerxes with a petition (4.11). However, after conversing with Mordecai, Esther becomes as pessimistic here as in the other texts by the conclusion of their exchange (4.16). But Esther's essential optimism returns. At a time when she is especially afraid, Esther hopes that she will find courage (14.12), and her high hopes are visible upon her face (15.5). And in general, Esther does not envision the result of Haman's edict on the Jews as being quite as devastating in the B text. Though this trait does not pervade the story, we can occasionally catch glimpses of Esther's outlook of optimism and hope.

Growth

Esther exhibits growth and change throughout the course of the story in all the three narratives.[1] But the degree of personal growth and change evidenced by Esther's character in the B text is the most striking. In this narrative, Esther is most clearly not the same person at the end of the story as she was before any of these events transpired. Her development is evident in several areas. First, before and during her initial approach to the king (episode 4), Esther is extremely fearful and upset. She is so intimidated by the sight of Artaxerxes and by being in his royal presence that she faints and is unable even to stand. But by the second time she approaches him with a petition (episode 7), she evidences none of the

---

1. Fox, for instance, outlines particular details of her development throughout the events of the story (*Character*, pp. 196-205). Though his focus is specifically upon the M text, much of what he observes can apply to the two other texts as well.

same fear or anxiety at all. She instead speaks to him confidently and coherently. Though her former awe is suggested when she requires assistance to stand, it is not nearly as debilitating as earlier. Esther has learned to overcome her terror, weakness, and hindering emotions. Secondly, Esther's response to others and her effects upon them also go through a transformation. She, at one point, describes how anxious and troubled she feels (15.13). But later she has the very same effect upon others (7.6), while she herself remains firm and unemotional. Esther has grown from being upset and feeling personally powerless to causing anxiety and fear in others.

Thirdly, Esther begins the story as a woman who has lived all her life under the influence of her foster-father Mordecai. She is the most obedient to him, and she even has difficulty separating her submission to him from her obedience to God (2.10, 20). However, by the end of the story, she has matured within their relationship. She no longer treats Mordecai as a father nor obeys him, but now relates to him as a co-worker. Esther has power over Mordecai (8.2), is generous in appointing him, and at last works with him as a partner rather than a subservient daughter in the production of her letter (episode 9). And finally, this narrative itself understands Esther's character to be one of change and growth throughout these events. In the interpretation of Mordecai's dream, it presents Esther as the one who grows from a tiny, insignificant stream of water into a mighty river (10.6). Though the other symbols of the dream are not similarly transformed, Esther's actions are interpreted as enlarging so that the people receive deliverance from the warring forces. In the B text, Esther's own growth is the most impressive, increasing in physical strength, control of emotion, and power over others from the beginning of the story to its conclusion.

Traits Particular to the M Text

Strength

The M text's Esther is a person of great strength, possessing both physical strength and strength of character. At times, her fortitude is particularly apparent, For instance, in their conversation, Esther is not as reliant upon Mordecai's persuasion when deciding to act; he does not attempt to convince her as completely (4.8). She later expresses her willingness to undergo hardship, her ability to withstand suffering (7.4), and at the end we see her issuing her letter with total strength (9.29).

The places at which the M text highlights Esther's strength is in its version of the approach scenes (episodes 4 and 7), especially in comparison with her greater weakness in the B text and, to a lesser extent, in the A text. During her first approach before Ahasuerus, Esther displays greater physical strength, but her mental strength is equally impressive. She needs neither the emotional support of attendants nor the king's assurance of safety to perform her task. During the second approach as well, Esther's strength is apparent, especially her physical fortitude. In the M text, Esther's spirit is strong enough to overcome all the pressures forced upon her.

Speech

The M text places greater emphasis upon Esther's speaking ability. She is one who speaks articulately and judiciously. First of all, Esther exhibits good discretion of when to speak and of when not to speak in the court system. She herself mentions making decisions about situations in which keeping silent is the best option, in contrast to others when one must speak up (7.4). We see her making such judgments in her two approaches before Ahasuerus. The first time she observes silence (episode 4), but the second time she determines that an appeal to the king's emotions is the best way to influence him (8.2, 5-6). Esther's action of speaking is presented as being of key importance for a successful outcome, for it is through her act of speaking that the Jews will be delivered (4.14).

And Esther knows how to speak well. She has mastered the art of rhetoric. This rhetorical ability is seen particularly in Esther's presentation of petitions to Ahasuerus. Esther here uses the most complete and most solid arguments for why the king should act as she asks.[1] She bases her arguments for the king's assent upon both Ahasuerus's good judgment and her favorability (5.4, 8; 7.3; 8.5). And in her final request, the M text alone portrays Esther as still speaking by means of persuasion. Esther furthermore understands how best to phrase her speaking to get the results she desires in the M text. Instances of her expertise are evident throughout the story. For example, Ahasuerus consistently asks Esther questions utilizing the same two words to refer to her desires, 'request' and 'petition'. She, in response, phrases her answers in a similar fashion, expressing her wishes in terminology

---

1. Fox further proposes that even the manner in which Esther phrases her speech to the king, downplaying her own influence and highlighting the king's initiative, is significant for her success (*Character*, p. 68).

consonant with the way in which he himself thinks (5.7; 7.3). In all, the M text shows Esther as able to influence people especially by means of her speaking abilities.

Balance

Esther exhibits a sense of balance on a variety of different levels, more so in the M text than in the other two texts. It characterizes Esther as one who does not go to extremes. She is moderate in her outward impression, the language and expressions she chooses to use, her manner of lifestyle, and her opinions and concerns. Most specifically, Esther is viewed by others in a balanced fashion. She is first introduced by both her Hebrew and her Persian names, and we are told that both her appearance, or face, and her form, or figure, are beautiful (2.7). Later, the king chooses Esther because she best fits his dual categories (2.14). And throughout the M text, Esther is also more frequently spoken of in terms of both her title and her personal name.

Esther's own behavior also gives the impression of a balanced person. The language she uses exhibits a certain sense of balance in her thinking. She speaks of all who know Ahasuerus's rule, both women and men, both inside and outside the court system (4.11), and she does not reveal both the Jewish people and her own family (2.10, 20). Most significant, however, is the balance Esther expresses in her petitions before the king. In the M text, she tends to base her arguments equally upon two reasons, his approval of her and his good judgment. Esther, furthermore, leads a more modulated lifestyle. When in the court, she, along with all the other women, divides her year of preparation evenly between two different types of cosmetic treatments (2.12), and later she knows the proper mixture of obedience and disobedience with which to respond to Ahasuerus (5.8). Esther is willing to undergo some degree of injustice and suffering, yet she will not tolerate abuse above a certain level (7.4).

More basic to Esther's being is the sense of balance she expresses in her concerns. She is not totally self-absorbed nor self-abnegating, caring that her own life as well as that of the people be delivered (7.3). She tries to juggle her concern about both aspects of her new identity, loyalty both to the king and kingdom and to the Jews. Esther finds these two areas of need equally important. Though her dual expressions and concerns sometimes make her appear almost divided in character, Esther integrates and balances her life, language, and concerns most self-consciously in the M text.

Continuity

The narrative of the M text describes its events in terms of continuity and discontinuity with past occurrences more so than do the other texts. This quality affects the characterization of Esther in particular ways. For instance, we see most clearly how Esther's early life is marked by discontinuity (episode 1). In particular, she experiences discontinuity in living situations and authority figures; Esther's early home life is not stable. She moves from one location to another, from her parents' house, to Mordecai's house, to the king's house. And even within the king's house she moves from the first house of women to a better place in the first house, and then to the second house of women. The persons who have responsibility for her care likewise shift numerous times, from her birth parents, to Mordecai, to Hegei, to Shaashgaz, and presumably to Ahasuerus. It is only when she is chosen queen that Esther's life of discontinuity ends. From that point on, the more frequent repetition of the locale of the house of the king, the palace, suggests that Esther finally experiences domestic stability.

The M text also highlights the continuity of events in the story through their repetitive nature. Certain actions of which Esther is a part are performed in explicit reference to actions done previously. The women gather a second time (2.19), Esther repeats Mordecai's actions (4.13, 15), she restates the same decree (9.13), the Jews gather for a second time (9.15), and Esther writes the second letter about Purim (9.29). And the language of description and direct speech used for the second banquet and Esther's second approach (episodes 6 and 7) make clear reference to the first times these actions occur. Some of these repetitions bear directly upon Esther's character and they help to elucidate her own actions and place within the continuity. For instance, that she repeats his actions during their conversation and writes a second letter to his first makes her appear equal to Mordecai. That the second banquet begins like the first makes Esther's new request seem that much more of a surprise. Esther consciously alters the second banquet in a manner that contrasts how with Ahasuerus and Haman expect the evening to progress. The M text presents Esther as living in a situation in which the sequence and timing of actions is important. Esther does not act totally autonomously, but the events and actions which she initiates have a place within a larger sequence.

Vashti and the Consequences of her Actions

At the beginning of the story, after queen Vashti and the king give their separate and elaborate banquets for the citizens of Persia, and after much wine and good spirits, the king requests his servants to bring Vashti to his banquet. Vashti chooses to forego the privilege, which makes the king angry. He consults with his advisers regarding Vashti's action, who foresee a gigantic influence upon women, officials, and marital relationships within the kingdom. They suggest that he banish Vashti, inform the kingdom by letter, and find a replacement for her. So, after a time, the king's advisers further suggest a procedure—beautiful young women are to be sought out and placed in the care of court servants, then the individual who pleases the king is to be proclaimed queen in Vashti's stead.

As numerous interpreters have noted, the first queen, Vashti, acts as a comparative figure for Esther, the second queen.[1] She is also the only other principal female character of the book. As the qualities and actions of characters in a narrative often affect how we view its other characters, so Vashti affects how we perceive Esther. What Vashti chooses to do, and the consequences of her actions in the king's and officials' decision to look for a new queen, set the stage for the arrival of Esther. In addition, the procedure and criteria established by the narratives for this new queen accentuate the degree to which Esther either fits with or is at odds with the expectations for this new ruler. Hence, these details provide two categories of comparison: Vashti as a counterpart character to Esther, and Esther as the type of queen that is desired.

As with the portrayal of Esther herself, the character of Vashti and the details about the proposed selection procedure vary among the three texts at certain points. These differences are, admittedly, not as crucial for attaining an accurate understanding of Esther as are the scenes in which she herself appears. Still, comparing her with Vashti serves to highlight certain aspects of Esther's character which are seen throughout the rest of the story and which have just been analyzed. This section will consider the effects of Vashti as read against the composite portrayal of Esther in each of the three texts.

1. Stanton and Chandler, *Women's Bible*, p. 89 (Part II); Laffey, *Introduction*, p. 217; Talmon, 'Wisdom', pp. 440-41, 449; Fuchs, 'Female Heroines', pp. 156-57; Gendler, 'Restoration, pp. 241-47; White, 'Esther', in Newsom and Ringe (eds.), *Women's Bible Commentary*, p. 127; Clines, *Story*, p. 244; Fox, *Character*, pp. 169-70.

This portion of the story is contained in 1.9–2.4. For ease of reference, a parallel presentation of the three texts and translations will first be provided, following the same format as that used throughout the previous chapter. However, as detailed notes on the text are not essential for this secondary analysis, they will not be included. To simplify the comparison, the translations and comments will not reflect the variations in the name of the first queen: Ουαστιν in the A text, Αστιν in the B text, and ושתי in the M text. She will be called 'Vashti' throughout.

Text

καὶ Ουαστιν ἡ βασίλισσα ἐποίησε δοχὴν μεγάλην πάσαις ταῖς γυναιξὶν ἐν τῇ αὐτῇ τοῦ βασιλέως·	καὶ Αστιν ἡ βασίλισσα ἐποίησεν πότον ταῖς γυναιξὶν ἐν τοῖς βασιλείοις ὅπου ὁ βασιλεὺς Ἀρταξέρξης·	גם ושתי המלכה עשתה משתה נשים בית המלכות אשר למלך אחשורוש	9

| And Vashti the queen gave a large banquet for all the women in the court of the king. | And Vashti the queen gave a drinking-party for the women in the palace where the King Artaxerxes was. | Also, Vashti the queen gave a drinking-party for the women of the house of the kingdom which was of King Ahasuerus. | |

ἐγένετο δὲ τῇ ἡμέρᾳ τῇ ἑβδόμῃ ἐν τῷ εὐφρανθῆναι τὸν βασιλέα ἐν τῷ οἴνῳ εἶπεν ὁ βασιλεὺς τοῖς παισὶν αὐτοῦ	ἐν δὲ τῇ ἡμέρᾳ τῇ ἑβδόμῃ ἡδέως γενόμενος ὁ βασιλεὺς εἶπεν τῷ Αμαν καὶ βαζαν καὶ θαρρα καὶ βωραζη καὶ Ζαθολθα καὶ Αβαταζα καὶ θαραβα, τοῖς ἑπτα εὐνούχοις τοῖς διακόνοις τοῦ βασιλέως Ἀρταξέρξου,	ביום השברעי כטוב לב־המלך ביין אמר למהומן בזתא חרבונא בגתא ואבנתא זתר וכרכס שבעת הסריסים המשרתים את־ פני המלך אחשורוש	10

| And it came to the seventh day, when the king was gladdened with wine, the king said to his servants | And on the seventh day, the king, when feeling pleasant, said to Haman and Bazan and Tharra and Boraze and Zantholtha and Abataza and Theraba, the seven eunuchs who served King Artaxerxes, | On the seventh day, when the heart of the king was pleasant with wine, he said to Mehuman, Biztha, Harbona, Bigtha, and Abagtha, Zethar, and Carkas, the seven eunuchs who served before King Ahasuerus, | |

ἀγαγεῖν Ουαστιν τὴν βασίλισσαν εἰς τὸ συνεστηκὸς συμπόσιον ἐν τῷ διαδήματι τῆς βασιλείας αὐτῆς κατὰ πρόσωπον τῆς στρατιᾶς αὐτοῦ.	εἰσαγαγεῖν τὴν βασίλισσαν πρὸς αὐτὸν βασιλεύειν αὐτὴν καὶ περιθεῖναι αὐτῇ τὸ διάδημα καὶ δεῖξαι αὐτὴν τοῖς ἄρχουσιν καὶ τοῖς ἔθνεσιν τὸ κάλλος αὐτῆς, ὅτι καλὴ ἦν.	להביא את־ושתי המלכה לפני המלך בכתר מלכות להראות העמים והשרים את־יפיה כי־טובת מראה היא	11

to lead Vashti the queen into the drinking-together in the diadem of her royalty, before his army.	to lead in the queen to him, to make her queen and to place upon her the diadem, and to have her show her beauty to the leaders and to the people, for she was beautiful.	to bring in Vashti the queen before the king, in the crown of royalty, to show the people and the leaders her beauty, for she was pleasant to see.

καὶ οὐκ ἠθέλησεν
Ουαστιν ποιῆσαι τὸ
θέλημα τοῦ βασιλέως
διὰ χειρὸς τῶν
εὐνούχων. ὡς δὲ
ἤκουσεν ὁ βασιλεὺς ὅτι
ἠκύρωσεν Ουαστιν τὴν
βουλὴν αὐτοῦ, ἐλυπήθη
σφόδρα, καὶ ὀργὴ
ἐξεκαύθη ἐν αὐτῷ.

καὶ οὐκ εἰσήκουσεν
αὐτοῦ Αστιν ἡ
βασίλισσα ἐλθεῖν μετὰ
τῶν εὐνούχων. καὶ
ἐλυπήθη ὁ βασιλεὺς καὶ
ὠργίσθη

ותמאן המלכה ושתי לבוא בדבר המלך
אשר ביד הסריסים ויקצף המלך מאד
וחמתו בערה בו

12

But Vashti did not wish to do the desire of the king through the hand of the eunuchs. And when the king heard that Vashti had refused his degree, he was made extremely distressed and anger burned within him.	But Vashti the queen did not listen to him, to come with the eunuchs. And the king was made distressed and angry.	But Queen Vashti refused to come at the word of the king which was by the hand of the eunuchs. And the king was extremely enraged and his anger burned within him.

καὶ εἶπεν ὁ βασιλεὺς
πᾶσι τοῖς σοφοῖς τοῖς
εἰδόσι νόμον καὶ κρίσιν
τί ποιῆσαι τῇ βασιλίσσῃ
περὶ τοῦ μὴ τεθεληκέναι
αὐτὴν ποιῆσαι τὸ
θέλημα τοῦ βασιλέως.

καὶ εἶπεν τοῖς φίλοις
αὐτοῦ Κατὰ ταῦτα
ἐλάλησεν Αστιν,
ποιήσατε οὖν περὶ τούτου
νόμον καὶ κρίσιν.

ויאמר המלך לחכמים ידעי העתים כי־
כן דבר המלך לפני כל־ידעי דת ודין

13

And the king said to all the wise persons who knew law and judgment, 'What is to be done to the queen concerning her refusing to do the desire of the king?'	And he said to his friends, 'This is how Vashti spoke. Therefore, present law and judgment concerning this matter.'	And the king spoke to the wise persons who knew the times, for this was the manner of the king towards all who knew law and judgment.

καὶ προσῆλθον πρὸς
αὐτὸν οἱ ἄρχοντες
Περσῶν καὶ Μήδων καὶ
οἱ ὁρῶντες τὸ πρόσωπον
τοῦ βασιλέως καὶ οἱ
καθήμενοι ἐν τοῖς
βασιλείοις·

καὶ προσῆλθεν αὐτῷ
Αρκεσαῖος καὶ
Σαρσαθαῖος καὶ
Μαλησεαρ οἱ ἄρχοντες
Περσῶν καὶ Μήδων οἱ
ἐγγὺς τοῦ βασιλέως, οἱ
πρῶτοι παρακαθήμενοι
τῷ βασιλεῖ,

והקרב אליו כרשנא שתר אדמתא תרשיש
מרס מרסנא ממוכן שבעת שרי פרס
ומדי ראי פני המלך הישבים ראשנה
במלכות

14

And the leaders of the Persians and the Medes, and who saw the face of the king and who were officials in the palace, came in to him.

And Arkesaeus and Sarsatheus and Malesear, who were leaders of the Persians and the Medes, who were close to the king, who were first in sitting beside the king, came in to him.

And those next to him were Carshena, Shethar, Admatha, Tarshish, Meres, Marsena, Memucan, the seven leaders of Persia and Media, who saw the face of the king and who sat first in the kingdom.

καὶ ἀπήγγειλαν αὐτῷ
κατὰ τοὺς νόμους ὡς δεῖ
ποιῆσαι Αστιν τῇ
βασιλίσσῃ, ὅτι οὐκ
ἐποίησεν τὰ ὑπὸ τοῦ
βασιλέως προσταχθέντα
διὰ τῶν εὐνούχων.

כדת מה־לעשות במלכה ושתי על אשר   15
לא־עשתה את־מאמר המלך אחשורוש
ביד הסריסים

And they reported to him regarding the law, which must be done to Vashti the queen, that she did not do that order by the king through the eunuchs.

'According to decree, what is to be done to Queen Vashti because she did not do the command of King Ahasuerus, through the hand of the eunuchs?'

καὶ παρεκάλεσεν αὐτὸν
βουγαῖος λέγων Οὐ τὸν
βασιλέα μόνον ἠδίκηκεν
Ουαστιν ἡ βασίλισσα,
ἀλλὰ καὶ τοὺς ἄρχοντας
Περσῶν καὶ Μήδων· καὶ
εἰς πάντας τοὺς λαοὺς ἡ
ἀδικία αὐτῆς ἐξῆλθεν,
ὅτι ἠκύρωσε τὸ
πρόσταγμα τοῦ
βασιλέως.

καὶ εἶπεν ὁ Μουχαῖος
πρὸς τὸν βασιλέα καὶ
τοὺς ἄρχοντας Οὐ τὸν
βασιλέα μόνον ἠδίκησεν
Αστιν ἡ βασίλισσα,
ἀλλὰ καὶ πάντας τοὺς
ἄρχοντας καὶ τοὺς
ἡγουμένους τοῦ
βασιλέως

ויאמר מומכן לפני המלך והשרים לא   16
על־המלך לבדו עותה ושתי המלכה
כי על־כל־השרים ועל־כל־העמים אשר
בכל־מדינות המלך אחשורוש

And Bougaios called upon him, saying, 'Not the king alone has Vashti the queen wronged, but also the leaders of the Persians and the Medes. And her wrongdoing has gone out to all the people, that she refused the order of the king.

And Muchaeus said to the king and the leaders, 'Not the king alone has Vashti the queen wronged, but also all the leaders and the officials of the king.'

And Memucan said before the king and the leaders, 'Not to the king alone has Vashti the queen acted subversively, but to all the leaders and to all the peoples who are in all the provinces of King Ahasuerus.

(καὶ γὰρ διηγήσατο
αὐτοῖς τὰ ῥήματα τῆς
βασιλίσσης, καὶ ὡς
ἀντεῖπεν τῷ βασιλεῖ).
ὡς οὖν ἀντεῖπεν τῷ
βασιλεῖ Ἀρταξέρξῃ,

כי־יצא דבר־המלכה על־כל־הנשים   17
להבזות בעליהן בעיניהן באמרם המלך
אחשורוש אמר להביא את־ושתי המלכה
לפניו ולא־באה

(For he had reported to them the speech of the queen and how she spoke against the king.) 'Therefore, as she spoke against King Artaxerxes,

For the deed of the queen will be known to all the women, to disdain in their eyes their husbands, while they say, 'King Ahasuerus said to bring Vashti the queen before him, but she did not come.'

οὕτως σήμερον αἱ τυραννίδες αἱ λοιπαὶ τῶν ἀρχόντων Περσῶν καὶ Μήδων ἀκούσασαι τὰ τῷ βασιλεῖ λεχθέντα ὑπ' αὐτῆς τολμήσουσιν ὁμοίως ἀτιμάσαι τοὺς ἄνδρας αὐτῶν.

18 וְהַיּוֹם הַזֶּה תֹּאמַרְנָה שָׂרוֹת פָּרַס־וּמָדַי
אֲשֶׁר שָׁמְעוּ אֶת־דְּבַר הַמַּלְכָּה לְכֹל שָׂרֵי
הַמֶּלֶךְ וּכְדַי בִּזָּיוֹן וָקָצֶף

so today the rest of the households of the leaders of the Persians and the Medes, when hearing that which was said to the king by her, will similarly dare to dishonor their husbands.

And this day the leading women of Persia and Media who have heard the message of the queen to all the king's leaders will speak, and there will be abundance of contempt and wrath.

εἰ δοκεῖ οὖν τῷ κυρίῳ ἡμῶν καὶ ἀρεστὸν τῷ φρονήματι αὐτοῦ, γραφήτω εἰς πάσας τὰς χώρας καὶ πρὸς πάντα τὰ ἔθνη, καὶ γνωσθήτω ἠθετηκυῖα τὸν λόγον τοῦ βασιλέως Ουαστιν· ἡ δὲ βασιλεία δοθήτω ἄλλῃ, κρείττονι οὔσῃ αὐτῆς,

εἰ οὖν δοκεῖ τῷ βασιλεῖ, προσταξάτω βασιλικόν, καὶ γραφήτω κατὰ τοὺς νόμους Μήδων καὶ Περσῶν, καὶ μὴ ἄλλως χρησάσθω, μηδὲ εἰσελθάτω ἔτι ἡ βασίλισσα πρὸς αὐτόν, καὶ τὴν βασιλείαν αὐτῆς δότω ὁ βασιλεὺς γυναικὶ κρείττονι αὐτῆς·

19 אִם־עַל־הַמֶּלֶךְ טוֹב יֵצֵא דְבַר־מַלְכוּת
מִלְּפָנָיו וְיִכָּתֵב בְּדָתֵי פָרַס־וּמָדַי וְלֹא
יַעֲבוֹר אֲשֶׁר לֹא־תָבוֹא וַשְׁתִּי לִפְנֵי הַמֶּלֶךְ
אֲחַשְׁוֵרוֹשׁ וּמַלְכוּתָהּ יִתֵּן הַמֶּלֶךְ לִרְעוּתָהּ
הַטּוֹבָה מִמֶּנָּה

Therefore, if it seems good to our lord and is pleasing to his mind, have it written to all regions and to every nation, and have it be known that Vashti has rejected the word of the king. And have the royal position be given to another who is superior to her,

Therefore, if it seems good to the king, have him issue royal command, and have it be written according to the laws of the Medes and Persians, so it may not be used otherwise, that the queen will no longer come in to him. And the king must give her royal position to a woman who is superior to her.

If it is good to the king, a royal word will go out from him and it will be written among the decrees of the Persians and the Medes, and it will not be transgressed, that Vashti will not come before King Ahasuerus. And the king will give her royal position to another better than she.

20

καὶ φαινέσθω
ὑπακούουσα τῆς φωνῆς
τοῦ βασιλέως καὶ
ποιήσει ἀγαθὸν πάσαις
ταῖς βασιλείαις· καὶ
πᾶσαι αἱ γυναῖκες
δώσουσι τιμὴν καὶ δόξαν
τοῖς ἀνδράσιν αὐτῶν
ἀπὸ πτωχῶν ἕως
πλουσίων·

καὶ ἀκουσθήτω ὁ νόμος ὁ
ὑπὸ τοῦ βασιλέως, ὃν
ἐὰν ποιῇ ἐν τῇ βασιλείᾳ
αὐτοῦ· καὶ οὕτως τᾶσαι
αἱ γυναῖκες
περιθήσουσιν τιμὴν τοῖς
ἀνδράσιν ἑαυτῶν ἀπὸ
πτωχοῦ ἕως πλουσίου.

ונשמע פתגם המלך אשר־יעשה בכל־
מלכותו כי רבה היא וכל־הנשים יתנו
יקר לבעליהן למגדול ועד־קטן

and let her be shown to listen to the voice of the king. And she will do good to all kingdoms. And all women will give honor and glory to their husbands, from poor to wealthy.'

And may the law, which is from the king, be heard— whatever is to be done in his kingdom. And thus all women will bestow honor upon their own husbands, from poor to wealthy.'

And the decree which the king made will be heard in all his kingdom (for it is large). And all the women will give honor to their husbands, from great to small.'

21

καὶ ἀγαθὸς ὁ λόγος ἐν
καρδίᾳ τοῦ βασιλέως,
καὶ ἐποίησεν ἑτοίμως
κατὰ τὸν λόγον τοῦτον.

καὶ ἤρεσεν ὁ λόγος τῷ
βασιλεῖ καὶ τοῖς
ἄρχουσιν, καὶ ἐποίησεν ὁ
βασιλεὺς καθὰ
ἐλάλησεν ὁ Μουχαῖος·

וייטב הדבר בעיני המלך והשרים ויעש
המלך כדבר ממוכן

And the message was good in the heart of the king, and he readily did according to this word.

And the message pleased the king and the leaders, and the king did just as Muchaeas had spoken.

And the message was good in the eyes of the king and the leaders, and the king did according to the word of Memucan.

22

καὶ ἀπέστειλεν εἰς
πᾶσαν τὴν βασιλείαν
κατὰ χώραν κατὰ τὴν
λέξιν αὐτῶν ὥστε εἶναι
φόβον αὐτοῖς ἐν ταῖς
οἰκίαις αὐτῶν.

וישלח ספרים אל־כל־מדינות המלך אל־
מדינה ומדינה ככתבה ואל־עם ועם
כלשונו להיות כל־איש שרר בביתו ומדבר
כלשון עמו

And he sent forth to all the kingdom, throughout regions according to their own language, so that respect would be given to them in their households.

And he sent out documents to all the provinces of the king, to province by province according to its script, and to people by people according to its language, so that each man would be the leader in his household and speak according to the language of his people.

1

Καὶ οὕτως ἔστη τοῦ
μνημονεύειν τῆς Ουαστιν
καὶ ὧν ἐποίσεν
Ασσυήρῳ τῷ βασιλεῖ.

Καὶ μετὰ τοὺς λόγους
τούτους ἐκόπασεν ὁ
βασιλεὺς τοῦ θυμοῦ καὶ
οὐκέτι ἐμνήσθη τῆς
Αστιν μνημονεύων οἷα
ἐλάλησεν καὶ ὡς
κατέκρινεν αὐτήν.

אחר הדברים האלה כשך חמת המלך
אחשורוש זכר את־ושתי ואת אשר־עשתה
ואת אשר־נגזר עליה

And thus he established remembrance of Vashti and what she had done to Ahasuerus the king.

And after these words, the anger of the king declined and he no longer remembered Vashti, recalling what she had said or how he judged against her.

After these matters, when the anger of King Ahasuerus declined, he remembered Vashti and what she had done, and what had been decreed against her.

καὶ εἶπον οἱ λειτουργοὶ τοῦ βασιλέως Ζητήσωμεν παρθένους καλὰς τῷ εἴδει,

καὶ εἶπαν οἱ διάκονοι τοῦ βασιλέως Ζητηθήτω τῷ βασιλεῖ κοράσια ἄφθορα καλὰ εἴδει·

ויאמרו נערי־המלך משרתיו יבקשו למלך נערות בתולות טובות מראה   2

And the servants of the king said, 'Let us seek out beautiful young women,

And the servants of the king said, 'Let virtuous, beautiful girls be sought out for the king.

And the servants of the king who ministered to him said, 'Let them seek for the king young virgins who are beautiful to see.

καὶ δοθήτωσαν προστατεῖσθαι ὑπὸ χεῖρα Γωγαίου τοῦ εὐνούχου τοῦ φύλακος τῶν γυναικῶν·

καὶ καταστήσει ὁ βασιλεὺς κωμάρχας ἐν πάσαις ταῖς χώραις τῆς βασιλείας αὐτοῦ, καὶ ἐπιλεξάτωσαν κοράσια παρθενικὰ καλὰ τῷ εἴδει εἰς Σουταν τὴν πόλιν εἰς τὸν γυναικῶνα, καὶ παραδοθήτωσαν τῷ εὐνούχῳ τοῦ βασιλέως τῷ φυλακιτῶν γυναι κῶν, καὶ δοθήτω σμῆγμα καὶ ἡ λοιπὴ ἐπιμέλεια·

ויפקד המלך פקידים בכל־מדינות מלכותו ויקבצו את־כל־נערה־בתולה טובת מראה אל־שושן הבירה אל־בית הנשים אל־יד הגא סריס המלך שמר הנשים ונתון תמרוקיהן   3

and let them be given to be assigned under the hand of Gogaios, the eunuch who is the guardian of the women.

And let the king establish village leaders in all the regions of his kingdom, and they will choose beautiful virginal girls, to be in Susa the city, in the women's quarters. And let them be given over to the eunuch of the king who is the guardian of the women, and let ointments and additional attention be given.

And let the king appoint overseers in all the provinces of his kingdom, and they will gather all the young virgins who are beautiful to see to Susa the fortress, to the house of women, to the hand of Hegai, the eunuch of the king, who is guardian of the women. And let their ointments be given.

καὶ ἡ παῖς, ἣ ἐὰν ἀρέσῃ τῷ βασιλεῖ, κατασταθήσεται ἀντὶ Ουαστιν. καὶ ἐποίησαν ἑτοίμως κατὰ ταῦτα.

καὶ ἡ γυνή, ἣ ἂν ἀρέσῃ τῷ βασιλεῖ, βασιλεύσει ἀντὶ Αστιν. καὶ ἤρεσεν τῷ βασιλεῖ τὸ πρᾶγμα, καὶ ἐποίησεν οὕτως.

והנערה אשר תיטב בעיני המלך תמלך תחת ושתי וייטב הדבר בעיני המלך ויעש כן   4

And let the child, whoever pleases the king, be established instead of Vashti.' And they readily did accordingly.	And let the woman, the one who pleases the king, be made queen instead of Vashti.' This matter pleased the king, and he did so.	And let the young woman who is good in the eyes of the king rule in place of Vashti.' And the word was good in the eyes of the king, and he did thus.

A Text

In the A text Vashti is not described as beautiful. There is only one reason for her coming to Ahasuerus's party, and that is to stand before his guests in her crown, to make clear her royalty and her authoritative status within the kingdom (1.11). Her decision to come is not as much in the realm of active disobedience, nor is the king's request described as an actual command. She is merely not willing to do what he desires her to do (1.12,13). There is also not any anticipated effect that Vashti's actions will have upon the kingdom or its women. Rather, it is the positive example that the new queen will be, instead of the negative example of Vashti, which will influence the women of the kingdom to respect their own husbands (1.20). In her behavior towards her husband, the new queen is described as actively doing good for the kingdom as a whole (1.20).[1] This text also does not emphasize the physical appearance of the women to be gathered for the selection process, as it refers to their beauty only once (2.2).

In this narrative Vashti's actions are less of strict obedience or disobedience, but more within the realm of her relationship with Ahasuerus. Her error is not respecting his wishes, not doing what he desires. And here there is even less of a logical reason why she should object to his request, as he does not ask her to parade her beauty before men but just to stand in front of them as their queen. Esther, in the A text, is portrayed more as the direct opposite of Vashti in terms of interaction with others. Esther has the best relationship with Ahasuerus and interacts more with him than in the other two texts. And in contrast to Vashti, she instead shows respect to him and to his desires. Esther has noted how Vashti has treated the king and decides to treat him

---

1.   In the context of this verse, 1.20, the one who does good to all kingdoms can be either the new queen or Ahasuerus. The verb form ποιήσει will allow for either the masculine or the feminine to stand as its subject. In contrast to Clines's understanding (*Story*, p. 221), it seems that this action most logically refers to the new queen, who has been described in the clause immediately preceding this one and whose corollary action upon the women is described immediately afterward.

differently. Though both of the queens' physical attractiveness is de-emphasized and their respective authority is emphasized, theirs is a different type of authority. Esther's authority is not against Ahasuerus, as Vashti expresses hers, but in ruling and making policy decisions *with* him. And we see that though Vashti is not willing to do for Ahasuerus what he desires, he is later quite willing to do what Esther desires, in granting her whatever she wants.

Two qualities are stated of the new queen: that she listen or obey the voice of Ahasuerus (1.20) and that she be beautiful (2.2). Esther is indeed initially introduced as beautiful, though this trait fades in importance during the rest of the story. However, Esther is not particularly obedient or submissive to the king in this text. Esther presents surprises to the kingdom, for she does not strictly perform as the type of new queen that is anticipated. She respects the king and obeys him, actions wanted in a queen. But he respects and even obeys her just as much, which is not anticipated. Esther thus acts as the positive example that the king and his advisers request, in the area of a woman's relationship with her husband (2.20). She, though, does not serve this purpose by being strictly obedient but by providing a model, in her own relationship with Ahasuerus, of how wives and husbands can share authority and practice mutual respect. It is in this way that Esther serves to do the good for the kingdom that is desired of the new queen, but hardly in the way that the king and his advisers anticipate.

B Text

This narrative stresses the importance of Vashti's action of speech. Her speaking is itself the basis of the king's displeasure with her (1.13), and also the reason that Artaxerxes's advisers find fault with her (1.17). Vashti's decision has the least ramifications, for it affects only the officials and their wives and not all the people of the area (1.16-17). And the king wants to emphasize her royalty as well as her beauty (1.11). As in the M text, this text provides certain requirements for the women being gathered for the selection process. They must be especially beautiful, young, and passive in the hands of the servants (2.2-3). But here alone the women must also be pure and virtuous (2.2).

The characterization of Esther exhibits the greatest contrast with Vashti, and the greatest conformity with the advisers' expectations for the new queen, in the B text. Whereas Vashti's crime is particularly in her speaking, Esther is less vocal and less rhetorically inclined than in the other two texts. It is especially against Artaxerxes that Vashti is here portrayed as talking, in insulting him (1.17). But Esther instead speaks to praise and honor Artaxerxes more readily. Esther's greater obedience and passivity throughout the bulk of this narrative is opposite to its interpretation of Vashti's decision as disobedience. Furthermore, Vashti's contentious relationship with the court servants, in not doing as they direct on behalf of Artaxerxes, is countered by Esther's congenial relationship with them. The characterization of Esther is contrasted with that of Vashti, but it is especially in Vashti's actions of strength and self-assertion that they differ the most. The only area in which the two queens are similar is in their beauty. However, Esther is the type of queen that is desired to take Vashti's place. She is described as particularly beautiful in this narrative, and she exhibits the greatest level of obedience to others in general. And as the new queen is expected to be virtuous, so Esther is, in her personal religious discipline within the court. The B text's Esther gives the advisers or their king no surprises. She succeeds in the court because she plays into their vision of the ideal queen.

M Text

The only reason that Ahasuerus wants Vashti to attend his party is to display her exceptional beauty before all his officials and even all the people (1.11). That she is wearing her crown is only incidental in this narrative. This presentation of events makes Vashti a more sympathetic character, for she refuses to be part of what would more likely be a degrading display. But she is also less important in her position as queen. She is portrayed as wrong in the specific action of refusing to come to the king, not as speaking amiss or acting disobediently in general (1.12, 17). Vashti's actions here affect the kingdom to the greatest degree, especially its women. She is described as wronging the entire kingdom, its general population as well as its leaders (1.16). And complete anarchy will be the result (1.18). With regard to the type of queen who is expected to replace Vashti, she is to be beautiful, as also in the B text, and willing to be under the servants' care, as in all three texts. But this text places more emphasis upon her virginal status (2.2, 3).

This narrative itself explicitly asks the reader to consider Esther in light of Vashti's earlier actions. It is only in the M text that Esther is directly compared with Vashti, as taking her place in rulership (2.17). Its greater emphasis upon Vashti's decision not to comply with Ahasuerus's request to appear before him and the more devastating results of her decision highlight Esther's choosing to do the opposite. Esther later dares to come before Ahasuerus, though unrequested. Audience with the king is emphasized, and there are, apparently, proper times to go to him and proper times to refrain. Because of Vashti's example, Esther knows what to expect if she makes the wrong move in her own decision to make request for her people. In this text, which already portrays Esther as quite confident when approaching Ahasuerus, Esther's courage in performing such an action is emphasized even more. Furthermore, Vashti is specifically faulted for going against the laws of the kingdom (1.13, 15). Esther notes this fact and is extremely careful to speak and act according to the law of proper Persian procedure with regard to the king when she likewise decides to break a law.

In contrast to Vashti, Esther is a more balanced person. Whereas Vashti is viewed, at least by Ahasuerus, as more important for her beauty than her regal position, Esther is important in both her role of queen and for being beautiful. But Esther does not have as great an influence upon the kingdom as Vashti. Vashti, in this narrative, is feared to have the potential for affecting the people to a larger degree. Esther's realm of influence, however, is the least in this text. Esther's actions affect only the Jews of the kingdom, and the anarchy she creates, in the form of the destruction of the Jew's enemies, is considerably less than in the A text. Thus, the portrayal of the former queen highlights Esther's degree of courage and her respect for Persian regulation, but it also makes Esther's degree of overall power to influence the kingdom appear less in comparison.

Chapter 4

THE IMPLICATIONS OF THIS STUDY

This final chapter will discuss what the study of the characterizations of Esther contributes to the larger questions of Esther scholarship and biblical interpretation. Three areas in which it does so will be considered. The first section will consider how the results of this study on characterization shed new light upon the book's relationship to other literature of the time. In the second section the topic of the possible origins of the three versions will be taken up. As Dorothy has been the only scholar who has provided concrete suggestions about the provenance of the versions, it will primarily entail a response to his conclusions. The third and final section will consider the implications of this study and its methodology for more broad-ranging areas of biblical scholarship and for possibilities of further work on biblical texts.

Relationship to Contemporaneous Literature

The book of Esther has frequently been viewed in light of other biblical and non-biblical literature. Within these comparisons, the figure of Esther herself has been seen as a primary means of relationship with two types of literature in particular: Hellenistic novels and the apocryphal book of Judith. In this section, the ways in which the results of this present analysis on characterization contribute to the discussion about the comparisons with these other Greek literary works will be briefly considered.

The Ancient Greek Novel
Some scholars already find in the Hebrew M text similarities to the genre of Hellenistic novel, or 'romance', as the genre is alternately termed. Certain general elements of the story itself have been noted to

exhibit an affinity with this secular Greek genre—its structure,[1] its descriptions of luxury,[2] its comic or satiric elements,[3] and its erotic concern with the king's love life.[4] The character of Esther, as the heroine of the story, and her situation also bear various similarities. Wills has noted parallels in Esther's being subject to impersonal, controlling forces and the elicitation of an emotional response on the part of the reader because of this coercion from outside circumstances.[5] Yet reservation has been expressed, with which I agree, about classifying the Hebrew Esther story as a full-fledged example of a Greek novel or romance.[6]

Some of those working with the Esther material have found in the sections not represented by the M text a movement towards the novel genre. Fox cites Esther's extended approach before the king, in which she faints, and the progress of the Greek story as making the story more closely resemble the Greek novel,[7] and Wills sees in this material a 'second editing towards romance'.[8] However, the connections between this newer version of the Esther story and its portrayal of its heroine with the Greek novels have not yet been considered in any depth. Nor have the differing details of the A text been considered at all when drawing such parallels. It is my contention that though the Esther of the two Greek texts indeed shares many characteristics with the female protagonists of the Greek novel as these scholars have suggested, there are also significant differences in their respective portrayals of the heroine.

Ancient novel writing occurred from around 100 BCE through the late fourth century CE.[9] Five ancient Greek novels are extant in complete

---

1.   Dorothy, 'Books', pp. 418-19.

2.   Fox, *Character*, p. 145.

3.   J.M. Sasson, 'Esther', in R. Alter and F. Kermode (eds.), *The Literary Guide to the Bible* (Cambridge: Harvard University Press, 1987), p. 339.

4.   LaCoque, *Feminine Unconventional*, p. 73; Fox, *Character*, p. 145; R. Stiehl, 'Das Buch Esther', *WZKM* 53 (1965), pp. 8-9.

5.   Wills, *Jewish Court Legends*, pp. 188-91.

6.   Fox, *Character*, p. 145; Wills, *Jewish Court Legends*, p. 189 (Wills classifies the book of Esther, along with the books of Tobit, Susanna, Joseph and Aseneth, and Judith, as 'proto-romances'); Gordis, 'Religion, Wisdom, and History in the Book of Esther: A New Solution to an Ancient Crux', *JBL* 100 (1981), p. 388.

7.   Fox, *Character*, p. 272.

8.   Wills, *Jewish Court Legends*, p. 191.

9.   E.L. Bowie, 'The Greek Novel', in P.E. Easterling and B.M.W. Knox (eds.), *The Cambridge History of Classical Literature* (Cambridge: Cambridge University Press, 1985), I, pp. 683-84; B.E. Perry, *Ancient Romances: A Literary-Historical*

texts: Chariton's *Chaereas and Callirhoe*, Xenophon's *An Ephesian Tale*, Longus's *Daphnis and Chloe*, Achilles Tatius's *Leucippe and Clitophon*, and Heliodorus's *An Ethiopian Tale*. In addition to these five, numerous papyrus fragments also exist of other examples of the genre. Distribution of these works was widespread, extending throughout the entire eastern Mediterranean region. The Greek novel is often considered to be literary prose of and for the educated popular culture. It is not a genre with a rigid structure, especially in comparison with classical Greek literature, but tends to be the least confined in what types of literary elements it can include.[1] The novel often includes components of drama, epic, historiography, and rhetoric. The plots, however, are essentially similar throughout the breadth of the genre. A young couple, each from an aristocratic family, falls in love. They are separated, either through the evil intention of others or through circumstantial accidents, and endure physical and psychological hardships which test each's fidelity to the other. After travel[2] and adventure, the two lovers are reunited with each other and to their home, and live happily ever after.

The female characters of the Greek novels have not themselves been the focus of study, either from a literary standpoint as characters in the stories or for the image they present of women.[3] The recent work of Brigitte Eggers is an attempt to fill this gap.[4] She considers the women of the novels from a variety of perspectives, including the types of female characters, their roles in the plot, the social world in which they exist, and the emotions with which they are portrayed. The figure of Esther will be compared with the results of her analysis of the types and

Account of Their Origins (Berkeley: University of California Press, 1967), pp. 153-54, 348-52; R.F. Hock, 'The Greek Novel', in D.E. Aune (ed.), *Greco-Roman Literature and the New Testament: Selected Forms and Genres* (Atlanta: Scholars Press, 1988), p. 128.

1. Perry finds this freedom of form an expression of literature of an 'open society' expanding in content to include the expanding interests of cosmopolitan Hellenistic society (*Ancient Romances*, p. 29).

2. Except for the case of *Daphnis and Chloe*, which does not utilize a travelling motif.

3. J. Helms's brief discussion of Callirhoe in his work on character portrayal in Chariton's novel is an exception (*Character Portrayal in the Romance of Chariton* [The Hague: Mouton, 1966], pp. 42-65).

4. B.M. Eggers, 'Women in the Greek Novel: Constructing the Feminine' (PhD dissertation, University of California, Irvine, 1990), pp. 39-367. She likewise notes the lack of attention paid to the female characters.

the typical qualities of the main female protagonists. The earliest extant complete representative of the ancient novel is later than the time of the formation of the Esther stories (Chariton's *Chaereas and Callirhoe*, dated from the mid first century BCE to the first century CE[1]), which precludes direct dependence. Therefore, the figure of Esther will be compared to the general characteristics of the Greek heroines rather than to any one novel or heroine in particular.

Women are central characters in the Greek novel. They typically include one female protagonist, the heroine. From early on in the story it is made obvious that she is the one who will be central to the action and with whom the reader is to identify. She is young and exceptionally beautiful, so much so that she is the object of awe and admiration from all she meets. The heroine also has a high social standing. She is a Greek citizen and from a family wealthy enough to be persons of leisure. The inner lives of characters in the novels, and especially their primary female protagonists, are reported and demonstrated in great detail, a quality of their characterization which enhances their importance to the plot and helps the reader become involved in their trials and victories.

Esther, in all versions, is similar to the Greek heroine most clearly in her centrality to the story. From the beginning, when she is first identified, we know that she will become important (even if we were not reading a book bearing her name!). And we can ascertain particular aspects of her emotions, either through direct narrative statements or from her actions. The A and B texts reveal much more of Esther's inner life, which is akin to the narrative technique of the novel. In both we are told considerably more about her emotional state as well as her being more subject to her emotions' power. In all versions Esther is similarly young, virginal, and beautiful. She likewise impresses other people immediately, the servants of the court and then the king himself, though her ability to do so is not entirely based upon personal attractiveness, and certainly not to the degree of the Greek heroines. Esther, however, differs in status. Though she is Jewish, which is equivalent to being Greek, the nationality of the work's own perspective, and though she is from a well-known family, as a female orphan Esther has no social rank.

---

1. Bowie, 'Greek Novel', p. 684; Perry, *Ancient Romances*, pp. 343-44; Hock, 'Greek Novel', p. 128; T. Hägg, *Narrative Technique in Ancient Greek Romances: Studies of Chariton, Xenophon Ephesius, and Achilles Tatius* (Stockholm: Svenska Institutet, 1971), pp. 5-6. Perry and Hock date the work to the later end of this spectrum.

Her status in all versions is raised only by her marriage. But the Greek versions go on to stress her acquired exalted position as one who is excluded from the general edict calling for the death of all the Jews.

In spite of all these similarities, the story of Esther does not have a counterpart to the central characteristic of the Greek novel. What is most stressed in the novel is the romantic and erotic nature of the heroine and her relationship with men. Her love and sensuality are those emotions around which the plot turns, and all other emotions are downplayed. The heroine is employed with fostering her relationship with her intended mate and warding off the amorous attention of other men. A main concern of the Greek heroine is to maintain her virginity or marital fidelity, and it is upon this quality that her honor depends. The reader is led to admire this aspect of her character.

An equal degree of the sensual and romantic is not a part of Esther's character. Though sexuality is an aspect of her characterization in all of the three texts, in none of them is Esther's sexuality of central concern to the story. And the sexual component of their relationship is not at all developed. Indeed, in the two Greek texts Esther makes it clear how much she dislikes sexual relations with the king. Esther's relationship with the king is indeed important for the plot, but because it allows Esther to gain success, not because of interest in its erotic element.[1] The B and M texts are the versions which are closest to the sensuality of the novel in general, in that they more fully detail the women's anointing treatments with perfumes during the selection process. But with regard to an actual romantic relationship between Esther and the king, the B text possibly goes the furthest towards such a direction, in that Esther tends to base her arguments upon his liking her. Though we are given a picture of a more mutually affectionate relationship between them by the A text, the sexual element is never accentuated. And the M text stands the furthest from the Greek versions in this regard, portraying their

---

1.   It is my opinion that LaCoque has misread the petition scenes between Esther and the king, when he speaks of the 'eroticization' of the Esther story in general. The language of all of the versions is very basic and simple; the narratives reserve their sensual descriptions for the lavishness of the king's banquets and the royal clothing given to Mordecai, not for Esther, her clothing, or her personal relationship with the king (as tends to be the case in ancient Greek novels). Furthermore, the texts themselves do not at all give the impression that Esther appears before the king as 'utterly powerless', throwing herself at the feet of the powerful male ruler, who feels towards her 'a dominance that is rapelike' (*Feminine Unconventional*, p. 73).

relationship as more professional than emotional.

The women of the Greek novel have very little real power within their environments. The heroine is subject to outside forces beyond her will and her fate tends to be controlled by others' decisions. Such coercion typically involves the woman being taken from her home to all places around the Mediterranean world, moved about by the desires of men who have designs on her, and being the victim of attacks on her chastity and her life. And the heroine usually responds with helplessness and passivity. It is only in the realms of the erotic and emotional that women have power of their own, and it is primarily by exerting their sexual power that they get the ones opposing them to do what they want. In so doing, they succeed not through forthright action but through indirect and emotional tactics.

The element of travelling through foreign lands is completely alien to the Esther stories. However, in general the figure of Esther shows certain similarities to the Greek heroine. She also, especially at the beginning of the story, is taken from her home by means beyond her control, and the entire situation of the Jews under decreed destruction decided by chance is one of powerlessness against larger forces. Yet, in response, Esther begins to take the situation into her own hands, to change actively the course of those outside forces. In so doing, though she uses somewhat indirect means, her tactics are not erotic. In all three versions, but especially in the A and B texts, Esther depends upon her emotional strength, as in the novel, but she also relies upon her rhetorical ability. It is the A text which presents a view of Esther's power which is the most divergent from that of the heroine of the Greek novel. By the end of the story, she has gained the most control over her circumstances and by the least indirect or emotional means.

The heroines of the Greek novels tend to have certain types of personal relationships, but to lack others. The female protagonist often lives a life isolated from any intimate contact except that of her beloved. She has no female or male friends and relies heavily upon female servants, who also sometimes act as confidantes. Family relationships and background are not of great importance. And the father is the dominant parent, with the mother being either dead or for some reason absent during the time of the story. The heroine is generally submissive and obedient to her parent/father, though she occasionally disagrees. And foreigners (i.e. non-Greeks) are often viewed negatively in the Greek novel.

It is in the two Greek texts of Esther that her personal circumstances correspond most strongly to these characteristics. In them, Esther both experiences isolation in the court and depends upon female servants for physical support (in both, but more pronounced in the B text) and emotional comfort (in the A text). In the B text Esther is closest to the Greek heroine in these qualities, for her loneliness is most extreme and she is in more frequent contact with her female attendants.[1] In all of the Esther stories she similarly has a father figure in Mordecai, but she lacks a mother. The M text is especially similar, for Esther is actually named as Mordecai's daughter and the death of her mother is explicitly recorded. However, foreigners are also viewed more negatively in the A and B texts during Esther's prayer, though overall the A and M texts are not as condemning. And in all the Esther stories, Esther perceives the Persians negatively not because they are not Jewish but because of what they have specifically done to harm the Jews.

Other general qualities of the Greek novel are pertinent for comparison with the Esther stories. The heroine is educated; she can read and write; and she is familiar with classical literature. She has no public occupation or profession and is involved only within the private sphere. However, even within the domestic arena, the heroine does not have her own tasks. This sphere is also dominated by men. She is also religious, praying to deities and a recipient of their interaction with her situation.

In every version Esther is similarly intelligent and educated. In the A text we know that she can read; in the B and M texts that she can write; and in the A and B texts she also appears to have been educated in the equivalent Jewish classical literature, the Torah. And in the two Greek versions, of course, she is explicitly dependent upon the intervention of the deity. At first, Esther is also not powerful in the private sphere of the court and is under the domination of men (the eunuchs), though the A text de-emphasizes her subjugation. It is, however, in the B text that Esther most explicitly transcends this situation of powerlessness in the private sphere, having more contact with servants and more responsibility over them and other parts of the domestic environment. Yet all three Esthers vary from the Greek heroine's lack of profession and influence in the public realm. Her position of queen and her ability to

---

1. And the B text more frequently uses the particular terminology (ἄβρα) that is typically found in the Greek novels (Eggers, *Women*, p. 98), in 2.9, 4.4, 4.16, and 15.2 (versus just 15.2 in the A text).

affect public decision are the details upon which resolution of the plot hangs.

To conclude, there are indeed certain similarities which the story of Esther shares with the Greek novel, as the various scholars have suggested. All three versions focus upon one woman who is young, attractive, and the victim of forces beyond her control from which she must extricate herself. And the two Greek versions go further towards presenting Esther with certain characteristics which resemble the Greek heroine. Both portray Esther's emotional life with greater detail, show her as reliant upon female servants but still feeling isolated and alone, and include recognition of a divine element in Esther's character and in her success.

Yet there is not enough direct correspondence to hypothesize that the redaction of the Esther story in either the M text or in one or the other of the Greek versions is an explicit reworking towards the Greek novel genre. The two aspects which are the primary focuses of interest in the ancient novels, the erotic/romantic relationship and the adventure motif, are almost completely absent in all three of the Esther stories. If it had been the purpose to rework one of the narratives closer to the Greek novel, or even if it was an unintentional reflection of the Greek popular literature of the time, the sexual aspect of Esther and her relationship with the king could easily have been amplified at numerous points within the existing plot line. And though the Greek versions show a greater similarity to the novel with respect to certain qualities in their female protagonists, the resemblance is not great enough or comprehensive enough to suggest dependency upon the Greek novel genre for their added details. The A text moves even further away from the Greek heroine, decreasing the importance of sexuality in Esther's relationship with the king and increasing her degree of power in the outside world.

The best conclusion with regard to a connection with the ancient novel genre is that the Esther story, and the traditions of its revision into the three texts we now have, are part of a general trend during the Hellenistic period to highlight female characters in literature. Women are made central to plot development, given more independence, and characterized with greater detail of inner life. By these means they become a focus for reader interest. The Greek novel, likewise, can be seen as part of this general trend, as are other Jewish stories of the time (for example, the stories of Judith and Susanna) and reworkings of biblical stories which expand the roles of female characters (for example, *Joseph and Aseneth*, the *Testament of Job*, and *Pseudo-Philo*).

The Book of Judith

The book of Esther has been compared to that of Judith in recent scholarship. Moore, Berg, LaCoque, and Gordis suggest similarities and differences between the two works in their discussions on the book of Esther,[1] as does Zeitlin in a commentary on the book of Judith.[2] All of these persons, excepting Gordis, consider the degree of similarity between the characterizations of Esther and Judith as well as the characteristics of the books which bear their names. Though there is not general agreement on this point,[3] I find these two heroines more alike than different. The similarities between them are striking and worthy of more detailed consideration. Both of these two women act in a situation of mortal danger to the Jews, perform with cleverness and courage in spite of risk to their own lives, and succeed almost singlehandedly in making a way for Jewish salvation and military victory. The results of this study on the characterization of Esther permit Judith to be compared to the multiple Esthers in the two Greek versions as well as the M text. Doing so allows us to see more points of agreement between the Esther of the B text and Judith,[4] and even greater similarities between the Esther of the A text and Judith.

The following are details of characters and action that are shared by Esther in the M text and Judith. They also, for the most part, reflect the ways in which the character of Esther in general (that is, Esther as she is portrayed in all three versions) is similar to the figure of Judith.[5]

---

1. Moore, *Additions*, pp. 220-22; LaCoque, *Feminine Unconventional*, pp. 71-74; Gordis, 'Religion', p. 388; S.B. Berg, *The Book of Esther: Motifs, Themes, and Structure* (Missoula, MT: Scholars Press, 1979), pp. 149-50.

2. Zeitlin, 'Esther and Judith', pp. 1-24.

3. Zeitlin, and also Berg, if I understand her correctly, on the whole find greater contrast in message and character between the two books than agreement.

4. An observation also, more generally, expressed by Moore and LaCoque. None of the recent studies of the A text have considered it in light of the story of Judith.

5. Numbers 1, 2, and 11 are also noted by LaCoque; 1, 2, 3, 7, and 8 are noted by Berg; and 1 and 3 are noted by Zeitlin.

1. Plot: women who interact with a powerful Gentile man to save Jews from destruction
2. Have low status in Jewish society
3. Possess beauty
4. Immediately win the favor of those with whom they come into contact
5. Do not rely upon leaders' advice but devise their own plan of action
6. Are not totally honest in dealings with king/general
7. Use rhetorical arguments to convince; display intelligence
8. Use their sexual desirability
9. Carry out strategy at banquets, with food and drink
10. Fast
11. Show greater practical insight into political situation and appropriate response than male characters
12. Actions are remembered throughout future generations

The B text goes even further in portraying Esther in similarity to Judith. All of these additional points of agreement between the heroines are in the extended material of the Greek texts but not in the M text. In addition to the details noted above, Esther and Judith share these features:[1]

1. Change into glorious attire for audience with king/general
2. Feel alone and/or without anyone else upon whom to depend, and express this situation in prayer
3. Depend upon God for success of actions
4. Are recipients of encouragement and assurance from king/general that they will not be harmed with other Jews
5. God influences their speech to king/general
6. Change into humble attire for prayer
7. Obey dietary laws and refuse to eat with Gentiles in court
8. Are reliant upon accompaniment of female servant(s) in carrying out plan
9. Pray before undertaking mission

---

1. Numbers 1, 2, 7, 8, and 11 are also noted by LaCoque. Numbers 4, 7, and 9 are noted (apparently) by Moore, who only rehearses points of the plot of the book of Judith, without discussing his reasoning for highlighting these portions. The correspondence is not always clear.

10. Express theological understanding about God and Israel's religious traditions
11. Appear especially beautiful immediately before approaching king/general
12. Flatter and/or honor king/general

The first five on this list are details which are indirectly suggested in the M text, though not outrightly stated. They are made explicit by the B text.

There are still more characteristics of Esther and her actions in the A text which have counterparts with those of the figure of Judith. I find Esther and Judith to be similar in the following respects, in addition to most of those listed above:

1. Act directly, more than through intermediaries, to bring about success
2. Are personally violent and command Jews to attack
3. Command/allow Jews to take plunder
4. Important to Jewish community particularly for this action alone; do not continue to act as its leader
5. Work independently; do not share power with the counterpart male character (Mordecai/Uzziah)
6. Appear more confident than weak and fearful
7. Speech is particularly important, and rely especially upon God for correct things to say
8. Intentionally deceive king/general
9. Recline at climax scene
10. Are more constantly prayerful
11. Desire all Jews to pray for deliverance before beginning actions
12. Great emphasis upon beauty when initially introduced to reader

The first seven of these details exist in the A text's version of the extended Greek sections of the story and in the portions of its ending which vary significantly from the ending of the B and M texts.

What has become apparent in this consideration of the portrayals of Esther and Judith is that the figure of Esther appears progressively more similar to Judith as we move from the M text to the B text to the A text. Based upon the agreement in details and the places at which they are found in each of the texts, it is possible to hypothesize that the heroine of the Esther story may have been made to look more like the heroine of the Judith story during the formation processes of the three versions.

In its core tradition, the essential plot of the Esther story shares certain similarities with Judith in character and actions. If we accept the predominant redactional theories, whereby the B text is dependent upon a textual tradition much like that of the M text, with the addition of the six extended passages, it is significant that the details in the B text which more closely resemble Judith are all in these extended passages. None of the similarities of the M text were removed, but instead descriptions of Esther and details in the events of the plot which make Esther appear more like Judith were added in this revision of the story. With regard to the A text, we can accept the theory that its final two chapters were added to an earlier core tradition of the story which differed from that which formed the M text. Also, at a time after this core had been formulated, the six extended passages were added. These additional passages were dependent upon the same or a similar source used by the B text for these passages. Then it is significant that many of the details in the A text which make Esther appear even more like Judith are in this later ending and the extended passages, both of which were added secondarily. There are, though, two details of likeness in the M and B texts which are changed in the A text, a situation we would not expect if its intentions were indeed to make Esther appear more like Judith. But at both of these places in the story, the A text's differing information reflects even more two other qualities of Judith's character, namely piety, in prayer and worship, and self-assurance.[1]

Hence, it is possible that when adding the extended material, a redactor in the history of the B text created the new form of the story in a way that highlighted the similarity of its heroine with the heroine of another Jewish story of the time, the story of Judith. And in the history of the A text, (a) redactor(s) may have shaped its new ending and its added passages, and possibly even altered other details within the core of its unique version of the Esther tradition, in order to make the presentation of Esther in the new form of the story appear yet more like the heroine of the Judith story.

---

1. At 4.16 Esther commands a fast and also fasts herself in the B and M texts; in the A text she commands and herself performs a worship service and prayer. And, in general, the B text emphasizes Esther's honoring of the king; the A text does not, and hence makes Esther appear more confident. But personal and community prayer, worshipping, and self-assurance are also all hallmarks of the character of Judith.

Intention and Provenance of the Greek Texts

The primary scholars who have worked extensively with one or both of the Greek versions, in addition to the M text, do not make suggestions about the place of origin of the final forms of the texts nor the concerns to which they may have been formulated to speak. The one exception is Dorothy, whose conclusions will be treated in detail below. Clines does not address the question of the historical setting of the various redactions of the stories nor the possible reasons for the changes in each version. In addition, he declines to contemplate the intention of the Greek sections or the Masoretic tradition. His only argument is that their effect is to move the story towards a scriptural norm. And in so doing, he does not distinguish between the A and B texts.[1] Fox, in his various discussions on the ideology of the redactions, likewise addresses only the specific results of the emendations made by the redactors, not their reasons for adding and changing the story or the locale at which they might have done so.[2] Moore suggests a provenance for only the six Greek extended sections as individual compositions: an Egyptian origin for the two edicts (because of their Greek original language), and a Palestinian origin for the others.[3]

Dorothy's recent dissertation on the versions of Esther will prove important to the field of Esther studies. Dorothy analyzes the versions, with particular attention to the A and B texts,[4] according to structure and literary form, and he draws conclusions about the genres of the components and formation of the Esther story. His work, on the whole, is quite detailed and carefully done. Though his purpose in working with the versions differs from that of the present study, the fact that he also works with the texts on the final level rather than at earlier stages of the story renders it more compatible and comparative in method than previous textual studies with primarily redactional objectives. However, the results of this present analysis of characterization lead to different conclusions about the possible intentions and provenance of the two Greek versions.

1. Clines, *Story*, pp. 168-74.
2. Fox, *Redaction*, pp. 127-33; *idem*, *Character*, pp. 269-73.
3. Moore, *Additions*, pp. 14, 166-67.
4. In discussing Dorothy's work, the terminology used by the present study for the two Greek texts will be continued rather than that which he actually uses (L, o´), to avoid any more confusion than necessary.

Dorothy has determined that though the cores of the two narratives are similar, the A and B texts exhibit differences in style.[1] He argues that the style of the B text is more detailed than that of the A text in terms of individual words, phrases, and entire thoughts. The B text is also longer in the sheer number of words. These greater details make the story more reportorial, historical, philosophical, and objective in character. They also make the author/narrator[2] appear more personally detached from the actions, not seeing herself or himself as much a part of the story. In contrast, Dorothy finds the A text to be more succinct, though it does not appear to be condensing the B text. Its style is more personal, exhibits socio-political concerns for the Jews as the chosen people, and shows the emotions of the characters at crisis points in the story. The A text also has a more pronounced disdain for Gentiles. Dorothy finds behind the A text an author who feels closer to the story and is more a part of its actions.

From these distinctive literary styles of the two texts, Dorothy hypothesizes a differing authorial intention and provenance for each. The final form of each narrative shapes a common core of tradition in the direction of disparate communities. In the B text he concludes that the author feels neutral, unattached to the events which she or he relates. The author's intention is to produce a didactic, historically-oriented version of the story, with emphasis upon objectively documenting events and upon feast observance. Therefore, Dorothy argues that the B text is a telling of the Esther story intended for a Hellenized diaspora audience. He contrasts the intentions of the A text with it. Lack of storytelling detail and greater interest in the inner lives of the characters lead Dorothy to conclude that the author of the A text is a Jew who is writing to other Jews. This version was created with ethnic, communal, and homiletical intentions for its community of origin. The author of the A text did not merely translate the story, but crafted it so that its readers would admire Mordecai, Esther, and the Jews, recognize God as the controller of all history, and appreciate it as their own heritage and life. From these conclusions, Dorothy argues that the A text arose from a more orthodox, less Hellenized community, possibly even in Palestine itself.

The conclusions of this present study encourage a re-evaluation of a

---

1. The conclusions regarding these issues of style, intention, and provenance which have been summarized are found on pp. 438-50.

2. Dorothy does not appear to make a distinction between the narrator in each final text and the author(s) who formed each story to be as it now appears.

number of Dorothy's general arguments.[1] It is in the following areas in which this close comparison of the portrayal of Esther calls into question his conclusions about the Greek versions:

1. The types of unique details in each of the two texts and the effects of their differing detail
2. The B text's attitude towards the Jewish community, religious orthodoxy, and Jewish heritage
3. The reason for the A text's greater representation of the inner lives of the characters
4. The degree of Jewish identification reflected by the A text and its view of Gentiles.

This section will address these areas. My response to Dorothy's work will not be comprehensive, but it will proceed from the specific perspective of the characterization of the figure of Esther in the stories. And as Dorothy considers only the two Greek texts in his conclusions, this response will similarly concentrate upon those versions.

1. Dorothy has noted that the B text presents more detail at certain places, including details about Esther. He is correct that the style of the B text has, on the whole, a tendency to be more detailed than the A text and that it is longer. However, sometimes the A text also exhibits certain details not in the B text, which Dorothy does not mention. And we must not only note the level of detail, but what type of information is given and at what points during the story. The greater density of details about Esther in the B text as compared to the A text tends to cluster in certain parts of the narrative. Such additional details occur towards the beginning of the story when Esther is in a position of lesser authority, in the descriptions of how Esther is selected as the new queen, and in her conversation with Mordecai. They also occur towards the end of the story, in her actions of approaching the king a second time and writing a letter about Purim. We are given more information about Esther's lineage, relationship to Mordecai, disciplined lifestyle, feelings about the fate of the Jews, and commands about the community's religious actions. In general, the effect of these details is to emphasize her relationship to the Jewish community and enhance her character towards the direction of greater passivity. Certain details are provided in the A text

---

1. These arguments should be considered in addition to the particular places in the texts at which I consider Dorothy's comments on individual verses. They have been cited previously in the notes to each episode.

at different points during the events of the story. The additional details unique to the A text are distributed more evenly throughout the story. Its details have the tendency to give more information about Esther's favorability to the king, her honor and queenship, conversations with the king, and the manner by which her desires are enacted.

The unique details of the A text highlight Esther's connection to the Gentile world, particularly that of the Persian court. She works more closely with the Gentile king than with other Jews to further her purposes, has more emotional concern for him and less for the Jews, and takes on a more Persian way of doing things. And as the Persians know of Esther's differing ethnic heritage and do not reject her because of it, the unique details of the A text portray a Persian government which does not discriminate against the Jews and is tolerant of different cultural and religious practices. Esther gets along best with Gentiles in this text, and she herself appears more Persian and less Jewish. Coupled with this information is the view of Esther as less personally concerned for the Jews; she sees herself as less a part of their community. She has a more detached or factual and a less personal knowledge of God's character and actions in history.[1]

2. In general, as Dorothy states, the narrative style of the A text shows its characters' emotional responses at key points in the story more than the B text. This tendency makes the times when the B text portrays emotions to hold that much more significance. At two different points in the plot we are told of Esther's concern and worry about the fate of the Jews, feelings not represented by the A text. Other information unique to the B text moves Esther's character towards religiosity and traditional Judaism, as has been argued earlier. For instance, Esther here sees herself within the Jewish heritage, follows religious discipline in lifestyle, and looks to God as a deliverer and one who is in charge. And Esther works primarily within (with Mordecai) and for (writing about Purim) the Jewish community.

3. Dorothy argues that the A text's more precise and personal presentation of the inner emotions of the characters reflects an author who feels a part of the story, one who is Jewish and wants to make other Jews see it as their story as well. If such is indeed the intention

1. Fox likewise finds the A text to be more tolerant of Gentiles, approaching the question from the standpoint of the redactor's actions to create the final form of the text. In his view, 'the redactor makes the world of the story a less hostile place. Gentiles are not fundamentally inimical to Jews' (*Redaction*, p. 87).

behind the narrator's more personal presentation of the characters, then one would expect greater emotion to be shown only on the part of the Jewish characters, Esther and Mordecai. This enhanced picture of their inner life would presumably create greater identification with the events of the story in Jewish readers. But the A text exhibits greater detail about the inner lives of *all* the characters, Gentile (Ahasuerus, Haman) as well as Jew. This characteristic makes it more likely that the narrative's greater closeness to the characters merely reflects the author's differing literary style in comparison to the B text. Thus, the author's increased attention to the inner life of the characters cannot be used to hypothesize that person's social location or intentions as readily as Dorothy suggests.

4. In further argumentation, Dorothy lists several ways in which he finds that the A text demonstrates increased Jewishness and lack of Hellenization.[1] But here his reasoning is inaccurate or incomplete.[2] The evidence he offers can be just as easily interpreted the opposite way,[3] or is simply not very compelling.[4] In particular, it is far-fetched to draw the

---

1. 'Books', pp. 448-49. The following number references reflect his numbered list on these pages.

2. Dorothy cites the A text's specifics of boundaries (his reason number 4), and the B text's purification rites and cutting of hair (number 6) and Mordecai's raising Esther to marry her (number 8). But, at other places later in the story, the A text instead gives *less* specific geographical distinctions. Furthermore, it is unlikely that a traditional Jew would see the B text's purification in a Persian court of women, with its secular intentions and very different setting, as similar to Jewish legal requirements. And the B text does not state at all that Esther cuts her hair, and, though mentioning it, does not in any way develop the idea that Esther is to be Mordecai's wife. Moreover, Dorothy's linkage of these actions to orthodox Jewish practices is unsubstantiated.

3. To support arguments for its Jewishness, Dorothy notes the Greek (rather than Jewish) names given for the court guards (number 3) and the lack of mention of Mordecai's Jerusalem origins (number 11) in the A text, and to support its hypothesized Hellenistic character, he notes the overnight hanging of Haman's body in the B text (number 7). However, Jewish readers would likely not object to Jews as guards for the Persian court any more than they would object to Esther and Mordecai's much higher positions in the court. And if the A text were the product of a traditional and orthodox Jewish community, as Dorothy maintains, it would be expected that Mordecai's Jerusalem origins would be emphasized, not ignored, to make him seem more pious, orthodox, and mainstream. The defilement of Haman's body (as assessed according to Jewish regulations) would serve to show greater antipathy towards this enemy, and thus reflect a more self-identified Jewish perspective.

4. Dorothy lists the A text's use of first person at one point in the dream (number 1) and terminology for menstrual cloth (number 6). But other possible

conclusions from the A text which he does regarding Esther's being proud of her heritage. He finds Esther's not concealing her nationality from the Persian court to be a demonstration of her pride in her Jewishness. But Esther's Jewishness when entering the court is simply not mentioned at all. It is not an issue for the author of the A text. Instead, the B text, which tells us not once but twice how Esther conceals her identity, presents an Esther who appears much more Jewish and expresses pride in it. Also with regard to Esther, the A text does not make the repeated reference to the covenant and inheritance that Dorothy states. She notes her connection with Abraham and Israel in her prayer not in the A text but in the B text. Therefore, on the whole, there remains little reason to see a tendency towards a greater Jewish perspective in the A text's telling of the story.

This present study has focused upon only one aspect of the Esther stories, that of the portrayal of Esther. For this reason, it is not appropriate to make definitive arguments about the provenance, date, or intentions lying behind these texts. There is simply too much of the story which was not analyzed in detail. Yet we can make some tentative suggestions.[1]

The A text presents Esther as the least traditionally Jewish and having less concern for the Jews. It sees Israel's traditions and history, as expressed by Esther, from a more detached and less personal perspective. Esther here appears to have integrated her Jewish and Persian identities, and the relationship of Jews with Gentiles, especially Persians, is positive. The character of Esther exhibits a type of Jewishness which works with the policies and rulers of other nationalities rather than striving to oppose them. A provisional consideration of the character of Mordecai in this text, as one who has more political power in the Persian government and is respected by its authorities, leads to similar conclusions about Jewish–Persian relations. The A text is possibly the product of a Jewish community within the diaspora setting which is more integrated with non-Jews and more Hellenized in thought and behavior. A concern of those who shaped the Esther tradition in such a way may have been to provide a model of how Jews might successfully live with others. Moreover, the A text may reflect the intention to prove that Jewish

explanations have already been given for the narrator's lack of distance from the story and for Esther's choice of terminology.

1. It might be noted that my suggestions (which are admittedly based particularly upon the portrayal of Esther) about the intentions and provenance of these two Greek texts differ from Dorothy's overall conclusions.

individuals, even women, might come to have great authority and respect in other governments and have control even over non-Jews as well as Jews.

In contrast, the B text characterizes Esther as having greater affinity with the religious community. She is concerned about religious observance and her Jewish identity is important to her. Yet Esther tends to be presented more as a traditional Jewish woman, even within the Persian court system. And a look at the character of Mordecai in the B text is similar; he appears to receive respect primarily from the Jews, and some from the Persians. The type of history this narrative promotes, through the viewpoint of Esther, is less distanced and more that of *heilsgeschichte*, of God continually working throughout time to help the Jews in an ongoing relationship. The B text may have been shaped by a Jewish community in Palestine itself or within the diaspora who maintained more traditional religious practices and views. This community may even have experienced increased tension or discrimination at the hands of non-Jews. The purpose of this version of the Esther tradition was possibly to demonstrate that working with Gentiles is a necessity, and one can even rise to high rank in so doing. Yet even when in a position of power in a foreign government, Jews should still maintain their primary allegiance to their own people.

With regard to general relationships between Persians and Jews suggested by the Esther stories, the M text travels a median route. In it, Esther has both strong connections to the Jews, particularly within the family of Mordecai, yet she is very much the queen in the Persian governmental setting. Both Jewish identity and governmental responsibility are important. In her roles of authority to both peoples, Esther appears as 'queen' to the Persians but as religious leader to the Jews. Dorothy is correct when he concludes that the M text is the most multivalent of the three versions.[1] Because of this quality, the M text could appeal to the greatest audience and could equally well be the product of a community in Palestine or throughout the diaspora. Perhaps the most that we can say is that it reflects a situation in which the Jews have a 'professional' relationship with the Persians. The Jews are cordial, work within the system, and obey the government's laws and observe its customs, but they also maintain a strong Jewish identity based upon religious observance.

---

1. Dorothy, 'Books', pp. 426-27.

The Books of Esther as Scripture: Canonical Concerns,
Multiple Literary Editions, and Feminist Hermeneutics

All biblical writings are the products of ancient communities. As simple as such a declaration may sound, it is essential to keep the personal and communal aspects in mind when dealing with biblical literature in any capacity. The texts, the final forms which we now have, did not arise of themselves. They were shaped by particular faith communities for the particular needs felt by those communities. Our biblical literature is the cumulative result of persons asking questions about identity and survival in terms of their past traditions and current situations. But these biblical works, in being given authoritative status, also include the dimensions of shaping community. As the literature ultimately developed into Scripture and canon, they were given the power to influence present and future communities.

Ideas about the formation of traditions into authoritative writings and the ways in which the writings function for ancient and modern communities may seem alien to the specific focus of this study on the characterization of Esther. Such considerations become relevant when we recall that canon was initially identified as a set of books, not a certain textual form of those books. That is, the authority of canonical status lies not in a single text (i.e. the Masoretic text), but in a book which might include a variety of textual forms. And the book of Esther is one that indeed evidences such a variety. Including thoughts about canon into Esther studies is not, by any means, to suggest that what was not considered 'canonical' by persons centuries ago is not worthy of study today. Rather, broadening our concept of what can be considered authoritative opens the possibility for the two Greek versions of the book of Esther, as well as the Masoretic version, to be used by today's faith communities.

Two proposals suggested by advocates of canonical criticism may be helpful when considering the books of Esther. The first is James A. Sanders's ideas about the adaptability, as well as the more typically emphasized stability, of the biblical canon. Sanders proposes a tension between the poles of adaptability and stability, and he suggests that we do not do justice to the process of the long and varied formation of the canon if we do not reflect both of these attributes.

The primary characteristic of canon, therefore, is its adaptability. Israel's canon was basically a story adaptable to a number of different literary forms, adaptable to the varying fortunes of the people who found their identity in it, adaptable to widely scattered communities themselves adjusting to new or strange idioms of existence but retaining a transnational identity, and adaptable to a sedentary or migratory life.

Canon, by its very nature is adaptable, not just stable. One must keep in mind all the texts and all the canons and all the communities.[1]

The second proposal is Donn E. Morgan's more particular suggestion about the formation of the Writings, of which the book of Esther is a part. He views the Writings as a whole as post-exilic responses to the Torah and the Prophets which were emerging as Scripture at the time. This dialogue between text and community reflects the cultural and religious pluralism of the diaspora communities which produced it.

What the Writings demonstrate—a dynamic interpretation of texts

within many different and diverse communities—continued. The canonization of this literature makes such diverse interpretation normative for all future biblical communities.[2]

And the resulting diversity found in the Writings, as representative of the pluralism involved in their creation, is a positive component of this part of the canon.

The first expression in what I hope will be a continuing discussion about multiple literary editions and how they should be treated was put forward recently by Eugene Ulrich. He defines them as such:

By double literary editions I mean a literary unit—a story, pericope, narrative, poem, book, and so forth—appearing in two (or more) parallel forms in our principal textual witnesses, which one author, major redactor, or major editor completed and which a subsequent redactor or editor intentionally changed to a sufficient extent that the resultant form should be called a revised edition of that text.[3]

---

1. J.A. Sanders, *From Sacred Story to Sacred Text* (Philadelphia: Fortress Press, 1987), pp. 19, 167.

2. D.F. Morgan, *Between Text and Community: The 'Writings' in Canonical Perspective* (Minneapolis: Fortress Press, 1990), pp. 3-4, and *passim.*

3. E. Ulrich, 'Double Literary Editions of Biblical Narratives and Reflections on Determining the Form to be Translated', in J.L. Crenshaw (ed.), *Perspectives on the Hebrew Bible: Essays in Honor of Walter J. Harrelson* (Macon, GA: Mercer University Press, 1988), p. 102. For the obvious reason that this study has dealt with what might be termed a 'triple literary edition', I prefer to use the term 'multiple literary

Some multiple versions encompass an entire book or story, but others only a smaller portion or a few chapters of a book. And they usually are found in variations between the Masoretic text and the Septuagint and other Greek texts. There are numerous examples of multiple literary editions within the Bible which have been recognized as such. For instance, we can note the double narrative tradition of the Hannah episode (1 Samuel 1-2), the David and Goliath story (1 Samuel 17-18), portions of Exodus, and the book of Jeremiah, and the triple versions of the book of Tobit, parts of the Daniel cycle, and, of course, the book of Esther.[1] And further consideration of the Qumran material may allow us to discern even more examples.

I would argue that multiple literary editions are concrete examples of Sanders's and Morgan's concepts. They serve as representatives of these concepts not on the scale of the canon as a whole or even the Writings portion of it, but on the smaller scale of one biblical book or even smaller sections of a book. The book of Esther, as reflected in its three versions, serves as an example as well. The very variety of the forms of the story, as well as their variant portrayals of its heroine, suggests the plurality of diaspora culture. If each of the versions of the book is indeed the product of different communities, we can see even in the books of Esther such a diversity of responses to ancient traditions in light of the practical concerns for successful diaspora living.[2] The Esther stories also display Sanders's poles of stability and adaptability within them. In one sense, the Esther tradition has remained stable. The story is recognizable as the same in all three versions. We can identify Esther from one version to the next as the same person, and the plot and other characters as constituting the same general story. Yet the significant differences among the versions, and even their presentations of Esther, demonstrate that this tradition was also considered adaptable for different situations and needs. The story has been tampered with, changed in divergent directions that we can suggest reflect different responses to questions

editions', leaving the precise number of representatives of these narratives unspecified.

1.   This is not an exhaustive list, but the primary examples of which I am presently aware.

2.   In an article more generally on individual problematic areas in the B text and M text versions of the book, W. Harrelson provides brief suggestions on how the former, as well as the latter, could be important in a diaspora community. He does not mention the A text's version of the story ('Text and Translation Problems in the Book of Esther', *Perspectives in Religious Studies* 17 (1990), pp. 204-206).

about identity and life. Not only the form but also the function of the Esther narratives were important in the formation of the book.

A few scholars have begun to consider how best to deal with multiple literary editions for faith communities today. There is a growing concern that the 'alternate' traditions of various biblical works must also be taken into consideration in biblical scholarship. In some cases, these alternate versions provide more original or otherwise preferable textual versions in relation to those represented by the Masoretic tradition. Movement has been away from considering these texts only as fuel for text critical consideration, for emendation of problematic spots in the Masoretic text, or as the consequences of careless translation. Scholarship has begun to move towards the recognition of these texts as intentional and deliberate formations of biblical traditions in divergent directions.

Ulrich and Sanders are two who have considered the general questions posed by the existence of multiple literary editions. Ulrich addresses the issue of what form of the text should be used for translations of the Bible. He suggests no universal guidelines but argues that we must systematically compare all the versions for each place at which more than one version exists. No one tradition, be it Masoretic text or Septuagint, should be given precedence over the other without careful analysis.[1] Sanders speaks of multiple literary editions within the broader context of the purpose of textual criticism in biblical studies. He argues that respect for the different versions must precede suspicion towards them. The full literary contexts of the versions must be analyzed. The texts should be treated with integrity in the forms in which they have been produced and with consideration of their mission for some ancient community before 'pillaging' them by pulling out individual readings for text critical purposes.[2]

The field is new, but already there are examples of the cautions of

1. Ulrich, 'Double Literary Editions', pp. 101-16.
2. J.A. Sanders, 'Hebrew Bible *and* Old Testament: Textual Criticism in Service of Biblical Studies', in R. Brooks and J.J. Collins (ed.), *Hebrew Bible or Old Testament? Studying the Bible in Judaism and Christianity* (Notre Dame: University of Notre Dame Press, 1990), pp. 57-65. The recent New Revised Standard Version translation is a step in Sanders's direction. The NRSV presents the entire B text (LXX) in its section of the Apocrypha, rather than the more typical presentation of just the six Additions out of their literary context. In contrast, Moore's decision to intersperse translations of the Additions of the B text into the overall framework of the M text distorts both versions and does justice to neither (Moore, *Additions*; see his argument for this procedure on p. 168).

these two scholars exemplified in recent work on multiple editions. For instance, Stanley D. Walters's work on the Hannah narratives, in his refusal to form a composite text of the two, demonstrates a treatment of both the Septuagint and the Masoretic text with integrity.[1] The dialogue of four scholars working with the David and Goliath stories provides an example of wrestling with the questions involved with multiple literary editions.[2] Manuscript evidence from Qumran and translation analysis have been used with regard to Daniel 4-6.[3]

This present study provides yet another way by which we can begin to look at multiple literary editions. It is an example of how we might indeed approach each such edition, be it an entire biblical book or only a smaller section, as a work of literature in its own right. My method has intentionally been not to supplement any of the versions with readings from one of the others, nor to remove parts of the final form to restore a more original reading. Rather, this study of the books of Esther demonstrates a hermeneutics of respect and integrity for each version of the work and a methodology which treats each holistically and structurally. I have approached the versions of the book from a differing perspective than other studies of multiple editions, that of literary rather than textual criticism. It is my hope that this analysis, with its focus upon characterization, will initiate new ways of working with such multiple editions in biblical interpretation.

One arena which has not yet been explored is the possibilities of multiple literary editions for feminist biblical interpretation. Feminist hermeneutics is a contemporary academic discipline which may be well served by the results of such study. The pluriform character of the Bible itself with regard to women's concerns has been long recognized. On the one hand, there is a diversity of biblical testimony about women. The Bible as a whole does not provide one view of 'woman' or her place in society and religious practice. The multitude of recent studies on particular biblical passages which address women and on the women presented in biblical narratives demonstrates that the Bible includes both positive and negative views of women within its texts. On the other

---

1. S.D. Walters, 'Hannah and Anna: The Greek and Hebrew Texts of 1 Samuel 1', *JBL* 107 (1988), pp. 385-412, especially pp. 408-12.

2. D. Barthélemy, D.W. Gooding, J. Lust and E. Tov, *The Story of David and Goliath: Textual and Literary Criticism* (Göttingen: Vandenhoeck and Ruprecht, 1986).

3. D.O. Wenthe, 'The Old Greek Translation of Daniel 1-6' (PhD dissertation, University of Notre Dame, 1991).

hand, the function of the Bible in contemporary communities has been similarly diverse. Its texts and their subsequent interpretation have worked both for the liberation and for the oppression of women. Hence, the biblical literature exhibits diversity in both form and function with regard to women. This multiform quality of the Bible, noted by feminist scholars, is evident also on a smaller scale within the diversity of variant versions of portions of the Bible.

Consideration of multiple literary editions has the potential to bring out of our religious tradition different views of, and different voices of, women.[1] In them, we see the self-critiquing aspect of Scripture necessary for women to find liberation from a work which is predominantly patriarchal, but on a smaller scale. To do justice to ancient texts, the community of women today needs to see a variety of perspectives on women and to hear a variety of voices, if it wishes to enable positive utilization of Scripture and find liberation in it. Study of multiple views of the same figure provides the contemporary community of women the freedom to look to other portrayals for a liberating portrait of these literary women in our religious traditions. In so doing, we do not seek to recover the lost or forgotten action of the real women who formed part of our tradition (i.e. a historical enterprise) but to recover ignored views of women in literature. The recent studies of Cheryl Anne Brown and Katheryn Pfisterer Darr are steps in the direction of such recovery. However, they have worked not with the literary women in multiple editions but in re-written Bible and midrash. Brown compares the portrayals of biblical women in Josephus's and Pseudo-Philo's re-tellings of biblical traditions,[2] and Darr outlines rabbinical understandings of biblical women as part of her work.[3]

The books of Esther exhibit two aspects important for feminist hermeneutics. First, they reflect the multivalency of our heritage. The pluralism in the books of Esther is a microcosm of the pluralism of the canon as a whole, a richness that should be celebrated.[4] We have been

---

1. For instance, Walters's delineation of the Hebrew Hannah and the Greek Anna in 1 Sam. 1–2 has, I believe, such potential to provide information useful for feminist hermeneutics, though he does not take his results in such a direction ('Hannah and Anna').

2. C.A. Brown, *No Longer Be Silent: First Century Jewish Portraits of Biblical Women* (Louisville: Westminster Press / John Knox, 1992).

3. Darr, *Far More Precious than Jewels*.

4. See Sanders's discussion on the plurality and self-corrective aspects of the

left with not one view of Esther but three. And all equally claim validity and the authority given to canon. The diversity of her characterization, as with the plurality of views presented by the Bible in general, allows us to ask new questions with regard to Esther and to utilize her as a model in different ways. With more than a single view of Esther, one understanding of her may be used to critique another. Or one Esther may prove to be a more useful portrayal of her than another for any given contemporary faith community.

Secondly, the original paradigmatic character of the story of Esther is connected to the search within feminist hermeneutics today for a liberating way to claim the Bible as authoritative. The story quite likely held a paradigmatic quality when it was formed in early communities. A purpose of the Esther stories was then to serve as a model for diaspora living, a quality which has been noted by others.[1] The figure of Esther herself functioned as an example for how the Jewish community might best act to succeed in its present situation. Morgan determines the story to be a part of the Writings which functioned as a response to other developments within post-exilic communities. He classifies the book of Esther as part of the edifying literature, a 'paradigm for faithful living'.[2] As the book of Esther, in its various forms, was re-worked, solidified in forms, and eventually considered authoritative, it also functioned in the communities that followed as paradigmatic. We continue this tradition through to present-day communities, who, viewing the books of Esther as Scripture, find in the figures of Esther models for faithful living.[3]

Elisabeth Schüssler Fiorenza has spoken of a way to view the authoritative nature of Scripture that is not dissimilar to the paradigmatic quality of the books of Esther. Because women cannot grant the Bible a type of authority that establishes universal and normative patterns (an

canon (J.A. Sanders, *Canon and Community: A Guide to Canonical Criticism* [Philadelphia: Fortress Press, 1984], pp. 46ff.).

1.   White, 'Esther', in Newsom and Ringe (eds.), *Women's Bible Commentary*; W.L. Humphreys, 'A Life-Style for Diaspora: A Study of the Tales of Esther and Daniel', *JBL* 92 (1973), pp. 211-17.

2.   Morgan, *Writings*, pp. 54, 85, and *passim*.

3.   Gendler has noted the paradigmatic power of the character of Esther within her present-day community, that of Jewish women. But because she does not find Esther to be an admirable model for contemporary women (as assessment with which I disagree), she laments the power that the figure of Esther has over young women ('Restoration', pp. 241-46).

'archetypal biblical paradigm'), she argues that we need instead to view the Bible as 'prototype'.

> Understanding the Bible as a historical prototype rather than a mythical archetype allows the church of women to make connections with our own experiences, historical struggles, and feminist options in order to create visions of the future from these interconnections ... In this process of feminist critical evaluation and assessment, the Bible no longer functions as an authoritative source but as a *resource* for women's struggle for liberation. [italics hers][1]

The character of Esther can function for women today as this type of prototype, as a Scriptural paradigm and a resource for determining how to live fruitfully in the world.

The varying characterizations of Esther are at the heart of a search for new models, for women and for all persons. In the three portrayals of Esther as in their books as whole, we find both the multivalency of our heritage and the paradigmatic quality of its literature. This present consideration of the views of Esther is part of a larger pattern of working with the biblical literature and its continuing traditions (re-written Bible, midrash, New Testament) to elucidate new views of its women. The search will lead us to other versions of literary works which particular religious communities found important enough to formulate and to preserve. It may force us to have a larger idea of what constitutes our 'canon' than the single textual form of any book. And we may need to broaden our definition of what types of literature are to be considered edifying or authoritative. Becoming more inclusive in our conceptions of Scripture will lead to liberation, the emancipation of new understandings of old stories and greater liberation for the communities today which continue to regard these stories as important for fostering their identity and life.

Sanders states:

> The western churches, Catholic and Protestant, all inherit Jerome's principle of *Hebraica Veritas* and must work with it in the best and improving text-critical mode possible. One might ask whether, as we move into the twenty-first century, those churches are not ready for a pluriformity of texts where double editions are available, even in translations.[2]

	1.	E.S. Fiorenza, *Bread Not Stone: The Challenge of Feminist Biblical Interpretation* (Boston: Beacon Press, 1984), p. 14; also pp. 1-22, which includes her discussion of these concepts.
	2.	Sanders, 'Hebrew Bible', p. 64.

To his question, I would answer a definitive Yes. But I would add that the feminist community, as well as Jewish communities and the church universal, would benefit from a re-acquaintance with all the books of Esther. We, as a community of women, or as biblical interpreters, or as readers who appreciate a good story, need to see all three Esthers.

BIBLIOGRAPHY

Ackroyd, P.R., 'Two Hebrew Notes', *ASTI* 5 (1966–67), pp. 82-86.

Adler, J.J., 'The Book of Esther: Some Questions and Reponses', *JBQ* 19 (1990–91), pp. 186-90.

Albright, W.F., 'The Lachish Cosmetic Burner and Esther 2:12', in H.N. Bream, R.D. Helm and C.A. Moore (eds.), *A Light Unto My Path: Old Testament Studies in Honor of Jacob M. Myers* (Philadelphia: Temple University Press, 1974), pp. 25-32.

Allis, O.T., 'The Reward of the King's Favorite (Esther vi.8)', *Princeton Theological Review* 21 (1923), pp. 621-32.

Alter, R., *The Art of Biblical Narrative* (New York: Basic Books, 1981).

Anderson, B.W., 'Introduction and Exegesis to Esther', in G.A. Buttrich *et al.* (eds.), *The Interpreter's Bible* (Nashville: Abingdon Press, 1954), III, pp. 823-74.

—'The Place of Esther in the Christian Bible', *Journal of Religious Studies* 30 (1950), pp. 32-43.

Anderson, G., *Ancient Fiction: The Novel in the Graeco-Roman World* (Totowa, NJ: Barnes & Noble, 1984).

—*Eros Sophistes: Ancient Novelists at Play* (American Philological Association American Classical Studies Series, 9; Chico, CA: Scholars Press, 1982).

Andrew, M.E., 'Esther, Exodus, and Peoples', *Australian Biblical Review* 23 (1975), pp. 25-28.

Bal, M., 'Lots of Writing', *Semeia* 54 (1991), pp. 77-102.

Baldi, D., and P. Lemaire, 'Esther Revised According to the Maccabees', *Liber Annuus (Studii Biblici Franciscani)* 8 (1962–63), pp. 190-218.

Baldwin, J.C., *Esther* (Tyndale Old Testament Commentaries; Leicester: Inter-Varsity, 1984).

Bankson, M.Z., *Braided Streams: Esther and a Woman's Way of Growing* (San Diego: LuraMedia, 1985).

Bar-Efrat, S., *Narrative Art in the Bible* (JSOT Supplement Series, 70; Sheffield: Almond Press, 1989).

Bardtke, H., 'Neuere Arbeiten zum Estherbuch: Eine kritische Würdigung', *Ex Oriente Lux* 19 (1965–66), pp. 519-49.

—'Zusätze zu Esther', in *Historische und legendarische Erzählungen* (Jüdische Schriften aus hellenistisch-römanischer Zeit Series 1; Gütersloh: Gütersloher Verlagshaus Gerd Mohn, 1973).

Barthélemy, D., D.W. Gooding, J. Lust, and E. Tov, *The Story of David and Goliath: Textual and Literary Criticism* (Göttingen: Vandenhoeck & Ruprecht, 1986).

Barucq, A., 'Esther et la cour de Suse', *Bible et Terre Sainte* 39 (1961), pp. 3-5.

Berg, S.B., 'After the Exile: God and History in the Books of Chronicles and Esther', in J.L. Crenshaw and S. Sandmel (eds.), *The Divine Helmsman* (New York: Ktav, 1980), pp. 107-27.

—*The Book of Esther: Motifs, Themes, and Structure* (SBL Dissertation Series, 44; Missoula, MT: Scholars Press, 1979).

Bergey, R.L, 'The Book of Esther: Its Place in the Linguistic Milieu of Post-Exilic Biblical Hebrew Prose' (PhD dissertation, Dropsie College, 1983).

—'Late Linguistic Features in Esther', *JQR* 75 (1984), pp. 66-78.

—'Post-Exilic Hebrew Linguistic Developments in Esther: A Diachronic Approach', *JETS* 31 (1988), pp. 161-68.

Berlin, A., *Poetics and Interpretation of Biblical Narrative* (Bible and Literature Series; Sheffield: Almond Press, 1983).

Besser, S.P., 'Esther and Purim—Chance and Play', *Journal of the Central Conference of American Rabbis* 16 (1969), pp. 36-42.

Bickerman, E.J., *Four Strange Books of the Bible: Jonah, Daniel, Koheleth, Esther* (New York: Schocken, 1967).

—'Notes on the Greek Book of Esther', *PAAJR* 20 (1950), pp. 101-33.

—'The Colophon of the Greek Book of Esther', *JBL* 63 (1944), pp. 339-62.

Booth, W.C., *The Rhetoric of Fiction* (Chicago: University of Chicago Press, 2nd edn, 1983).

Botterweck, G.J., 'Die Gattung des Buches Esther im Spektrum neuerer Publikationen', *Bibel und Leben* 5 (1964), pp. 274-92.

Bowie, E.L., 'The Greek Novel', in P.E. Easterling and B.M.W. Knox (eds.), *The Cambridge History of Classical Literature. I. Greek Literature* (Cambridge: Cambridge University Press, 1985).

Brooke, A.E., N. McLean and H. Thackeray (eds.), *The Old Testament in Greek* (London: Cambridge University Press, 1940).

Brown, C.A., *No Longer Be Silent: First Century Jewish Portraits of Biblical Women* (Gender and the Biblical Tradition Series; Louisville: Westminster Press/John Knox, 1992).

Brownlee, W.H., 'Le Livre Grec d'Esther et la Royaute Divine', *RB* 73 (1966), pp. 161-85.

Buttrick, G.A. *et al.*, *The Interpreter's Bible* (Nashville: Abingdon Press, 1954).

Cazelles, H., 'Note sur la composition du rouleau d'Esther', in H. Gross and F. Mussner, *Lex Tua Veritas: Festschrift für Herbert Junker* (Trier: Paulinus Verlag, 1961), pp. 17-29.

Chatman, S., *Story and Discourse: Narrative Structure in Fiction and Film* (Ithaca, NY: Cornell University Press, 1978).

Clines, D.J.A., *The Esther Scroll: The Story of the Story* (JSOT Supplement Series, 30; Sheffield: JSOT Press, 1984).

—*Ezra, Nehemiah, Esther* (New Century Bible Commentary Series; Grand Rapids: Eerdmans, 1984).

—'In Quest of the Historical Mordecai', *VT* 41 (1991), pp. 129-36.

—'Reading Esther from Left to Right: Contemporary Strategies for Reading a Biblical Text', in D.J.A. Clines, S.E. Fowl and S.E. Porter (eds.), *The Bible in Three Dimensions* (JSOT Supplement Series, 87; Sheffield: JSOT Press, 1990), pp. 31-52.

Cohen, A.D, '"Hu Ha-goral": The Religious Significance of Esther', *Judaism* 23 (1974), pp. 87-94.

Collins, A.Y. (ed.), *Feminist Perspectives on Biblical Scholarship* (SBL Biblical Scholarship in North America Series, 10; Chico, CA: Scholars Press, 1985).

Cook, H.J., 'The A Text of the Greek Versions of the Book of Esther', *ZAW* 81 (1969), pp. 369-76.

Craghan, J.F., 'Esther: A Fully Liberated Woman', *Bible Today* 24 (1986), pp. 6-11.

—'Esther, Judith, and Ruth: Paradigms for Human Liberation', *BTB* 12 (1982), pp. 11-19.

Crenshaw, J.L., 'Methods in Determining Wisdom Influence upon "Historical" Literature', *JBL* 88 (1969), pp. 129-42.

Darr, K.P., *Far More Precious than Jewels: Perspectives on Biblical Women* (Gender and the Biblical Tradition Series; Louisville: Westminster Press/John Knox, 1991).

Daube, D., 'The Last Chapter of Esther', *JQR* 37 (1946–47), pp. 139-47.

Davies, T.W., *Ezra, Nehemiah, and Esther* (New Century Bible Series; New York: Henry Frowde, no date provided).

Docherty, T., *Reading (Absent) Character: Towards a Theory of Characterization in Fiction* (Oxford: Clarendon Press, 1983).

Dommershausen, W., *Die Estherrolle: Stil und Ziel einer alttestamentlichen Schrift* (Stuttgarter Biblische Monographien Series, 6; Stuttgart: Verlag Katholisches Biblewerk, 1968).

—*Ester* (Die Neue Echter Bibel; Stuttgart: Echter Verlag, 1985).

Dorothy, C.V., 'The Books of Esther: Structure, Genre, and Textual Integrity' (PhD dissertation, Claremont Graduate School, 1989).

Duchesne-Guillemin, J., 'Les noms des eunuques d'Assuérus', *Muséon* 66 (1953), pp. 105-108.

Edwards, R.K., 'Reply to "Ahasuerus Is the Villain"', *JBQ* 19 (1990), pp. 33-39.

Egger, B.M., 'Women in the Greek Novel: Constructing the Feminine' (PhD dissertation, University of California, Irvine, 1990).

Elliger, K., and W. Rudolph (eds.), *Biblia Hebraica Stuttgartensia* (Stuttgart: Deutsche Bibelgesellschaft, 1977).

Feldman, L.H., 'Hellenizations in Josephus' Version of Esther', *Proceedings of the American Philological Society* 101 (1970), pp. 143-70.

Fewell, D.N., "Feminist Reading of the Hebrew Bible: Affirmation, Resistance, and Transformation', *JSOT* 39 (1987), pp. 77-87.

Fiorenza, E.S., *Bread Not Stone: The Challenge of Feminist Biblical Interpretation* (Boston: Beacon Press, 1984).

Fisch, H., 'Esther: Two Tales of One City', chapter in *Poetry with a Purpose* (Bloomington: Indiana University Press, 1988).

Forster, E.M., *Aspects of the Novel and Related Writings* (Abinger Edition of E.M. Forster; ed. O. Stallybrass; London: Edward Arnold, 1974), XII.

Fox, M.V., *Character and Ideology in the Book of Esther* (Columbia: University of South Carolina Press, 1991).

—*The Redaction of the Books of Esther* (SBL Monograph Series, 40; Atlanta: Scholars Press, 1990).

—'The Redaction of the Greek Alpha-Text of Esther', in M. Fishbane and E. Tov (eds.), *Sha'arei Talmon: Studies in the Bible, Qumran, and the Ancient Near East Presented to Shemaryahu Talmon* (Winona Lake, IN: Eisenbrauns, 1992), pp. 207-20.

—'The Structure of the Book of Esther', in A. Rofé and Y. Zakovitch (eds.), *Isac Leo*

Seeligmann Volume: Essays on the Bible and the Ancient World (Jerusalem: E. Rubinstein, 1983), pp. 291-303.

Fox, N.S., 'In the Spirit of Purim: The Hidden Hand of God', *JBQ* 18 (1990), pp. 183-87.

Fuchs, E., 'Status and Role of Female Heroines in the Biblical Narrative', *Mankind Quarterly* 23 (1982), pp. 149-60.

Fuerst, W.J., *The Books of Ruth, Esther, Ecclesiastes, The Song of Songs, Lamentations* (Cambridge Biblical Commentary Series; Cambridge: Cambridge University Press, 1975).

Gaster, T.H., 'Esther 1:22', *JBL* 69 (1950), p. 381.

Gehman, H.S., 'Notes in the Persian Words in the Book of Esther', *JBL* 43 (1924), pp. 321-28.

Gendler, M., 'The Restoration of Vashti', in E. Koltun (ed.), *The Jewish Woman* (New York: Schocken, 1976), pp. 241-47.

Gerleman, G., *Esther* (Biblischer Kommentar Altes Testament, XXI; Neukirchen-Vluyn: Neukirchener Verlag, 1973).

—'Studien zu Esther: Stoff–Struktur–Stil–Sinn', *Biblische Studien* 48 (1966), pp. 1-48.

Goldman, S., 'Narrative and Ethical Ironies in Esther', *JSOT* 47 (1990), pp. 14-31.

Gordis, R., *Megillat Esther* (New York: Rabbinical Assembly, 1974).

—'Religion, Wisdom, and History in the Book of Esther: A New Solution to an Ancient Crux', *JBL* 100 (1981), pp. 359-88.

—'Studies in the Esther Narrative', *JBL* 95 (1976), pp. 43-58.

Grasham, W.W., 'The Theology of the Book of Esther', *Restoration Quarterly* 16 (1973), pp. 99-111.

Greenstein, E.L., 'A Jewish Reading of Esther', in J. Neusner, B.A. Levine and E.S. Frerichs (eds.), *Judaic Perspectives on Ancient Israel* (Philadelphia: Fortress Press, 1987), pp. 225-43.

Haelewyck, J.-C., 'Le texte dit "Lucianique" du livre d'Esther: Son etendue et sa coherence', *Muséon* 98 (1985),pp. 5-44.

Hägg, T., *Narrative Technique in Ancient Greek Romances: Studies of Chariton, Xenophon Ephesius and Achilles Tatius* (Stockholm: Svenska Institutet, 1971).

—*The Novel in Antiquity* (Berkeley: University of California Press, 1983).

Hallo, W.W., 'The First Purim', *BA* 46 (1983), pp. 19-26.

Hanhart, R. (ed.), *Septuaginta* (Göttingen: Vandenhoeck & Ruprecht, 1983).

Harrelson, W., 'Text and Translation Problems in the Book of Esther', *Perspectives in Religious Studies* 17 (1990), pp. 197-208.

Harvey, W.J., *Character and the Novel* (London: Chatto & Windus, 1965).

Haupt, P., 'Critical Notes in Esther', *AJSL* 24 (1907–1908), pp. 97-186.

Helms, J., *Character Portrayal in the Romance of Chariton* (The Hague: Mouton, 1966).

Herrmann, W., *Ester im Streit der Meinungen* (Beiträge Zur Erforschung des Alten Testaments und des Antiken Judentums Series, 4; Frankfort am Main: Verlag Peter Lang, 1986).

Herst, R.E., 'The Purim Connection', *USQR* 28 (1973), pp. 139-45.

Hochman, B., *Character in Literature* (Ithaca: Cornell University Press, 1985).

Hock, R.F, 'The Greek Novel', in D.E. Aune (ed.), *Greco-Roman Literature and the*

New Testament: Selected Forms and Genres (SBL Sources for Biblical Study Series, 21; Atlanta: Scholars Press, 1988), pp. 127-46.

Horbury, W., 'The Name Mardochaeus in a Ptolemaic Inscription', *VT* 41 (1991), pp. 220-26.

Horn, S.H, 'Mordecai, a Historical Problem', *BR* 9 (1964), pp. 14-25.

Hoschander, J., *The Book of Esther in Light of History* (Philadelphia: Dropsie College, 1923).

Huey, F.B., 'Irony as the Key to Understanding the Book of Esther', *Southwestern Journal of Theology* 32 (1990), pp. 36-39.

Humphreys, W.L., 'A Life-Style for Diaspora: A Study of the Tales of Esther and Daniel', *JBL* 92 (1973), pp. 211-23.

—'The Story of Esther and Mordecai: An Early Jewish Novella', in G.W. Coats (ed.), *Saga, Legend, Tale, Novella, Fable: Narrative Forms in Old Testament Literature* (JSOT Supplement Series, 35; Sheffield: JSOT Press, 1985), pp. 97-113.

Hyman, R.T., 'Who Is the Villain?', *JBQ* 20 (1992), pp. 153-58.

Jacob, B., 'Das Buch Esther bei den LXX', *ZAW* 10 (1890), pp. 241-98.

James, H., 'The Art of Fiction', in M. Roberts (ed.), *The Art of Fiction and Other Essays* (New York: Oxford University Press, 1948), pp. 3-23.

Jones, B.W., 'The So-Called Appendix to the Book of Esther', *Semitics* 6 (1978), pp. 36-43.

—'Two Misconceptions about the Book of Esther', *CBQ* 39 (1977), pp. 171-81.

Kellogg, R., and R. Scholes, *The Nature of Narrative* (London: Oxford University Press, 1966).

LaCoque, A., 'Haman in the Book of Esther', *HAR* 11 (1987), pp. 207-22.

—*The Feminine Unconventional: Four Subversive Figures in Israel's Tradition* (Overtures to Biblical Theology Series; Minneapolis: Fortress Press, 1990).

Laffey, A.L., *An Introduction to the Old Testament: A Feminist Perspective* (Philadelphia: Fortress Press, 1988).

Lagarde, P. de, *Liborum Veteris Testamenti Canonicorum Prior Graece* (Göttingen: Arnold Hoyer, 1883).

Lebram, J.C.H., 'Purimfest und Estherbuch', *VT* 22 (1972), pp. 208-22.

Levenson, J.D., 'The Scroll of Esther in Ecumenical Perspective', *JES* 13 (1976), pp. 440-51.

Lewy, J., 'Old Assyrian puru'um and pūrum', *Revue Hittite et Asiatique* 5 (1939), pp. 117-24.

—'The Feast of the Fourteenth Day of Adar', *HUCA* 14 (1939), pp. 127-51.

Lichtenberger, A.C., 'Exposition to Esther', in G.A. Buttrich, *et al.*, *The Interpreter's Bible* (Nashville: Abingdon Press, 1954), III, pp. 832-63.

Loader, J.A., 'Esther as a Novel with Different Levels of Meaning', *ZAW* 90 (1978), pp. 417-21.

Loewenstamm, S.E., 'Esther 9:29-32: The Genesis of a Late Addition', *HUCA* 42 (1971), pp. 117-24.

McBride, W.T., 'Esther Passes: Chiasm, Lex Talio, and Money in the Book of Esther', in J.P. Rosenblatt and J.C. Sitterson, Jr (eds.), *'Not in Heaven': Coherence and Complexity in Biblical Narrative* (Bloomington: Indiana University Press, 1991).

McCarthy, C., and W. Riley, 'The Book of Esther: Banquet Tables are Turned', chapter in *The Old Testament Short Story: Explorations in Narrative Spirituality* (Wilmington: Michael Glazier, 1986).

McGee, J.V., *Esther: The Romance of Providence* (Nashville: Thomas Nelson, 1982).

McKane, W., 'A Note on Esther IX and I Samuel XV', *JTS* 12 (1961), pp. 260-61.

Magonet, J., 'The Liberal and the Lady: Esther Revisited', *Judaism* 29 (1980), pp. 167-76.

Martin, R.A., 'Syntax Criticism of the LXX Additions to the Book of Esther', *JBL* 94 (1975), pp. 65-72.

May, K.M., *Characters of Women in Narrative Literature* (New York: St Martin's, 1981).

Mayer, R., 'Iranischer Beitrag zu Problemen des Daniel- und Esther-Buches', in H. Gross and F. Mussner (eds.), *Lex Tua Veritas: Festschrift für Hubert Junker* (Trier: Paulinus Verlag, 1961).

Meinhold, A., *Das Buch Esther* (Zürcher Bibelkommentare Altes Testament Series, 13; Zürich: Theologischer Verlag, 1983).

—'Die Gattung der Josephgeschichte und des Estherbuchs: Diasporanovelle', Part I: *ZAW* 87 (1975), pp. 306-24; Part II: *ZAW* 88 (1976), pp. 72-93.

—'Theologische Erwägungen zum Buch Esther', *TZ* 34 (1978), pp. 321-33.

—'Zu Aufbau und Mitte des Estherbuches', *VT* 33 (1983), pp. 435-45.

Millard, A.R., 'The Persian Names in Esther and the Reliability of the Hebrew Text', *JBL* 96 (1977), pp. 481-88.

Miller, C.H., 'Esther's Levels of Meaning', *ZAW* 92 (1980), pp. 145-48.

Moore, C.A., 'A Greek Witness to a Different Hebrew Text of Esther', *ZAW* 79 (1967), pp. 351-58.

—'Archaeology and the Book of Esther', *BA* 38 (1975), pp. 62-79.

—*Daniel, Esther, and Jeremiah: The Additions* (Anchor Bible Series, 44; Garden City, NY: Doubleday, 1977).

—*Esther* (Anchor Bible Series, 7B; Garden City, NY: Doubleday, 1971).

—'Esther Revisited: An Examination of Esther Studies over the Past Decade', in A. Kort and S. Morschauser (eds.), *Biblical and Related Studies Presented to Samuel Iwry* (Winona Lake, IN: Eisenbrauns, 1985), pp. 163-72.

—'Esther Revisited Again: A Further Examination of Certain Esther Studies of the Past Ten Years', *HAR* 7 (1983), pp. 169-86.

—*The Greek Text of Esther* (PhD dissertation, John Hopkins University, 1965).

—'On the Origins of the LXX Additions to the Book of Esther', *JBL* 92 (1973), pp. 382-93.

Moore, C.A. (ed.), *Studies in the Book of Esther* (New York: Ktav, 1982).

Morgan, D.F., *Between Text and Community: The 'Writings" in Canonical Perspective* (Minneapolis: Fortress Press, 1990).

Morris, A.E., 'The Purpose of the Book of Esther', *Expository Times* 42 (1930–31), pp. 124-28.

Mosala, I.J., 'The Implications of the Text of Esther for African Women's Struggle for Liberation in South Africa', *Semeia* 59 (1992), pp. 129-37.

Niditch, S., 'Esther: Folklore, Wisdom, Feminism, and Authority', chapter in *Underdogs and Tricksters: A Prelude to Biblical Folklore* (San Francisco: Harper & Row, 1987).

—'Legends of Wise Heroes and Heroines', in D.A. Knight and G.M. Tucker (eds.), *The Hebrew Bible and Its Modern Interpreters* (Chico, CA: Scholars Press, 1985), pp. 445-63.

Paton, L.B., *A Critical and Exegetical Commentary on the Book of Esther* (International Critical Commentary Series; New York: Charles Scribners & Son, 1908).

Pelling, C. (ed.), *Characterization and Individuality in Greek Literature* (Oxford: Clarendon Press, 1990).

Perry, B.E., *The Ancient Romances: A Literary-Historical Account of Their Origins* (Berkeley: University of California Press, 1967).

Pervo, R.I., 'Aseneth and Her Sisters: Women in Jewish Narrative and in the Greek Novels', in A.-J. Levine (ed.), *'Women Like This': New Perspectives on Jewish Women in the Greco-Roman World* (SBL Early Judaism and Its Literature Series; Atlanta: Scholars Press, 1991), pp. 145-60.

Phelen, J., *Reading People, Reading Plots: Character, Progression, and the Interpretation of Narrative* (Chicago: University of Chicago Press, 1989).

Portnoy, M.A., 'Ahasuerus Is the Villain', *JBQ* 18 (1990), pp. 187-89.

Raleigh, A., *The Book of Esther: Its Practical Lessons and Dramatic Scenes* (Edinburgh: A. & C. Black, 1880).

Reardon, B.P., *Courants littéraires grecs des IIe et IIe siècles après J.-C.* (Paris: Les Belles Lettres, 1971).

Re'emi, S.P., 'The Faithfulness of God: A Commentary on the Book of Esther', chapter in *Israel Among the Nations: A Commentary on the Books of Nahum, Obadiah, Esther* (International Theological Commentary Series; Grand Rapids: Eerdmans, 1985).

Ringgren, H., 'Esther and Purim', *SEÅ* 20 (1955), pp. 5-24.

Ringgren, H., and O. Kaiser, *Das Hohe Lied/Klagelieder/Das Buch Esther* (Das Alte Testament Deutsch Series, 16.2; Göttingen: Vandenhoeck & Ruprecht, 1981).

Roiron, F.X., 'Les parties deutérocanoniques du Livre d'Esther', *RSR* 6 (1916), pp. 3-16.

Rosenthal, L.A., 'Nochmals der Verglieich Ester, Joseph-Daniel', *ZAW* 17 (1897), pp. 125-28.

Rudolph, W., 'Textkritisches zum Estherbuch', *VT* 4 (1954), pp. 89-90.

Russell, L.M. (ed.), *Feminist Interpretation of the Bible* (Philadelphia: Westminster Press, 1985).

Sakenfeld, K.D., 'Feminist Perspectives on Bible and Theology: An Introduction to Selected Issues and Literature', *Interpretation* 40 (1986), pp. 5-18.

Sanders, J.A., *Canon and Community: A Guide to Canonical Criticism* (Philadelphia: Fortress Press, 1984).

—*From Sacred Story to Sacred Text* (Philadelphia: Fortress Press, 1987).

—'Hebrew Bible *and* Old Testament: Textual Criticism in Service of Biblical Studies', in R. Brooks and J.J. Collins (eds.), *Hebrew Bible or Old Testament? Studying the Bible in Judaism and Christianity* (Christianity and Judaism in Antiquity Series, 5; Notre Dame: University of Notre Dame Press, 1990), pp. 41-68.

Sasson, J.M., 'Esther', in R. Alter and F. Kermode (eds.), *The Literary Guide to the Bible* (Cambridge: Harvard University Press, 1987), pp. 335-42.

Schötz, P.D., 'Das hebräische Buch Esther', *BZ* 21 (1933), pp. 255-76.

Segal, E., 'Human Anger and Divine Intervention in Esther', *Prooftexts* 9 (1989), pp. 247-56.

Stanton, E.C., and L.B. Chandler, 'Comments on the Book of Esther', in *The Woman's Bible* (New York: European Publishing Company, 1898; repr. Seattle: Coalition Task Force on Women and Religion, 1974).

Sternberg, M., *The Poetics of Biblical Narrative: Ideological Literature and the Drama of Reading* (Bloomington: Indiana University Press, 1985).

Stiehl, R., 'Das Buch Esther', *WZKM* 53 (1965), pp. 4-22.

Streane, A.W., *The Book of Esther* (Cambridge: Cambridge University Press, 1922).

Streidl, H., 'Untersuching zur Syntax und Stilistik des hebräischen Buches Esther', *ZAW* 55 (1937), pp. 73-108.

Talmon, S., '"Wisdom" in the Book of Esther', *VT* 13 (1963), pp. 419-55.

Tolbert, M.A., 'Defining the Problem: The Bible and Feminist Hermeneutics', *Semeia* 28 (1983), pp. 113-26.

Torrey, C.C., 'The Older Book of Esther', *HTR* 37 (1944), pp. 1-40.

Tov, E., 'The "Lucianic" Text of the Canonical and Apocryphal Sections of Esther: A Rewritten Biblical Book', *Textus* 10 (1982), pp. 1-25.

Ulrich, E., 'Double Literary Editions of Biblical Narratives and Reflections on Determining the Form to be Translated', in J.L. Crenshaw (ed.), *Perspectives on the Hebrew Bible: Essays in Honor of Walter J. Harrelson* (Macon, GA: Mercer University Press, 1988), pp. 101-16.

—'Jewish, Christian, and Empirical Perspectives on the Text of Our Scriptures', in R. Brooks and J.J. Collins (eds.), *Hebrew Bible or Old Testament? Studying the Bible in Ancient Judaism and Christianity* (Notre Dame: University of Notre Dame Press, 1990), pp. 69-85.

Van Uchelen, N.A., 'A Chokmatic Theme in the Book of Esther: A Study in the Structure of the Story', in M. Boertien *et al.* (eds.), *Verkenningen in een Stroomgebied* (Amsterdam: [publisher not given], 1974), pp. 132-40.

Walcutt, C.C., *Man's Changing Mask: Modes and Methods of Characterization in Fiction* (Minneapolis: University of Minnesota Press, 1966).

Walters, S.D., 'Hannah and Anna: The Greek and Hebrew Texts of 1 Samuel 1', *JBL* 107 (1988), pp. 385-412.

Wehr, H., 'Das "Tor des Königs" im Buche Esther und verwandte Ausdrücke', *Der Islam* 39 (1964), pp. 247-60.

Wenthe, D.O., 'The Old Greek Translation of Daniel 1-6' (PhD dissertation, University of Notre Dame, 1991).

White, S.A., 'Esther', in C.A. Newsom and S.H. Ringe (eds.), *The Women's Bible Commentary* (London: SPCK, and Louisville: Westminster Press/John Knox, 1992), pp. 124-29.

—'Esther: A Feminine Model for Jewish Diaspora', in P.L. Day (ed.), *Gender and Difference in Ancient Israel* (Minneapolis: Fortress Press, 1989), pp. 161-77.

Wills, L.M., *The Jew in the Court of the Foreign King: Ancient Jewish Court Legends* (Harvard Dissertations in Religion Series, 26; Minneapolis: Fortress Press, 1990).

Wright, J.S., 'The Historicity of the Book of Esther', in J.B. Payne (ed.), *New Perspectives on the Old Testament* (Waco, TX: Word Books, 1970), pp. 37-47.

Yahuda, A.S., 'The Meaning of the Name Esther', *JRAS* (1946), pp. 174-78.

Yamauchi, E., 'Mordecai, the Persepolis Tablets, and the Susa Excavations', *VT* 42 (1992), pp. 272-74.

Zadok, R., 'Notes on Esther', *ZAW* 98 (1986), pp. 105-10.

Zeitlin, S., 'The Books of Esther and Judith: A Parallel', introduction to M.S. Enslin, *The Book of Judith* (Dropsie University Jewish Apocryphal Literature Series, VII; Leiden: Brill, 1972), pp. 1-37.

INDEXES

INDEX OF REFERENCES

INDEX OF AUTHORS